CELEBRATING ETERNITY NOW

CELEBRATING ETERNITY NOW

A Study in the Theology of St Alphonsus de Liguori (1696–1787)

Hamish F. G. Swanston

Published by Redemptorist Publications
Alphonsus House Chawton Alton Hampshire GU34 3HQ

Copyright © The Congregation of the Most Holy Redeemer

Text: Hamish F. G. Swanston
Design: Rosemarie Pink

Cover photographs:
  Portrait of Alphonsus de Liguori
  (The Redemptorists, Pagani)
  Troughton's Orrery
  (The Science Museum/Science & Society Picture Library, London)

Published September 1995

ISBN 0 85231 155 9

Printed in Britain by:
Bourne Press Limited
Bournemouth
BH1 4QA

CONTENTS

Acknowledgements

My putting together this response to Alphonsus' theology was first suggested in a conversation with two members of the London Province of the Redemptorist Congregation, Fr Denis McBride and Fr Frank Goodall, when I was teaching a course on Doctrine and History at Hawkstone Hall; the project has been further encouraged by the London Provincial, Fr James McManus, and by Fr Michael McGreevy, its kindly enabler, with Mrs Rosemarie Pink, at Redemptorist Publications.

I should next thank some self-effacingly anonymous helpers: the Brother at Marianella who, having taken me on a gracious tour of Alphonsus' birth-place, worried lest I should board the 'bus without a sufficient supply of oranges for the forty-minute journey back to Naples, the Redemptoristine at Scala who rose from her Sunday lunch to take me up to the house in which Alphonsus and the first Redemptorists established their community, the retired Father at Pagani who, directing me along the corridor to Alphonsus' rooms, talked so shamingly of the Founder's practice of poverty, and the young street-football player in Foggia who would not cease his pleadings at the convent inter-com until the Sisters opened their chapel out of hours so that I might pray at the glass casket of the Venerable Celeste.

I have had particular helps in my researches from Sr M. Bernadette, O.SS.R., Redemptoristine Prioress at Liverpool, the Rev Dr Brian Davies, O.P., Regent of Studies, Blackfriars, Oxford, the Rev Prof. Edward R. Callahan, S.J., at Boston College, Fr T. G. Holt, S.J. Archivist of the English Jesuit Province, Br Anthony McCrave, C.SS.R., and from the Rev Fathers C.SS.R., Carl Hoegerl of the Baltimore Province, Brian V. Johnstone of Canberra, Frederick M. Jones of Dublin, Henry Parker of London and, in the Redemptorist Generalate archives, Fr Raul Campos of Buenos Aires who, on any appeal being made for assistance, at once put aside his own work to attend to my problems with friendly efficiency. But then, I was, while conducting my researches, everywhere courteously received by the Very Rev Fathers Rector and the Redemptorist communities at Canterbury, Clapham, Hawkstone, Marianella, Pagani, Rome and Scala.

Most especially, I would thank my friend the Very Rev Fr James Casey, C.SS.R., the General Secretary of the Congregation, who has for many years now kept up a pawky commentary on me and all my doings. It is right and pleasant to dedicate this book to him.

Hamish F. G. Swanston

1

Foreword

One evening in the first week of September, 1728, a school usher, Pietro Barbarese, and a roast-chestnut seller, Leonardo Cristagno, known as "Nardiello", were arrested by the Naples Police. Taken in the morning from the guard-room at Porta San Gennaro for examination by the Viceroy's magistrate, they were questioned about their membership of an unauthorized association of working men. Others of their group had been forewarned of the police raid by their leader, the priest Alphonsus de Liguori. He was the son of Don Giuseppe, the flamboyant captain of the newly-refitted *Padrona*, and Donna Anna Caterina who had a couple of judges and a bishop among her kinsmen, and on his representations to Cardinal Pignatelli the men were released. Alphonsus had explained that their group met in the corner of a piazza or in the back room of a barber's shop not to plot the downfall of the government but for prayer, elementary religious instruction, and hymn-singing. Barbarese and Nardiello and others had been given some training as catechists so that they might help with the numbers of uneducated men and boys, soap-makers, street hawkers, discharged soldiers, stevedores, who came after work to hear the good news of Jesus. An attempt to form a women's group had failed. Their work did not, after all, cease at the sounding of the evening *Angelus*, and anyway, Neapolitan men were made uneasy by the thought of their women going out at night.

Barbarese and Nardiello had to teach the young priests of good family, Giuseppe Panza, Giovanni Mazzini, Gennaro Fatigati, and half-a-dozen others working with Alphonsus, something about such social realities. They had to teach them, too, that there was a need for some translating of the latinate formulations of university and seminary study into a language of the poor. Alphonsus, certainly, was learning to think and speak clearly, popularly, attractively, at these evening meetings. And to write, too. It was for these *Cappelle serotine* that he put together his *Maxims of Eternity*, 1728. Cheaply printed, poorly sewn, small enough to be shoved into a coat pocket, thousands of copies of this manual of daily devotions were distributed in the city and, later, in the country towns of the Kingdom.

Looking among the range of possible models for such a manual, Alphonsus had learnt enough at least to know that he should not simply reproduce the nice instances from Seneca and Plutarch which Jeremiah Drexel (1581-1638), proposed for educated young men like Alphonsus in his *Portent of Eternity*, 1628. He would assuredly find little to his purpose in the more extended Greek and Roman parallelisms of the five-volume *One Thing Necessary*, 1697, of Benedetto Rogacci (1646-1719). Alphonsus was a young man in a hurry. He told the reader of his *Visits to the Blessed Sacrament* in 1745 that he had wasted the first twenty-six years of his life before realizing what he should be doing. In 1728 he was certainly thinking of himself as a late starter. He wanted, in his *Maxims*, to warn others not to waste time as he had done. They'd soon be dead. "You'll then see the value of the time you're losing, but it will be too late"; "put your affairs in order"; "do not wait"; "it is time"; "what are you doing?" The youthful impetuosity of these exhortations contrasts, however, with the general dullness of what Alphonsus had selected from the run of manualists. Much of what he says of the man who is at the point of expiring, of the naked body eaten by worms, of the blessed entering the bliss of heaven, could have been said, indeed had been said, in a score of middle-class handbooks. Alphonsus had evidently gone trawling among the pieties of the *Gospel Light* of Heinrich Engelgrave, d.1670, and the *Sweet and Holy Death* of Jean Crasset (1618-1692), and the *Eternal Truths* of Carlo Gregorio Rosignoli (1631-1707). Much of it was then being said by St Leonard of Port Maurice (1676-1751), in his *Holy Handbook*, 1734. And would be said again by Alphonsus' great friend, Gennaro Maria Sarnelli (1702-1744), in his *Easy Way to Paradise*, 1738.

His keeping within the conventions of such handbooks may suggest a becoming modesty in the young man, but we read *Maxims of Eternity* now not for what in it was conventional but for promises of some distinctive element in Alphonsus' later theology. There are, certainly, hints of Alphonsus' abiding enthusiasm for story-telling as he recounts the death-bed regrets of Cardinal Wolsey, of his favourites among the blessed as he works in a reference to St Maria Maddalena de Pazzi, of his theological sensitivity as he frames an "an act of contrition" so that it shall affirm the vital connection in our appreciation of the Trinity, the Eucharist, and the Immaculate Conception. The very title of his little book must seem now to presage Alphonsus' later determination to place all our experiences within the context of eternity. He is making repeated efforts to express "this great thought of eternity". Twenty-eight uses of "eternity" and "eternal" in the twenty-four page booklet, and another eighteen of "always" in sentences which suggest it is synonymous here with "eternity": "Always, always! Oh for ever! Oh

4

always! Oh eternity! Oh hell!" The excitable young man announcing an imminent everlasting death would take twenty years or more to put his ideas into decent order, discipline his prose, and get his meaning across. But he had all that while a consistent meaning. Working from a steadfast understanding of his experiences, he would become the great elucidator of the relation which obtains between our present condition, the celebration of the eucharistic liturgy, and eternal life. This was his chief concern. To his expression of this relation, therefore, I shall turn in Part One of my account of Alphonsus' theology.

That it proved no easy matter for him to maintain his intellectual hold on what it meant to be living eternally now is evident not only from some sad lapses into a merely futurist language of "eternity after death" in the writings of his extreme old age, but in his acute sensitivity all his working life to the charge of being merely "a pious author". "To say", he fumed on receiving one censor's permission to publish, "that my opinions are dictated more by the heart than the head is really to discredit the whole work". It meant, he thought, that "I have written like an imbecile".[1]

Alphonsus is certainly not an imbecile. He is, in his sermons and his more than a hundred books and pamphlets, shaping an intelligent account of all that seems important for him and his fellows, and he proves in this endeavour to be a civilized and civilizing Christian. In *Maxims of Eternity*, Alphonsus exhibits all the young man's eagerness to slough off his past enthusiasms and to celebrate the excitements of the present. "Fancy", he says on Sunday, "preferring a bagatelle, banqueting, holidaying, having a good time, to eternity." He was still quite quick to denounce such things in 1745. "Going to parties, watching farces, gossiping, card games, all is folly; believe me, I've done it all and weep."[2] He could slip into such revilements of his old self every now and again, but he came, also, to appreciate that his recollections of youthful diversions and employments, of astronomy, modern music, and the literatures of antiquity, together with what he had learnt in the university lecture hall and the law courts, might be put to less tearful theological use. Generally, Alphonsus manages these things by allusion rather than plain statement. But something may be learned of both the experiences and Alphonsus' way of converting them by standing in his places, in Naples, Scala, Foggia, Benevento, and Pagani. Something more by listening to the theatrical music of Scarlatti, Handel, and Leo. If he would later speak of hell, it would be as a cacophony of "singing with discordant voices".[3] And more again, by reading the same books. Or some of them, at least, for Alphonsus was an eager reader, careful borrower, and great buyer of books. He was ever urging Redemptorist Rectors to spend whatever they could manage on the house libraries. I am, in Part Two, exploring half-a-dozen instances of such allusions to his earlier education, for these enable his reader to identify what is most personal in Alphonsus' language.

His writing *Maxims of Eternity* for those who came to the evening meetings is a sign that he recognized even so early that it was his vocation to be a manager of language. He was not only, with his brothers Dom Antonio and Cajetan, to read out the Gospel, pronounce the given words of consecration and absolution, he was to be the maker of sermons and of books. These were elements of an integrated vocation. "Not to multiply books, labour and expense", as he says in the foreword to his *Preparation for Death*, 1758, he was hoping that these considerations "on the eternal Maxims" would provide matter for personal meditation and for the mission sermon. His effort to find the words for others brought Alphonsus to an ever-increasing appreciation of what it might mean for him to follow Christ as priest and bishop. In Part Three, I shall hope to suggest how Alphonsus' imitation of Christ was actualized as an announcement for forgiveness, in the confessional and in the *Moral Theology*, as a story-telling which offered contemporary parables to the learned nun taking up one of his books and the man saying the rosary, and as a lively proclamation of the Kingdom of God among us, in a discussion upon papal infallibility as in sermons exhorting villagers to salute their "Holy Queen".

Alphonsus recognized that he would have to manage language according to the diverse capacities of his hearers and readers. He remarked more than once, in the *Exercises of the Missions*, 1760, for instance, and, in shorter form, in the *Letter to a Religious* 1761, that a sermon should be "less encumbered with Latin quotations" when delivered to a country congregation. It may be, as I have been told more than once, that only a Neapolitan could truly appreciate Alphonsus' mind. It would have to be a very well-educated Neapolitan. At any rate, when preaching in the city, Alphonsus supposed he should keep his learning within charitable bounds. While it would be good to quote the Latin texts of the Fathers, the preacher would do well to concentrate on explaining one or two knock-down quotations rather than confuse the people with a great many. On the other hand, his writings were liberally laced with citations from the Scriptures in the Vulgate translation and from the Latin Fathers. Cicero, Lucretius, Ovid, and Virgil, he quoted in Latin, and, though he read Greek, Plato, too. Alphonsus recognized that even in his day "the priests are not much in love with the Latin language",[4] and he produced in 1758 an Italian Compendium of his moral theology. Then again, in 1759, to get a hold in Transalpine markets he turned this into a Latin *Homo Apostolicus*. So, ultramontanely, I have throughout used the Latin form of his Italian name. He read French, and Spanish, but cited Rousseau and St Teresa of Avila in Italian. He did not read English, so he must have made use of others' translations for his Italian citations of Tindal, Hobbes, and Locke. I have, reciprocally, cited Alphonsus himself only in English translation. Not always in Grimm's English. Thus *Selva* appears as the *Treasury* and, with merely a modernist's excuse, *Vera Sposa* as *True Bride*.

The distinction Alphonsus makes about the uses of Latin in preaching and writing may still seem sensible, even if readers are not now, for the most part, entirely at their ease with the Vulgate. What he recommended about scholarly apparatus seems somewhat odder. He acknowledged that when historical facts are alleged in a sermon "it will be proper to support them by indicating the author, the time, and the place",[5] but he did not care for such things, and that support was rarely offered in his literary work. Alphonsus was at his footnoting best for the *Moral Theology*, but even so the indefatigable Gaudé mutters protectingly about there being unfortunate carryings-over of inaccuracy from Hermann Busenbaum's *Medulla Theologiae*, 1650, of places where the even more careless printer had mis-set Alphonsus' annotations, and of Alphonsus' having to employ inadequate editions of ancient authors. Alphonsus felt freer, as he reviewed supporters and opponents in his dogmatic, controversialist, writings, to make more generalizing references to "the opinion of scholars" like Monsignor Bossuet, to "what the philosopher Newton wisely says", to "the most pernicious system" of Bayle and to the pesky Chillingworth "with his Oxford theologians".[6] And he was, on occasion, cheerfully content with "as a learned man once observed" or, not much more satisfyingly to donnish readers, "as St Ambrose or some other saint says"[7] in that great body of writing, from *Visits to the Blessed Sacrament* through the *Glories of Mary*, 1750, to the *Brief Reply to the Abbate Rolli*, 1776, in which he was making his consistent declaration of the present offer of eternal life.

I too, have denied myself the immodest fun of reference-laden, witty, and opponent-slaying, annotations. But I have placed at the end of each part a largish number of notes declaring the sources of my quotations from Alphonsus' writings so that any who wish may deconstruct what I have put together from my readings of his books and pamphlets, and may then enjoy a like excitement in making the attempt to reconstruct the relations of Alphonsus' experiences, ideas, and expressions.[8] I have tried, likewise, to provide a book-list at the end which shall rather further the researches of an interested reader than make a pleasant display of my own. And since I have been making some attempt to follow Alphonsus' example in these bookish matters, perhaps I may close my Foreword with his usual proposition that author and reader make an exchange of charity.

NOTES

1 Letter to Don Giulio Selvaggio, April 1772.

2 *Visits to the Blessed Sacrament*, Introduction, I.

3 *Treasury*, Pt. I, vii.

4 To Remondini, 13 July, 1764.

5 *Exercises of the Missions*, VII, I. 2.

6 *Conduct of Providence*, cap.11, Marietti, 789b, *Truth of Faith*, Pt I, cap. VI, Marietti, 557a, Pt I, cap. I, Marietti 538a, and Pt III, cap. VI, Marietti, 701a.

7. *On the Passion*, XI,ii.

8. At the beginning of June, 1761, Alphonsus wrote to his "dear friend", Giambattista Remondini, that, since he was an old man, "every day expecting death", he probably would not write another book, and suggesting that "it might be a good thing if all my spiritual works were published together in one complete edition". In September that year he was already deciding that he would have to go through them all revising them "one by one, page by page" for this *omnia opera*. By January, 1762, he was working on a general index for "this new uniform edition". But the project stalled. In March, 1773, Alphonsus was clearly less confident of publication: "Of the *Collected Ascetical Writings* we shall speak later when God enlightens us on the subject". A month later he was no longer thinking in terms of some great retrospective collection: "I have taken up my work on the *Passion* again and two other little treatises...". These things are always the same. The standard edition, begun at Rome with the *Practica de Amar Gesu Cristo* in 1933, halted in 1939, re-started in 1960 with an *Introduzione* volume, and is uncompleted yet. So references cannot be made consistently to this authoritative *Opere Ascetiche*. And since there is also a design to publish a new edition of the *Lettere*, it does not seem sensible to refer readers to the 1887-90 edition which is long out of print. If English-readers suppose that annotations to both ascetical works and letters could be uniformly attached to the volume and page numbers of the great Grimm

translation for the "Centenary Edition", they would have to allow that this might prove a rather arcane exercise since these volumes have become rarities on second-hand book-sellers' shelves. And those who have produced paper-back editions of Alphonsus' works in the last thirty years have not in every case reproduced the Grimm pagination. I am thus persuaded that the only useful references are to those divisions into Part, Chapter, Section and Sub-section, set up either by Alphonsus himself or by a tidying Grimm. It must at least be a gain that, on this procedure, the checking reader will encounter a quotation in its original context. References to the *Theologia Moralis* are, of course, to Gaudé's weighty edition, but Alphonsus' dogmatic works equally with some of the ascetical await their modern editor and I offer column references to the volume in the Marietti edition without much hope of this being on any local bookshop shelf however dusty.

PART ONE
"In remembrance of me"

"Putting together this little treatise, at the age of seventy-seven, and near to death", Alphonsus anticipates the complaint "that I have repeated here what I have already repeated in my other works." But he claims for these *Reflections on the Passion of Jesus Christ*, written in 1773, when he had another fourteen years to live, that licence which is allowed to "authors of mischievous books". Such persons constantly repeat their immodest jests in their efforts to excite the jaded reader. Alphonsus' reader will surely give better words, however often repeated, a better welcome. And since, again and again, the very hints that he is offering here have proved helpful to Alphonsus himself "as I make my own poor meditations", it may not be unprofitable to devout souls if he write of them once more. His reader and he may meditate again together. "Now, let us make a start."

Alphonsus is entirely right to admit to a charge of repetitiveness. In that little treatise he does return to the characteristic expression of his feeling. "How pleasing it is to Jesus Christ that we should often remember his Passion and the shameful death he suffered for us" and "I feel a great longing to love thee" and "With thy grace I desire to be thine through all eternity". And he returns to the range of his characteristic references. There are, in these contemplations of the suffering Lord, the usual disclosures of Alphonsus' interest in astronomy, in contemporary music, in the relations of myth with gospel. There are the reminders, too, of his unhappy involvement with the Amatrice lawsuit and the obsessions of the three aristocratic litigants with property and the getting of money. And these reflections are sustained, as ever, by a clutch of quotations from *Hebrews*, his favourite among New Testament epistles, and by repeated citations of all his chosen saints, John Chrysostom, Teresa of Avila, Aquinas, and Maria Maddalena de Pazzi.[1] This little treatise contains, too, that pleasant example of those familiar references to his wider reading in the works of great women and men which have made dry-as-dust scholars so wary of him. Anyone addicted to footnotes is left to rummage among the sources as Alphonsus observes easily that he is merely repeating what "St Ambrose, or some other saint, says". Such carefree things recur in the consistently personal tone of Alphonsus' writing. And, in his ordinary way, he returns to the language of Thomas à Kempis to make his announcement of the full scope of his enterprise: "Imitate Jesus", he tells his reader, and "become like Jesus".

Alphonsus returns, also, to the characteristic expression of his thinking. It is apparent, at a reading of this or any of his writings, that, as he remarked of *Prayer, the Great Means of Salvation*, 1759, each "is not only an ascetical work, a book of spirituality, but a theological work".[2] It is apparent that each in turn represents an intensification of Alphonsus' understanding of a recurring pattern of ideas. Alphonsus makes his start in these reflections *On the Passion* as, explicitly or implicitly, he makes a start in the more than a hundred pieces of ascetical, moral, and dogmatic writing of his fifty years of doing theology, from a question about the celebration of the eucharistic liturgy.

Paul, when he told the Corinthian community that at the Eucharist "you show forth the Lord's death", well knew that Christ had risen from the dead, so "Why does he speak of the Lord's death, rather than of his incarnation, birth, or resurrection?", and "Why, then, did he say that he would know nothing but Jesus crucified?"[3] Less wide-ranging, it might seem, than the starting question of Anselm, "Why did God become man?", less academic in tone, certainly, than Aquinas' question, "What sort of thing is holy teaching?", less peremptory than the "Who made you?" of the old Catechism, Alphonsus' question gets a great answer. "It is because," he replies, "Jesus dying on the cross most moved him to love him."

Who, "on seeing a young man of noble blood, innocent and holy, die, tormented on a shameful tree", would not be filled with compassion? And if that young man were dying to obtain forgiveness for the guilty? And if that young man were the Son of God? That is the sight, Alphonsus understands, most feelingly, which confronts Paul in the liturgy of his Corinthian community. This is the sight which confronts the present eucharistic community. We may appreciate, Alphonsus says at the start of his 1773 reflections, just how intensely Christ desires us to live in awareness of his shameful death by recognizing that he instituted the most holy Sacrament of the altar to this very end, "that there might ever dwell in us the lively memory of the love which he bore to us". The Eucharist is always celebrated "in remembrance of the Lord's death".

Remembrance of things present

Alphonsus has, therefore, to ensure that he and those who depend on him shall have a true understanding of what "remembrance" means in this context, and of the relation of this eucharistic remembrance to "the Lord's death". The line of his theological investigation is already laid out for him on his taking his place in the celebrating community. This is his constant professional occupation in his writing and the constant theme of his most popular preaching. It is also the constant topic in what might, for others, be opportunities of recreational conversation. It is entirely according to this pattern that the musical sequence of his 1760 *Duet between the soul and Jesus Christ* should be brought to a climactic recitative and aria of the suffering Christ in which the Lord makes an immediate linkage of his death with the Eucharist:

> And when my life is ended,
> O then, remember me.

Another might connect "remembrance" with "separation" and "cenotaph" and "nostalgia". But in Paul's mind, Alphonsus is sure, memory is the power by which images, places, incidents, sensations, and, most affectingly, people that we had thought gone and dead, are made present and alive to us. We, like the members of Paul's Corinthian community, have to make this sense of memory our own. And this may take some doing. For we start from the experience that even our most lively memories have been poor substitutes for the presence of those we love.

There are two sorts of remembering being noticed here. Alphonsus is aware of an energy in human remembering which, now and again at least, can make things live. "Though some time has elapsed since my stay at Scala", he wrote to Mother Angiola del Cielo in late October 1730, "my remembrance of you is as vivid as if I had departed only yesterday", and "I hope that this memory will always be the same".[4] But to express a hope is to acknowledge a fear. Alphonsus is, disappointedly, as aware that our poor memories, after "departure", too often fade, get muddled with one another, do not remain always the same. And they quit us altogether just when we should be bringing them to mind. "We are men", Alphonsus apologised to his publisher, Giuseppe Remondini, when a fine proof sheet from the Venetian printer had to be altered, "and cannot think of everything at the right time."

So, making our effort to understand the relation of the Eucharist with the Lord's death, we have also to acknowledge that we quite quickly cease to remember the dead. "Your relatives will at first be afflicted at your death, but it will not be long before they will console themselves with the portion of your property which may fall to them." Sadly, humanly, "we barely remember the Passion of Jesus Christ".[5]

From this reflecting on human remembering and forgetting, we may come to a distinct appreciation of the eucharistic remembrance. Our memories of the dead may come back to us for a moment, prompted perhaps by "their portraits", by "letters in their hand-writing", by "the rooms, the beds, the clothes, they used", but they come back to us only to make us more terrifiedly aware of the death which waits for us also.[6] Human remembering generally brings with it the weary acknowledgement of the exhaustion of human energy. Contrastingly, the liturgy is a remembering which is informed by inexhaustible vitality. For it is a remembering which springs out of the will of the Lord. "Do this in memory of me." In the eucharistic celebration, we are divinely assured that Christ "is not dead, indeed, but living" for us. Alphonsus brings forward the express witness of the liturgy itself to what is happening among us. He repeats the exultant Passiontide chant: "Life endured death, and by death brought forth life". Keeping this lively memory of Christ's love for us, we remember in the Eucharist not as if it were yesterday but as it is today. This remembering is "always the same".

Alphonsus' 1774 translation of the Psalms and Canticles suggests that he had a weekly experience of the distinction of these rememberings which informs his interpretation of the Corinthian epistle. His commentary on the psalms shows that, reciting Lauds on Saturday, returning in thankful memory to some kindness shown him in the past week, Alphonsus knows what the psalmist means by the just man's "living in the memory" of his fellows. Even this memory, however, may fade as the just man's heirs unpack his boxes. Alphonsus knows, too, at Sunday Vespers, the thrust into the next week's work at the affirmation that "he hath made a remembrance of his wonderful works". The Lord, Alphonsus explains here, had "left a memory" in the manna which he gave the Hebrews to keep them alive in the desert.[7] This memory is not left behind in the past. The manna is a forwarding, vigorous, figure of the Eucharist. The divine energy within that Old Testament memorial has now burst upon us in the New Testament

14

celebration. In the Eucharist, the Lord's death is, he says, "left as a memory" for us, not as we so often remember and forget, nor even as the Hebrews preserved their Passover memory of the Exodus, but as a life-giving power.

Sometimes, as he celebrated Mass, as he made his further thanksgiving after Communion, as he meditated before the Tabernacle, Alphonsus was caught up in this enlivening memory of the Passion. He experienced, overwhelmingly, a sharing in the mysterious order centred at Jesus dying on the cross. These ecstasies are reliably recorded. At Modugno, in February 1745, he was seen after the Consecration prayer to be raised quite off the ground. Such things disquieted his contemporaries at least as much as they would ourselves. One Friday in March 1770, his assistant at the altar, Canon Cesare Mechella, was so alarmed at the prospect of Alphonsus' rising from the floor that he took a firm hold of Alphonsus' cassock. On 14th October 1784, Alphonsus' ecstatic transports before the Blessed Sacrament so perturbed the congregation at Pagani that the Rector forbade him to come down to the church any more. In the house, the members of his community learnt to endure such disturbances.

What Alphonsus sometimes felt, he always knew. As he repeats, at the start of the liturgy, the psalm "Judge me, O God", there should come again to the priest's mind, Alphonsus wrote in a little book on *The Rubrics of the Mass*, 1769, "the aim of everything he does". Life would declare its meaning for the priest through his celebration of the eucharistic mystery. For this remembering is purposeful. It is not some poor regretful substitute for what is gone and dead. This remembering of Jesus Christ enables the vital presence of Jesus Christ. The short prefatory note to his treatise *On the Sacrifice of Jesus Christ*, 1775, says plainly that "we encounter at the altar the same victim and the same priest who offered himself on the cross that day". This is a real encounter. Alphonsus insists always on the most literal and comprehensive significance of this "presence" of the Lord. He is eager, throughout his preaching and writing, to effect a conversion of whatever might seem formal in the doctrine of "real presence" into an immediately realizable intimacy. His *Visits to the Blessed Sacrament*, c.1745, begins with the short scholastic statement that "we are bound to believe that in the consecrated host Jesus Christ is really present under the species of bread". "But", he at once goes on to say, there is more to understand, "he is present on our altars to show the love he bears us", and to show this love "by living night and day among us". Forty years later, when he was no longer strong enough to celebrate the liturgy himself, his lively sense of "real presence" broke through again and again at Holy Communion in his cry to the priest, "Give me Jesus Christ". And always the liturgy is a celebration of the presence of Jesus crucified. In his very first sermon, which he preached as part of the "Forty Hours" eucharistic devotions at the parish of San Giovanni in Porta in April 1726, Alphonsus, pointing towards the host in the monstrance, had declared to the little congregation that "this is our dear Jesus" and that "he who is now calling to you from the altar" is "the Victim of Calvary". It is in such an announcing of the coincidence of the moment of Jesus' dying and the moment of the community's eucharistic liturgy that the priest may disclose the meaning of all our lives.

These moments cannot be appreciated truly except in reciprocity with one another. Alphonsus would have us always imagine and feel and think of them together. For the instructive frontispiece of *Visits to the Blessed Sacrament*, which became his most popular piece of writing, Alphonsus had the engraver show a Benediction monstrance floating above the hill of Calvary. Arrows pointed the connection of the one with the other. In an ascetical work like the masterly *Practice of the Love of Christ*, 1768, Alphonsus is exclaiming "what two great mysteries of hope and love are the Passion of Jesus Christ and the Sacrament of the altar", asking "should not these two mysteries consume with love the hearts of all people?"[8] Certainly, the hearts of those who enjoy a share of the priesthood: "To advance in perfection, the priest must entertain a great devotion to the Passion of Jesus Christ and to the Blessed Sacrament". The priest is to encourage that same devotion in lay women and men, he is to "fire hearts with a love of Jesus crucified", so that those who come to Holy Communion may make their own the merits of the Passion of Christ. This ought to be, as he wrote in the *Letter to a Religious*, 1761, which he sent to all the local bishops as well as to the superiors of religious orders in the Kingdom of Naples, the constant, coupling, theme of the parish sermon. "I entreat you to speak often of the love that Jesus Christ has shown us in his Passion and in instituting the most holy Sacrament, and of the love we should bear in our turn towards our most blessed Redeemer, by often calling to mind these two great mysteries of love." And if the language of "fire" and "hearts" be not congenial, Alphonsus is equally ready with the drier pronouncement of that coinciding celebration that he has found in Chrysostom: "The celebration of a Mass has the same value as the death of Christ on the cross", and the even more restrained statement of Aquinas in his *Commentary on John:* "Whatever is the effect of the Passion of our Lord is also the effect of this sacrament".[9] In this imagining, feeling, thinking of them together, Alphonsus is, as ever, "still more assured", and he intends his priest-reader of *The Treasury,* 1760, to be more assured too, by the witness of the liturgy itself; at the Collect for the ninth Sunday after Pentecost, he is delighted to announce with the Church everywhere that "As many times as this commemorative sacrifice is celebrated, so often is this work of our redemption performed".[10] This is the witness of the authoritative, worshipping, community, from Corinth to Naples, that in the one act, "remembering", "celebration", and "redemption" are performed together.

Alphonsus cannot speak of "the work of our redemption" without at once seeing the Lord on the cross, and he cannot see the Lord on the cross without at once being brought to meditate upon the wonder of the sacrament. "I died for you, I died upon the tree of shame...what more could I do?...my love has found out a way of doing more. After my death, I have chosen to stay with you in the most Blessed Sacrament." And on Alphonsus' making this meditation, he comes into an all-inclusive appreciation of the aim of everything that Christian women and men are doing: "If he has given you all, as he has in his Passion and in the holy Eucharist, you are to give all yourself to him".[11] If this still seems too limitedly liturgical and para-liturgical in its declaration of the opportunities of grace, Alphonsus kept up a simple human remembering of the supper of the Lord and of his death at the most sluggish time of the ordinary Neapolitan's day. The members of his Congregation were to observe the afternoon silence after their community meal in memory of the three hours that Jesus was hanging on the cross.[12]

It was usual for the missioners of the Kingdom of Naples to encourage the poor to the practice of contemplating the poor, suffering, Christ on the cross. This was a common exercise of the members of the Congregation of the Apostolic Missions, founded in 1646 by Sansone Carnevale, to which Alphonsus' theology tutor, the redoubtable Giulio

Torno (1672-1756), and his mother's kinsman, the volatile seminary Rector, Pietro Gizzio (1662-1741), both belonged. It was the practice, too, of the Pious Workers founded in 1602 by the Venerable Carlo Carafa (1561-1633), of which another uncle, Emilio Cavalieri, was a distinguished member, and in which Alphonsus' "dear Father" Tommaso Falcoia (1663-1743), first enjoyed the experience of being in authority. It was a custom, too, in the little local Congregation of the Assumption, the *Conferenza*, founded in 1611 by the Neapolitan Jesuit, Francesco Pavone (1569-1637), whom Alphonsus much admired. He made a careful study of the missionary methods of each of these groups, and, particularly, the ways in which they promoted devotion to the crucified Lord. He read Pietro Gisolfo's *Life of Carlo Carafa*, 1667, and the Pious Workers' edition of their founder's manual of *Instructions for Missioners*, 1673; he read both Pavone's *Instructions for the Congregation of the Assumption*, 1629, and, most attentively, his *Meditations before the Blessed Sacrament*, 1622. And in November, 1724, he began his probationary period with the Congregation of the Apostolic Missions. But Alphonsus is distinguished among all these contemporary missioners by his insistence that the "exercise of the devout life" in honour of the crucified Lord should be practised within a eucharistic context. The Pious Workers, for example, had placed their contemplation of the crucifix alongside devotion to the eucharistic Christ, but Carafa had not brought these devotions to any integrating expression. They remained as distinct from each other as each was from Carafa's equally intense devotion to the Blessed Virgin. Pavone's *Meditations* provided matter for a variety of affective considerations before and after the reception of Holy Communion whose tone and content were generally intended to encourage a more personal apprehension of Jesus' love for the communicant. There was little in them to bring about a specific apprehension of the love of Jesus as the love of the crucified Lord. Alphonsus possessed the theological energy required for a popular declaration of the singleness of the suffering and eucharistic Lord in a single devotion.

Alphonsus' missioners were to encourage the villagers to form themselves into informal groups, even regular sodalities, so that they should sustain one another in continuing, after the missioners had departed for another village, the vital contemplation of crucifix and tabernacle together. The country folk learnt that they, too, were called to enjoy those silent moments of mental prayer which they might have supposed the prerogative of the more sensitive enclosed Religious. Among Alphonsus' first companions, Gennaro Sarnelli (1702-1744), became a most enthusiastic and effective advocate of this practice for ordinary lay women and men. *The Sanctified World,* which Sarnelli published in 1738 let others know of Alphonsus' hopes for these praying groups. It was quickly reprinted and reprinted. Not everyone approved. The encouragement of such silent prayer in village churches seemed a little too advanced, heretical perhaps, to the Dominican preacher Gesualdo Dandolfo. In 1746, he attacked Alphonsus as "a simple rustic" encouraging equally simple rustics into "laxist" practices and devotions which were "not approved by Rome". Alphonsus was not persuaded to make a change. He simply added an "explication" to the 1748 edition of his *Notes to Busenbaum,* and went on his way. In his first week as bishop of Sant' Agata dei Goti, 1762, he established this practice in his cathedral parish and kept it going there and across the diocese until his retirement in 1775.

The living memory of the Passion of Christ at the present Eucharist provides a hitching-post for every one of Alphonsus' assessments of our human experience. Confident in the enlivening power of this memory, he conducts a wide-ranging review of our physical environment, our living together with angels and animals, our moral stance towards our neighbour human beings, our proper service of God. There could be no other hitching-post. Alphonsus could not, for example, however greatly he venerated her spiritual gifts, employ the language of Maria Celeste Crostarosa (1696-1755), when she spoke of her community as "a living remembrance" of the work and love of Christ. Alphonsus never placed the Redemptorist Congregation at the centre of his experiencing. It was, indeed, the eucharistic centering of his imagining and feeling and thinking which got him through the terrible experience of Pope Pius VI's declaring in 1780 that Alphonsus and his Neapolitan brethren had "ceased to be members of the Congregation" that he had founded.

"That ever-fixed eternity"

In the remembering Eucharist, that present experience of being in the presence of the redeeming Lord, Alphonsus discovers how insubstantial are our little notions of chronology. The temporal priority of the past is put aside in this present. The moment of the Cross is not "before" the moment of our sharing in the eucharistic celebration. "St Teresa of Avila is astonished", Alphonsus tells the congregation at a mission sermon preparing them for Holy Communion, "that so many envy the happiness of those who lived in the time when Jesus Christ was seen on earth, when everyone could enjoy his presence, speak to him face to face, and ask him for favours."[13] Alphonsus shares the astonishment of "my dear patroness". He repeats her question to his congregation. "Have we not in the Blessed Sacrament this same Jesus?" Our appreciating the irrelevancy of the past tense for any true expression of this moment of coincidence allows us to recognize an irrelevancy in the future tense also. The moment of our enjoying the wonder of Paradise is not "after" the moment of our eucharistic celebration. The moment of Paradise is already realized. Meditating in his *Reflections on the Truth of Divine Revelation*, 1773, upon the great declaration, "I am the way, the truth, and the life", Alphonsus is quietly assured that the one word "life" reveals the one life. Christ, he says, enables us to live a life of "contentment on earth and blessedness in Paradise". It is of those who "live contentedly" that the Lord says "theirs is the kingdom of heaven". Alphonsus points out that the Lord does not say "Theirs will be the kingdom of heaven" but "theirs is".[14] To be before the Blessed Sacrament is, indeed, Alphonsus exclaims rejoicingly, time and again, to be in Paradise.[15] "Behold, then, our Paradise on earth — the most Blessed Sacrament!"

The wondrousness of being in Paradise is simply an intensification of that enjoyment of the presence of the eternal Lord which is offered to us now as we contemplate the Blessed Sacrament. It pleased Alphonsus to recall, also, that St Teresa had come from heaven to tell one of her reformed nuns that the sisters should be "the same in love" with the angels and saints, for "what we do in heaven before the divine essence, you should do before the most holy Sacrament".[16] Alphonsus' first biographer, Antonio Maria Tannoia (1727-1802), caught just Alphonsus' sense of the possibilities of present life in the Church when he observed that at Alphonsus' first taking up his curacy at Sant' Angelo a Segno, he found himself "already in Paradise", in *un Paradiso anticipato*.[17]

Alphonsus has made his own way, as he meditates on what is offered in the Eucharist, to that understanding of time as expressed in the later books of Augustine's *Confessions*. While others may let their hearts turn this way and that between the motions of things past and to come, Alphonsus catches with Augustine at the fineness of "that ever fixed eternity" which is "all at once present". It became a matter of philosophic devotion for Augustine to ask lengthy questions about where the past and the future are, and to worry it out that such a language for times has meaning only in the present. Alphonsus is not troubled about such things. It is his experience in the liturgy that temporal categories simply fall away. The suffering Christ, present in the Eucharist, opens the gates of perception, and Christians may go in to eternal life.

Alphonsus is a Christian of his times and circumstances. He is, as Frederick Jones makes delightfully plain in his recent biography, "The Saint of Bourbon Naples". There must therefore be occasions, in the early *Maxims of Eternity*, 1728, and the late *Theological and Moral Dissertation pertaining to Eternal Life*, 1776, and between, when Alphonsus recognizes the conventional usage of Bourbon Neapolitans and others, and takes "eternal" to describe a future life with the Lord after death. But Alphonsus is not a merely representative Christian of those times and circumstances. Certainly not in the most personally imagined and felt and thought passages of his writing. While he does not disregard the conventional usage, he is consistently shifting attention from an enjoyment of future happiness to a start of eternal happiness now. There is, perhaps, no disputing about these things, but it seems to me that even in those early *Maxims of Eternity*, in which he is making use of material from a common stock of contemporary devotion, Alphonsus was, most delicately, making personal modifications to the tone of this material. Though he does repeat the sort of thing that Leonard of Port Maurice says in his *Holy Manual*, about "the two eternities" of a future heaven and a future hell, and though he does anticipate what the imaginative Gennaro Sarnelli says in *The Way to Paradise*, 1738, about the threat of being sent to "an eternal hell" after death, he positions such things so that they have rather different emphases. He is surely intending to put himself at a little distance from the conventional futurist usage when, by a very neat reversal of every reader's every expectation, he brings the gospel language of eschatological judgement straight into this present: "The man who sins is saying to God, if not in words then at least in effect, 'Depart from me'."[18] The sinner is determining a present hell for himself.

This is a characteristic turn in Alphonsus' explanations of what is happening in our lives. He does not care to leave things in past or future tenses. In those 1773 reflections *On the Passion*, he resolves all the difficulties of past and future in a present appeal to the Redeemer: "I have well known" that by sinning "I would condemn myself" to live far from the Lord in hell, but "I turn to say, 'Thy blood is my hope'." Eternity starts now. To be a sinner now is to be in hell now. And we can have now a starting share in the happiness of the blessed. "So that he who often rejoices in the joy of God begins in this life to do that which he hopes to do in heaven."[19] It is only, perhaps, when he is tired or a little out of sorts, that Alphonsus slips into the futurist conventions of contemporary piety. It is when he is making a deliberate effort to recapture, for a moment of imitative verse-making, the old-fashioned conceits of Giambattista Marini (1569-1624), the Naples poet of yesteryear, that Alphonsus lets go his personal hold on what he has in the present and sighs towards the remote future: "O Paradise! O Paradise!" The great body of his theological work is distinguished by his consistent use of "eternal" and "Paradise" to denote the quality of life in the presence of the Lord.

When we say "It seemed eternity", or "I'll be eternally grateful", the expressions have the quantitative sense of "endless" or even merely "a very long time". On occasion, even the theologian who really knows better may lapse into uses of "eternity" in this temporal sense. "Naturally", as Alphonsus acknowledges in his *Brief Dissertation*, 1756, against the errors of modern unbelievers, "the word eternal means endless." But he sees that the gracious quality of the divine "eternal" must be kept from confusion with that natural quantity of the human "endless".[20] There are, evidently, two senses of eternal, just as there are two ways of remembering. So when, in a translation of *Psalm 111:6*, it is suggested that "the just shall be in eternal memory", Alphonsus is careful to make the necessary distinction. Since this is a reference to human fame, the psalmist must mean that "the just shall live 'endlessly' in human memory". The translation must be altered accordingly. Contrariwise, reading in *Psalm 54:20* that the wicked will be humbled by God "who is before all ages", Alphonsus is quick to take steps to separate the divine from all talk of times. He proposes the better translation of "who is eternal". He was always on the lookout for instances of this confusion of "eternal" with "endless". Putting together that *Brief Dissertation*, he had judged it to be important for his contemporaries that someone should deal with those fashionable materialists who, taking it for granted that their world was endless, were asserting that it was also eternal, giving the word the merely temporal sense of "having no beginning". Ten years later, in *The Truth of the Faith,* 1767, Alphonsus had felt it necessary to return to these impertinent challengers of "the common belief" of mankind and to put them right about both the proper use of "eternal" and the proper reverence towards the Creator.[21] Perhaps such impertinence should be expected in such philosophic persons. But it was peculiarly distressing that the Catholic apologist, Giovanni Vincente Patuzzi (1709-1769), should suggest, in his *Study of Probabilism,* 1764, that even if there were no formally promulgated law to regulate some specific instance of human conduct, there would always be a "natural law" to apply to the case, and that this law was "virtually" promulgated by God "from eternity". Alphonsus moved with some speed to point out that, leaving aside this "virtually", there is a most improper use of language here, and a most slip-shod management of idea. "I assert" and "I will prove" that such a natural law could have been promulgated only on the creation of the natural world. It must, therefore, be a temporal law, not to be confused with anything "eternal". Patuzzi re-wrote his argument for his *Theological Observations,* 1765, but his re-formulation showed that he, like those all over Europe who were trading in "everlasting" and "from eternity" and "for ever and ever", had missed the point. Not until F.D. Maurice (1805-1872), in a controversy with the cleverer, more philosophic, H.L. Mansel (1820-1871), about "eternal punishment", was there any evidence of a theologian's taking anything like Alphonsus' care for the peculiar wonder of divine presence expressible in the language of "eternal".

Even in our domestic use, "I'll be eternally grateful" has, of course, some qualitative intensity. We are suggesting that we are now as grateful as we can be. But these are not matters which can be fitted easily into a paragraph of a popular meditation manual. That Alphonsus brings them forward so regularly in his ascetical writing is an indication of the theological impulse which shapes his pastoral care. It is noticeable that where the longer text of *The Way to Paradise* parallels the *Maxims of Eternity,* Gennaro Sarnelli has omitted everything that Alphonsus says about "this great thought of eternity". Perhaps Sarnelli was simply acknowledging that most of us find thought rather tiring, and the great thought of eternity more tiring than most. Alphonsus knew as well as Sarnelli how easily the temper of his ordinary reader might be dulled by theological disputation. In *Prayer, the Great Means of Salvation*, he ends one section about efficacious grace with a nod towards any readers who "might wish that I had given more space to the distinct examination of a question so much controverted". They might be eager to learn more about the different Schools' accounts of "physical premotion", "congruous grace", "concomitant grace", and the two sorts of "delectation", but these had not been his chief concern in this little book. He was, he says, simply recommending the use of prayer as the most powerful and necessary means of grace. But, while he avoided the jargon of the Schools even here, whenever he came to "this great thought of eternity", the precision of what he says makes it clear that Alphonsus reckoned every Christian to be called to think the great thought and to be quite capable of appreciating the difference of the experience of the eternal from all other experiencing.

We experience the eternal now, but we have to react to this experience of what is time-free under the conditions of our time-bound existence. He who rejoices in the joy of God now is doing "what he hopes to do" through the eternity of heaven, but that very hoping is a recognition of the conditions of our present enjoyment: "That hope is accompanied by fear". As well as a presence which is eternal, there may be an absence equally eternal. We may, "at any time", fail.[22] We may "put up the barriers of sin against grace". We may depart from Christ. Our happiness now is distinguished, in Alphonsus' 1773 *Pious Reflections*, from the Paradise of the saints by reference to the real possibility of our losing this share in joy. We should not presume on our enjoying eternal happiness nor on our escaping eternal horror. This possibility is manifest both on the Lord's saying "Come, ye blessed" and on the sinner's saying "Depart from me". Those who make their meditation on these matters with Alphonsus will learn, assuredly, that the pain of hell is as properly-termed "eternal" as is the happiness of heaven, not because either starts at death and goes on for ever, but because hell is the deprivation of that presence of the Lord which gives heaven its quality. Hell is the absence of all that makes human life worth living. "Separated from him and incapable of loving him; this would be the hell of our hell." And those who make their meditation with Alphonsus in the consciousness of such a hell, will learn, too, where they may receive the gracious prompting to love him now. "You tell me that sometimes you believe that you are lost", he wrote in 1782 to a despairing cousin, "Let us encourage one another, for I am passing

24

through the same trial."[23] Alphonsus knows how to encourage this devout soul. He knows how he must make his own poor meditations. "Let us, therefore, cling to the cross, and try always to keep our eyes fixed on our dying Saviour."

This is the sight that most moved Paul to love him, and the sight he encountered in the Corinthian eucharist. This liturgy opens upon eternal happiness. And if we find it too difficult to express the great thought of the eternal in words then we may do so in effect at the liturgical action. We are, Alphonsus wrote to Pope Clement XIV, in our celebrating, "companions of the angels who celebrate the glory of the Saviour in heaven".[24] We are, in this celebrating, companions, too, of the whole human race. We may, Alphonsus says in his *Rubrics of the Mass*, at this remembering, bring with us to the celebration we share with the angels of heaven not only the living saints but also "the pagans, the heretics, and the unbelievers".[25] We may bring with us not only the dead saints but those in Purgatory. Still keeping the memory of the death of the Lord, we may "hear Mass for them" and "recommend them to God by the merits of the Passion of Jesus Christ". We may bring with us, also, those who are shifting beyond the present hope: "It is a very charitable act to recommend at the same time those who are at the point of death". That way, we will come ourselves to a clearer understanding of this shareable eternity.

A Christian's language

The experience of the eternal enjoyed by those who share the eucharistic liturgy is to be communicated to all other women and men. Alphonsus received the vocation to speak of these things. He had to find words. He listened for a theological language which should express his distrust of every suggestion that this sharing in eternal presence could be described in the terms of what is "new" or what is "old" in the world.

He can find no use for the vocabulary of those "modern" and "innovative" persons who would sell us a "contemporary" lampshade or cook us "today's special" breakfast. He does not resort to that salesman's talk when he is describing anything of which he approves or would have others approve. He knows, of course, that there is scriptural warrant for talk of God's making all things new. But he is convinced that the scriptural "new" is not the merely temporal "new" of our ordinary usage. He stops only for a moment in his 1773 reflections *On the Passion* to explain that the *Hebrews* declaration of Christ's making "a new and living way" for us refers to "a new way" precisely because it is the way to Paradise.[26] "New" has here, and elsewhere in the scriptural witness to the work of our redemption, a qualitative sense beyond its usual temporal sense and this qualitative sense derives from its association in the minds of the scriptural authors with that eternal wonder revealed to them as "Paradise". So he has to stop only for another moment to explain again, in his *Pious Reflections*, as the joyful angels and saints are singing in Paradise "a new canticle" to the Lord, that the delights of Paradise, including this singing, "seem ever new, as though they were being enjoyed for the first time" by the blessed, but they are, indeed, eternal delights. What is "new" in Paradise is "always the same". Scripture gives him the pattern for the elucidation of Tradition. So, admitting to Cardinal Giuseppe Spinelli (1691-1754), the Archbishop of Naples, that it must surprise a good Christian, their King Charles, say, to hear that the Holy See is being asked in 1748 to approve a "new" Institute, Alphonsus assures him that acceptance of the Redemptorist proposal would not really be acceptance of anything new. Eternal God is always raising up such institutes to maintain regular observance in the unchanging Church. What seems "new" is to be appreciated, again, as "always the same".

There are, on the other hand, enterprises that are merely temporally new. These have nothing to do with the eternal Paradise. *The Truth of Faith* is directed against "all those pestilential modern books" by which "the opinion of the innovators" is being spread through Europe.[27] Contrariwise, recommending the *Mystical Directory* of Giambattista Scaramelli (1688-1752), Alphonsus is quick to distinguish the book as "modern, but learned and pious".[28] New projects were not, generally, either. There were, for example, as Alphonsus observes in his *Psalms and Canticles*, some "modern commentators" who were suggesting that the literal sense of Psalm 2, "The princes met together against the Lord", refers not to Christ but to King David. This is "a novel opinion", "prevailing among Protestants", and "worthy of our condemnation". There was, too, an eighteenth century modernism within the Church. Whatever surprised Alphonsus about the Abbate Rolli's objections to the bestowing of "Tower of David" and "House of Gold" as titles in the litany of the Blessed Virgin, it cannot have surprised him that the objections should have been put forward as a "New Project" in the Church.[29] It is, however, entirely characteristic that Alphonsus should identify, among all those "modern unbelievers" outside the Catholic community and proponents of "the new theology" within, those French and Netherland Jansenists for his particular condemnation. They have, in their "pernicious system", been proposing a new and restrictive relation of the Passion of the open-armed Christ to those who now come to the Eucharist. They have been denying the will of the Lord that all of us should share in his Paradise. They have set their "new" notions against that which is "ever new".

Those who run after novelties, confidently announcing that the future will be unlike the present, are likely to get the future wrong. This is the ordinary case with pagans, false religionists, and heretics. Alphonsus does not need much room to demonstrate this unhappy fact in his *Evidence of the Faith*. Not one of the famous prophecies of Apollonius of Tyana was fulfilled. Luther announced that the world would end in 1583, but it didn't. No one thinks much about either prophets or prophecies now. Those who look to some new thing in the future must, inevitably, come themselves to seem very old-fashioned. Alphonsus is particularly happy to demonstrate that John Chrysostom, Augustine himself, and Aquinas, had already dealt with the Propositions of Jansen before he had made them. Not everyone of these pagans, false religionists, and heretics will come to look as foolish, perhaps, as Jansen and the Jansenists, but, in time, all their notions will fall into a like disuse. They will all have their mere history of beginning, middle, and end. Alphonsus' *History of the Heresies*, 1772, is replete with exemplars of this temporal sequence. He talks consistently of "starting up", "process", and "decay", of "beginning", "course", and "dissipation", of "birth", "progress", and "collapse". This sequence is "according to the temporal order of things". The *True Bride* evidences his knowing that others, most famously the Jesuit, Bernardino Rossignoli (1547-1613), in his *On the Rule of Christian Perfection*, 1600, had staged the Christian life as "beginning", "proficiency", and "perfection",[30] but he could never think this a helpful way of declaring the actual wonder of life in the Church.

Alphonsus has no greater sympathy with those who do theology in a language of the past, and express their ecclesiastical confidence by an articulation of some long recessive line of historical precedent. "Men are by nature inclined to want to hand on to posterity a memory of themselves and of their ancestors."[31] Alphonsus had met with clergy who were always talking of their coats of arms and their old family honours. It is not their memory or the memory of their noble ancestry which is celebrated in the shared liturgy. There must be nothing of that sort in his Congregation. "Let everyone be on his guard not even to mention the word 'honour'."[32] But, in thus putting to one side the boasted crest and shield and motto of those who lay claim to an endless authority in the arrangements of civil and ecclesiastical society, Alphonsus has to make plain what he means when he uses the language of "tradition".

What, by nature, women and men call "our tradition" is not, he knows, at all like that realization, by grace of "Tradition" in the Church. When Alphonsus is talking of an inherited tradition, he is very aware of how dead a weight such tradition may heap upon its inheritors. How effective a distraction it may be when there is some question to be decided about the present life of the community. He has, indeed, taken our general enthusiasm for receiving legacies to be an indicator of the general failure of our human memory. The benefactor is forgotten as we busy ourselves with the inheritance.[33] There is nothing of this sort in his talk of Tradition and the memory of the Church. Alphonsus refers Tradition not to the past as past but to the past as present. The ecclesial Tradition is to be recognized as the handing-on of the liturgical community. "I received from the Lord what I also delivered to you." What the Corinthians receive is the living memory of the night of the Lord's death. The Tradition is revealed to be that time-released life which present Christians enjoy in the company of Christians of the temporal past and future as they celebrate that memory. Such a Tradition could never in its liveliness be confused with a time-bound, merely old-fashioned, way of doing things.[34]

Alphonsus sees clearly enough that it is the persecutors who are traditional. Those "princes" of Psalm 2, meeting together to plot against Christ, stand at the beginning of a temporal line whose middle is occupied by "Herod and Pilate and the chief priests of the Jews", and whose end is exampled by "all the emperors and all the kings of the gentiles who have persecuted the Church of Jesus Christ". With the tradition of persecution we may take a tradition of heresy. They very often go together. There is an historical handing-on of malice,

Alphonsus notes, as the Jews crucify Jesus, the Romans kill Christians in the arena, and the contemporary Cartesian Modernists perpetrate "their innumerable crimes" against poor deceivable people. But the heretics can, sometimes, keep their tradition going without recourse to the persecutors. From Lucidus at the Council of Lyons in 490, through Gotheschalcus at Quercy in 853 and Michel Baius at the Sorbonne in 1560, there is, as Alphonsus describes it at length in both the 1759 *Prayer, the Great Means of Salvation* and the 1772 *History of the Heresies,* a line of tradition, a handing-on of false doctrine, which reaches its horrid end in Jansen and the five Propositions condemned by Pope Innocent X in 1653. Alphonsus can set about writing that *History of the Heresies* with some enthusiasm, the book's getting bigger and bigger as he revises his list of contents. But he never attempted to write a parallel history of the Church. The Church has no history.

It is quite evident, however, that the Church does have historians. Alphonsus could take down from his own shelves the large twelve volume folio edition of the *Ecclesiastical Annals,* 1588-1607, of the Oratorian Cardinal, Cesare Baronio (1538-1607), and the even fatter six volumes, packed with documents by the indefatigable Giovanni Domenico Mansi (1692-1769), of the *Acts of the Sacred Councils,* 1748-1752. Alphonsus was properly congratulatory when Mansi became Archbishop of Lucca in 1765, but perhaps he had acquired Mansi's rather haphazardly arranged and badly edited *Acts* from some feeling of the comradeship of moralists. He certainly thought the *Epitome* which Mansi had made of the writings of the great canonist, Pope Benedict XIV, truly "a beautiful book". He had Remondini bind it into the fourth edition of his own *Moral Theology,* 1761, persuading him, not without difficulty, that it would give "an extra value" to the work. But the annalist's method of describing the life of the Church, adopted by Baronio and supported by the apparatus of Mansi, came close to putting the Church into the alien temporal order of beginning, middle, and end. Alphonsus had a theological preference for the more anecdotal version of ecclesiastical experience. He took down more often the third edition, Venice, 1703, of the four volume folio *Library of Moral Preaching* of Giuseppe Mansi, which is a rich source of improving stories, and he had a reprint of his *Studious Cleric,* 1673, and perhaps the Latin edition of his *Holy Storehouse,* 1685. He delighted in these collections himself and recommended them to others. "Mansi should be available in each of our houses." His enthusiasm for the story collections of this Oratorian anecdotalist betrayed Alphonsus into at least one rash judgement: "I would much rather", he told a superior of a Redemptorist house who had sent a Brother to buy Augustine's sermons, "that you had spent the money on a set of Mansi."

Alphonsus' sense of the proper occupation of the historian becomes apparent to the reader as Alphonsus offers, in paragraph after paragraph, the results of his scouting for both quick-fire anecdotes and quite long-winded narratives in the community records of Benedictine Abbeys, the Dominican *Diary*, the *Great Introduction* to the holy members of the Cistercian Order, and the more scholarly hagiography of the Jesuit Bollandists which was suspended on their suppression in 1773. These collections, and a clutch of other *Acts* of patron saints and venerable predecessors, martyrologies, equally with the bed-time stories of aunts, and popular "lives of the saints" read in the parlour and remembered round the farm hearth, constituted for Alphonsus the properly achronological witness to the vitality of Tradition in the Church.[35] He read them himself. "It is related in the *Lives of the Fathers* ..." "We read of a large community of nuns who never tasted fruit or wine..." "We read", again, of "this lady in Vienna" who was so disappointed at the cancellation of a ball that she joined the Carmelites. "For many years", he wrote to Pope Clement XIII, "I have admired the great servant of God, Leonard of Port Maurice," but now, in 1762, "I have been reading his wonderful *Life*", and feel "impelled to beg your Holiness to proceed with his beatification". Alphonsus feels that the *Life* has shown him the venerable man's true place in the wider community. His beatification "will prove to be of great consolation and profit to the whole Christian world" and especially "to all those provinces where the Servant of God was preaching the divine word". That sense of the Christian world is the effect that a Christian history should have in the mind of the reader. Alphonsus uses such material through all his ascetical and dogmatic writings, through all his sermons and missioner exhortations, to assist him in the reconstruction among the deprived people of his provincial congregations of an appreciation of their enlarging Christian culture. He wrote such lives himself. The *Notes* on the life of the Redemptorist lay-brother, Vito Curzio, who died in 1749, which were designed to be read with his other *Notes on the Life of Father Gennaro Sarnelli*, 1752, and *The Life and Death of the Servant of God, Teresa Maria Liguori*, 1761, and *Notes on the Life of the Reverend Father Cafaro*, 1767, and the great collection of the *Victories of the Martyrs*, 1776. These lives, as he re-tells them, prompt the reader and the hearer, and, indeed, the re-teller himself, to enjoy the happy sense of belonging in a remembering Church whose memory is not like that made available to the world's researchers and whose records are not like those put together by the world's annalists.

If the researcher and the annalist have their use in the Church, it is that they can be turned on the researchers and annalists of the world. Baronio can be turned on the historians of the "enlightenment", on Edward Gibbon (1737-1794), for example. He can be brought forward to defend the reputation of the Neapolitans' own great patron. Alphonsus' narrative of the life and martyrdom of St Januarius begins with a nice antithesis, perfectly expressive of his characteristic evaluations. "There are no historical records" of the first years of our saint, but "it is certain" that his parents were devout Christians. He sustains this antithesis of unimportant temporal fact and matters of continuing significance through the length of his narrative. Thus he does not worry who was Pope "at that time", it could have been Caius, or then again, Marcellinus, what matters is that there was a Pope, as there always is, a diocese of Benevento, as there is, and that its bishop was converting pagans and encouraging the faithful, as bishops do. This antithesis propels the narrative along at a fine pace. The climax of the story, as Alphonsus manages it, is not the decapitation of the saint, which is, consistently, roughly dated as "towards the close of the third century" and more exactly and pleasantly fixed as occurring on 19th September, the day when the Church makes the liturgical commemoration of the martyrdom. The decapitation is, of course, recorded in the *Acta* of the saint, but it is more important to Alphonsus that "the Offices of Puzzuoli" and "the tradition of Nola" should give accounts of these events their liturgical warrant. This is the way the Church remembers. The climax of the story, as Alphonsus intends his reader to read it, occurs at the announcement of the miracles wrought by St Januarius from that time to this, and especially "the most stupendous miracle" of the liquefying of the blessed martyr's blood in the two vials kept in the cathedral at Naples. This happens now.[36]

It is against this paradigmatic miracle of the liquefying blood that enlightened historians, even Catholic historians, like Sébastien Tillemont (1637-1698), in his *Notes towards a Church History*, 1693, and Adrien Baillet (1649-1706), in his *Lives of the Saints*, 1701, have raised objections along with "some other modern authors". They have done so with some pretence of pastoral, ecumenical, purpose. "They say that the account of these miracles only makes heretics laugh at the too great credulity of the Catholics, and for this reason they refuse to be united to our Church." Alphonsus knows, however, that it is, rather, "precisely because they do not wish to unite to our Church, and to submit to her, that they refuse to believe in the miracles". So he comes to state the true case of the matter against such persons. "Allow me to make here a painful reflection. The present age is called 'the age of light' because it has a better taste and a more correct judgement of things." It has not justified its claim to better taste and more correct judgement. Alphonsus takes his faithful stand on the persistent character of the gospel. "The Christian faith was propagated and maintained by means of miracles" at all times, "just as Jesus Christ and the Apostles propagated it." He has no need to go into the historical evidences of this. "They know." He will simply say that "miracles wrought, more or less frequently, by God through his servants, have never been lacking in our Church". Things are just the same now.

Then Alphonsus recollects that he is conducting this little aside in the *Victories of the Martyrs*, 1775, not so much to defend St Januarius, who evidently requires no defending, but to put these men of taste out of countenance. "Let us return to our subject." And he gives a final flick in their direction. Even modern scholarship fails the modern sceptic. Professor Xavier Rossi had recently written a learned dissertation proving that the manuscript on which these enlightened historians were relying dated only from the sixteenth century. And Alphonsus is not unpleased to note that the guardians of taste have trusted a chronicler who, on Rossi's description, was clearly "an ignorant person" who committed "many faults in Latin grammar". Better that they had trusted Baronio, who had, at least, worked from better versions of the *Acts* of the miracle-working saint.

Even the most distinguished ecclesiastical historians, even Baronio, seemed to Alphonsus to be disappointingly content with the mere logging of people, events, places, as over and done. "Bare-footed Friars were singing Vespers in the temple of Jupiter", but still the ecclesiastical historians were reaching for a command of the language of the secular historian which, as Gibbon showed in 1776, was fit only for talk of "decline" and "fall". If one of the Congregation's preachers must refer to the past, Alphonsus warned in the 1760 *Brief Instruction for the*

Exercises of the Mission, he should content himself with setting out "the facts of Scripture" in short form; "as for other historical facts" and all that apparatus of "supporting reference to the author, the time, and the place", well, he told his Redemptorists, "these should be rarely supplied". He himself, certainly, supplied them very rarely. Only once, in the *True Bride of Jesus Christ*, is found anything of that sort. The exception occurs when he refers to a gruesome story of a self-disfiguring Abbess told by St Antoninus "as having happened in 1291, in Palestine, in a convent of the Poor Clares". It is apparent that Alphonsus feels uncomfortable with such drastic mutilations. The Abbess who cut off her nose to spite her face and make herself unattractive to marauding brigands is to be put at a safe distance from the congregations of nuns to whom he is writing. She is placed very firmly in an historical tradition and is thereby removed to the very fringe of the ecclesial Tradition: "It would not be lawful for others to imitate this heroic conduct".[37]

It would be lawful, and laudable, for them to imitate the conduct of those Redemptorists whose lives he remembered in his *Notes*. These were certainly not composed according to any temporal order observed by historians. In the first of the *notes* that Alphonsus made to keep the memory of the lay Brother, Vito Curzio, suddenly, between notices of the young, hot-headed, Curzio's exaggerated sense of his own honour and his dreaming of climbing a steep mountain with Redemptorist guides, Alphonsus puts in a sentence about the death of Cesare Sportelli. "His tomb was opened four months after his death, when it was found that his body was quite flexible, and blood issued from an incision that was made in his foot." But if these *Notes* do not fit the order of the historian, they exactly fit the order of the theologian. In the midst of nicely realistic suggestions of the actualities of life in the community, of how bad a cook Curzio was and of his muttering to himself at being given too much to do, we are confronted in the third *note* with successive sentences telling us that Curzio "could not help bursting into tears" while making his meditation upon the Passion of Christ, and that, after Holy Communion, "his tears and sighs also lasted a good while". Alphonsus puts Gennaro Sarnelli into the same theological pattern. He, too, in successive sentences, is said to have been "specially devout towards the Passion of Jesus Christ" and to have had "no less great devotion to the holy sacrifice of the Mass". And in these Sarnelli *Notes* the unseen dimensions of such devotion are made more apparent than had seemed possible within the frame of the Curzio remembrances. After some lively recollections of mice jumping up and down on Sarnelli's tattered bed-cover and of his regularly making up small packets of tobacco for poor men, a demon steps into the room of the dying priest to mislead him with fulsome praises of such virtue. Sarnelli is seen to be struggling himself to get out of the limiting conditions of temporal experience: "When he was on the point of death, he said to Canon Sersale, 'Canon, I wish to go on preaching until the Judgement Day'." But this was, however right-feeling and right-thinking, mere wishing. The *Notes* on Paolo Cafaro take things further, showing just how these limits may be transcended by the Christian.

By the time Alphonsus was writing his *Notes* on Cafaro, in 1767, he had become remarkably skilful in making a pen portrait, and in making the pen portrait do his theological work. At the start, the reader is thrown into the ecclesial context of Cafaro's existence. We are told in what diocese he was born before we are told what town or the names of his parents. And the first thing we learn about Cafaro's father is that he belonged to a sodality which sustained him in mental prayer, "and he also taught his family how to practise it". There is evidently, an apologetic motive for all this. And for Alphonsus then showing just what God can make of Cafaro who seems at first to have something of the male supremacist and the sneak about him. He, too, is to be set in Alphonsus' characteristic pattern. Once he has become a member of the Redemptorist community, he is shown to have "great devotion towards the Passion of Jesus Christ", and once he has mounted into the pulpit and is "preaching on the love of Jesus Christ" in the presence of the Blessed Sacrament, he is caught into an ecstasy. By this time, Alphonsus has found his way of bringing to clearest expression that eternity upon which such devotion is opening. Cafaro becomes an effective sign of the eternal for the community. He recalls that "One of our Fathers, who was a man of great virtue and discernment, said that if he had to depict Father Paolo , he would represent him on a marble pillar with this inscription: *Semper idem* — Always the same."

Alphonsus has learned, too, how to bring the things of eternity home to his reader. He can use these *Notes* now to show how all such *Notes* should be read. These are not to be mistaken for idle anecdotes. These are not concerned with what is gone and dead. Paolo Cafaro knows this. "When the servant of God read the *Lives* of the saints that gave themselves up wholly to God, he shed tears of joy." We may know it, too. Across the barriers of time, we may identify with Cafaro, make the same response to *Lives* and life as he. Be always the same with him. Alphonsus has been looking for a language which shall place what may seem "the historical facts" of the Church into their true historical context. He has discovered the language of identity.

Redeeming the time

If the activities of the princes and Herod and the emperors, or of the priests and the Roman soldiery and the Cartesian philosophers, have quite properly to be set out, like all other historical facts, in a temporal sequence, the facts of the Church resist the historian's listing devices. The facts of the Church are not "historical" facts.

Alphonsus' *Victories of the Martyrs* may seem at first read to be a history of those who were put to death by the emperor Diocletian, followed by a history of those who were put to death in Japan in the late sixteenth and early seventeenth centuries. But Alphonsus is making, in the careful design of the book, an effort to avoid the categories of the historian. "It is not our intention", he says in one of those explanatory prefaces which anyone who wishes to know Alphonsus' mind should not skip, "to give, in this work, a history of all the martyrs who have glorified the Church, but, without subjecting ourselves to any order of time or of persons, simply to relate the victories of some saints". In Alphonsus' design, the book proves to be a diptych which, at each critical moment of the narrative, declares the Church of the Roman Empire to be the Church of Japan. Christians in Rome and Nagasaki offer the same estimate of human experience to Caesar and Mikado. They are members of the same eucharistic community. They enjoy the same life with Christ. They suffer the same martyrdom. St Laurence was placed on a red-hot grid-iron, under which a slow fire burned, and he, perceiving that one side was completely roasted said "Turn me, this side is done". Simon Keisaiemon boldly stretched himself upon the grate of burning coals, "and even turned himself now upon one side, now upon the other". Thomas Soxin was stretched on a grid-iron and "they turned his body until it was entirely roasted". And the same signs follow upon their martyrdoms. After the beheading of St. Theodotus, his body was "surrounded with a light so supernaturally resplendent that none dared approach it". It was therefore left to be guarded by soldiers. After the beheading of Simon Taquenda, the soldiers who guarded his body testified to having seen a great light, descending from heaven, and resting above the house of the martyr.[38] The reality of the Church, which is always the same but which we do not always recognize, is manifest at such gracious moments. It is on this basis of identity that, towards the end of the book, Alphonsus deals with a difficulty which may occur to those who are used to putting their trust in history. The experience of the Church in Japan may look for a moment uncomfortably like the sort of process which is described by historians, having its beginning, middle, and end. "Our European priests who undertook to evangelize Japan were at first very successful; but in the year 1586 God made known by several signs the approach of a long and bloody persecution", and now, "to sum up", we know that "the mission of Japan lasted only eighty-four years since St Francis Xavier opened it in 1549", and "it ceased about the year 1633". A sympathetic reader will be at once alerted by the oddity of Alphonsus' alleging so many dates. He is up to something more than the repetition of "what the best historians say". The characteristic antithesis is about to be brought into play. "It is certain" that we and peoples everywhere belong in one community with those Japanese martyrs and that they join us at the commemoration of the living in prayers for the excommunicated, the heretics, and the infidels. "They will not cease to intercede for their countrymen."[39] There is no call to talk of temporal endings. Not in the case of Japan any more than there was in the case of Rome.

In *The Truth of the Faith*, Alphonsus makes the more complicated identification of those Japanese martyrs with both "the martyrs of antiquity" and "our Catholics in England" during the reign of Elizabeth I. Each of these witnesses was made the same offer of freedom by the persecutor and each returned the same faithful answer.[40] He manages this complex of persons and places and dates with practised skill. He has learnt over a long career as a writer how to rid his text of the historian's apparatus in order to make his theological point. Alphonsus' earlier writings show as keen a sense of this identity of Christian life in divers times and places. They show, too, in the sequence of those *Notes* for the remembrance of the Redemptorists, for example, how very hard he had worked to construct the truly communicative language for his theological insights. Even after the experiments of the Curzio and Sarnelli *Notes*, he had not, in 1760, been quite able to bring off his projected identification, in the *True Bride of Jesus Christ*, of the endurance of the three Levantine women, Faith, Hope and Charity, tortured in the reign of Antiochus, and the endurance of the Japanese Maxentia, on her professing Christian faith, hope and charity, under the persecution of Taidono. But whether he managed things elegantly or clumsily, it was Alphonsus' consistent theme that these different Christians offer, in their different ways, the same witness to the Lord who is eternally present to them and to us in the same way, *sempre uniforme*, "always the same".

In this present

To be always the same is, as historians and heretics know, not the natural state of things. Historians spend their time and energy establishing the origin, development, and collapse of things. Heretics insist on getting back to primitive observance or calculating the date of the end of the world. And indeed, we are, by nature, creatures of time as the historians and heretics keep saying. By nature, we are conceived, we mature, we disintegrate. By nature, all our works must collapse, all our powers wither. By nature, we trudge towards death. That we are presently released from the natural confines of time is a gracious mystery.

Alphonsus saw very well that time was once the determining context of experience, and history its proper record. He accepted the chronology of Archbishop James Ussher (1581-1656), in his *Annals of the Old Testament*, 1650, and 1659, and the confident assertion there that "4000 years passed after the transgression of Adam" before the event of the Redeemer.[41] Alphonsus was prepared to look into the relation of events in Ussher's chronology to what is alleged in "the false annals" of the reign of Yaco in China and "the invented memories" of the Egyptians. He consulted historians about such things, because events fell naturally, in that long time before Christ, into the past tense: "Plato said...", "the Jews solemnized", "Alexander dressed up as...", "Holy Job was struck by wonder", and "Lucretius killed himself at the age of forty-four years". The most significant and interesting of the women and men of the past quite understood their limiting, historical condition. Alphonsus could talk easily of the Sibyl of Cumae, of Virgil looking forward to the birth of a lovely boy, of Confucius, whose words he had been reading in Prospero Intorcetta's anthology, *The Chinese Wisdom*, 1662, waiting for the reign of the Holy One. And he knew that Isaiah, Jeremiah, and Job, had been precisely reported as propelling their words forward as they themselves sank back into the past. Their words were prophetic. They were reaching and still reach into the present of Jesus. It is, indeed, only now that their words are clearly appreciable as what they always are. These are Jesus' words. Alphonsus prefaces citations of these old scriptural writers by "Jesus Christ says..." and "Jesus Christ continues to say...", placing the words which we usually, naturally, in our historical way, fix in the past, into their true context. He places them in the present. Whatever Plato said or the Jews solemnized in the past, the prophets witness, as they declare words that belong to Christ, to what is "always the same". We quite misunderstand them, if we do not interpret their words and their lives as signals of Christ for us. So the manna of the Exodus journeyers only finds its proper meaning in the Eucharist of the Corinthian community. So "the work" of the Lord in the Canticle of Habakkuk, which once referred to the liberating of the Jews from their Babylonian captivity, is "better understood in a figurative sense" having its clear application to "the work of our redemption". So the brazen serpent of Hezekiah is "an express figure" of the cross of Jesus. And the furnitures of the Jerusalem Temple are "signs and figures of the promised redemption". And "Rebecca was a figure of Mary", pointing towards her distributing the charity of Christ not only to the just, of whom Abraham's servant is a figure, but to sinners "who are signified by the camels". The stories of those women and men and animals come into meaning only as they are being read now. How beautifully St Albert the Great applies to Mary's intercedings for us the story of Esther, "who was herself a great type of our Queen". Such a reading of these Old Testament signs is most powerfully encouraged by the exegetical example of *Hebrews*. In his 1773 meditations on the Passion, the wondrous assurance at *Hebrews* 5:9 that 'He became the cause of eternal life' enables Alphonsus to appreciate just what was happening when the Hebrew priest took the blood of calves and goats with water and with scarlet wool, *Hebrews* 9:19, for "as wool is by nature white and becomes red by being dyed" so the innocent Jesus appeared all red upon the cross. What was happening when the High Priest entered the Holy of Holies, *Hebrews*, 9:11, for Jesus opens the doors of eternity for us. What was happening when the blood was sprinkled on the unclean people, *Hebrews* 9:19, for, as St Maria Maddalena de Pazzi was divinely instructed, the blood of Jesus "does not call for vengeance like the blood of Abel, but for mercy only".[42] There is in this epistle a paradigm for all our reading of the biblical narratives. The meaning of what occurred "before the work of our redemption was accomplished" is perfected, *"consummatus" Hebrews* 5:9, in Jesus' exercise now of "an eternal priesthood", *Hebrews* 7:4. Alphonsus responds in his scriptural exegesis as everywhere in his work to what is for him the irresistible invitation to employ present tense verbs where others would opt naturally for historic tenses.[43]

For the prophets, Jesus will be in the future, for the heretics, Jesus was in the past, but for Alphonsus, Jesus is present. "Jesus Christ says." And Alphonsus is in his presence. At the *Ecce Homo* of Pilate, Alphonsus is among the crowd below the governor's balcony. "I see thee." On the hill of Calvary, Alphonsus is among the women and men of Jerusalem as they watch Jesus stretch himself out on the cross. It is in Alphonsus' present that Jesus is "leaning his weight now on his hands, now on his feet".[44] It is in this present that he sees Jesus dying. And it is in this present that the lively remembering in the Church of the Lord's death makes plain the eternal significance of what Alphonsus sees. It is this which most moves him to love Him.

Each Christian, giving thanks at the climactic celebration of the Eucharist, stands in the same time-free relation to Christ as each Christian at all other dates. The Christian of today is not further from Christ than the Christian of yesterday, of the thirteenth century, or the second century, or the very first. Not further from Christ than those who stood at the foot of the Cross. It is this mystery, effected at the Cross and manifest in the Eucharist, at which not one of the dead is forgotten, nor one of the living neither, that Alphonsus is most fit to declare.

A woman's place?

"Every human being wants to be happy", Alphonsus generalised fairly, adding, characteristically, "and to be happy always."[45] His considerations of eternal presence suggest a deep-down temperamental response to experience. He had looked for signs of that "always" in the offers of happiness made by the world and been staggered by the "eternally" of the Church. Coming from the celebration of the Eucharist, from the Forty Hours devotions, or his meditation before the Blessed Sacrament in the Tabernacle, and having to find the words for his sense of how things are with us, Alphonsus seizes on hints of what is "always the same" in our ecclesial life. On the identity of martyrdoms, on the re-statements of doctrine from Creed to Creed, on the Papacy. These become, as he clarifies his meaning, elements in an account of the inward eternal liveliness of the Church. Of course, he was as likely as the rest of us to be led by temperament into mistakes as well as into enhancing realizations of how things are. Alphonsus was temperamentally assured, for example, that *Mark*, written in Rome, must have been written originally in the Latin of that eternal city.[46] But he was led into rather fewer mistakes than many of us, and into more interesting appraisals of what is happening. He was enabled, by temperament, to say something about the teaching office of the Church, for example, which provides a helpful counter to what others, of a different temperament, say about an historical "development of doctrine". The interest of Alphonsus' enterprise resides in our being confronted by what an intelligent, sensitive, civilized, human being can manage within the confines of temperament. As it does on our being confronted by the theological work of any woman or man, or by a poem, a painting, or an opera. Such confrontations show us, if only for a while, the limitations of our own temperamental visions of the world. They prompt a just evaluation of our lesser talents and achievements, and, maybe, suggest, on our coming to know ourselves that little better, that we may do something more worthwhile in our turn.

We may, of course, as he repeats yet again his announcement of the eternal, think for a while that we are more realistic in our estimates of experience than he. We may judge that what is interesting about ourselves, and even about other people, is not what is merely the same but what is distinctive. We may think it a great thing to require that he make some greater recognition that the fire which burned St Laurence had its individual heat, that he felt an individual pain, that it was not the same fire which burned Simon Keisaiemon, nor the same pain that he suffered. That it was a different fire again which tormented Thomas Soxin. But if Alphonsus is insisting so repeatedly on the eternal significance of what St Laurence and Simon Keisaiemon and Thomas Soxin and we are experiencing in the Church, it is because he judges that we do not usually attend sufficiently to the shareable life, not that he has not noticed our individualities. There is nothing impersonal in Alphonsus' account of Thomas Soxin, the good old man who seemed invigorated by his arrest and imprisonment, or of Vito Curzio's shooting an unsatisfactory physician, or of Teresa Maria's fondling the bambino in the Christmas crib, or in Alphonsus' accounts of their meaningful deaths. He proves as interested in the value of an individual as any of us. It is precisely in his insistence on the manifestation of what is "always the same" through the Christian lives of the Roman martyr and the Japanese grandfather and his own Italian contemporaries that Alphonsus is declaring their individual value, and declaring the individual value of the members of his congregation. It is within the context of what is eternal that any individual has meaning. And only in that context. The women, at least, in his congregation, should recognize the truth of that.

Alphonsus was much distressed by the condition of working mothers on the farms in the Kingdom of Naples. The peasant's wife would have to clean the house, wash the clothes, cook, see to the children, and work in the fields. Civil authority not yet having thought of providing a creche for the children, Alphonsus did his unofficial best for them. On his retiring as bishop of Sant' Agata, one oppressed wife singled out Alphonsus' care for them as the outstanding episcopal virtue: "Whenever we went up in the hills, we'd leave the children at the palace, quite sure that Monsignore would give them something to eat".[47] He was distressed not only for working mothers. And not only for those on the farms. He had a good idea of what his own mother had had to endure, along with other wives of the petty nobility of the Kingdom. "The husband demands her attention; if his directions be neglected, or his commands be not immediately executed, he breaks out into complaints and reproaches." And there are the children who "if small, are a perpetual source of annoyance, either by their cries and screams, or by the endless variety of their wants", and, he went on, "if grown up, they are an occasion of still greater disquietude, fears and bitterness, by association with bad companions".[48] The true bride of Jesus Christ should remember all this as she went in to the eucharist. "For myself, I do not remember ever to have found among married women a single pious person who was content with her state of life."[49]

It is on account of their continual endurance of these awful lives, in patience and cheerfulness, that these mothers are to be recognized as having the value that is more usually reserved by pious authors for St Januarius and Simon Keisaiemon. In the usage of Alphonsus' contemporaries, "martyr" and "martyrdom" were almost always restricted to considerations of Christians who had died violent deaths at the hands of persecutors.[50] Alphonsus revives here, as at other of his recognitions of Christian living, the New Testament, patristic, and even mediaeval, use of "martyr". He refers "martyr" to a "witness", and "martyrdom" to the testimony given by a witness to the wonder of Christ. He had begun his revision of contemporary usage in 1750 in the *Glories of Mary*. There, Mary is presented as "a true martyr", as the Litany of Loreto's "Queen of Martyrs", and her martyrdom as "surpassing all others". The Tradition of the Church comes forward to make this affirmation, breaking all time barriers, converging on present reality. Richard of St Laurence points to Mary, "the martyr of martyrs", just as Isaiah points forward, saying as he turns towards Mary, "He will crown thee with a crown of tribulation". And with these come many others. The Tradition is again manifesting the identity of the Church's response in every age to the wonders of divine love. What Isaiah means, "that is to say, that suffering itself, which exceeded the suffering of all the other martyrs united, was the crown by which she was shown to be the Queen of martyrs", is meant by a great concourse of saints and theologians.[51] So "Jeremiah seems unable to find anyone with whom he can compare this Mother of Sorrows...", "Wherefore Cardinal Hugo says...", "Hence St Anselm asserts...", "St Bernardine goes so far as to say..." and, declaring again the singleness of earth and heaven in praise, St Agnes comes to tell St Bridget the same thing. Even Erasmus is brought forward from the edges of the Church to suggest that parents generally are more cruelly tormented by their children's sufferings than by their own. "This", Alphonsus comments, with a short glance at the world about him, "is not always true", but, "in the case of Mary, it evidently was so." Mary's martyrdom "consisted in her seeing and pitying her innocent and beloved Son suffer so greatly". From the moment the sword pierced her heart she endured a life-long witness to her Son. After this, whether she ate, or worked about the house, or however she occupied herself with the things that women have to do, her heart was always occupied with sadness and suffering.

This appreciation of an endurance of suffering, a continuity of witnessing to Christ, along with dying at the hands of an executioner, as each representing a true martyrdom informs Alphonsus' accounts of a diversity of Christians. In the first part of the *Victories of the Martyrs*, he proposes that his great favourite among theologians, John

Chrysostom, "should be styled a martyr", even though, Alphonsus has to allow, "this great saint did not actually die for the faith". And Brother Vito, too, was "as it were, a martyr", on account of his having been so obedient a Religious right up to his dying day. Alphonsus does not suppose that he is making a rhetorical flourish here. He has already alleged Aquinas' observation that "to have the glory of martyrdom it is sufficient to exercise obedience in its highest degree". He does not, in his description of the lives of married women, put any emphasis on the pains of childbirth that they endure, terrible though these may be, nor, in his account of their especial martyrdom, on "the danger of death which is always attendant on childbirth"; he identifies, rather, a martyrdom in their continuing to live Christian lives amidst oppressive circumstances: "there are some who sanctify themselves in the world by suffering a continual martyrdom".[52]

Even at his first declaring the martyrdom of Mary, Alphonsus had used the language which he would use again in his description of Paul's response to the Corinthian liturgy: "The sight of the Passion of the Redeemer was always present to her mind".[53] There is a eucharistic reference for each element in Alphonsus' considerations of Christian witness. The sight which is "always present" to Mary is the sight which always confronts Paul at the eucharist and which is seen by Alphonsus to give present significance to the lives of Neapolitan women. They will come into the eucharistic celebration as members of a community with all martyrs. Alphonsus has read that women in the Netherlands were quite commonly authorized by local ordinaries to make the responses at Mass when no man or boy was available. He has himself met with convents in Italy in which a nun has done the like at a proper distance from the sanctuary gates. Alphonsus makes no comment when noting this substitution in his *Moral Theology*.[54] In his meditation upon martyrdom in the Church, and the individual value of those members of the community who are called to be martyrs now, he has greater things to say. The women in the fields and in the little palaces of Naples are called to stand round the altar with St Januarius and Maxentia, with St John Chrysostom and the daughters of Sanniemon, at the time-free liturgy.

The nun, too, is to realize the eternal as present. Alphonsus has said nothing of the unhappiness of many women in the convents of the Kingdom. Perhaps the sister reading the *True Bride of Jesus Christ* could be expected to supply her own instances. He knew, of course, that nuns have their own crosses to carry. Superiors reprove them, refuse permissions, assign them to unsuitable jobs, members of the community contradict them, gossip about them, despise them, until they may feel that there is no one who has any respect for them and their desires. Such frustration, too, may be a martyrdom: "A martyr dies for the faith; a religious for perfection".[55] And assuredly, the nun, like Brother Vito, "by a vow of obedience or total renunciation of self-will" must be ranked "amongst those who die in the Lord". So, while it may be true that "there are some discontented souls even in the cloister", such sisters had better think again. They have an eternal choice to make now. The Venerable Cesare da Bustis described religious life as a Purgatory where many just souls suffer in peace with a certain hope of eternal life. This is too futurist a notion for Alphonsus. "For my part, I have been accustomed to say that a religious in her convent enjoys a foretaste of Paradise or suffers an anticipation of hell." Everything depends on the nun's attitude. "There is nothing either good or bad, but thinking makes it so." Alphonsus had used Hamlet's principle to effect the elucidation of some tricky problems in his *Moral Theology*, here, he is developing what Hamlet says about Denmark's being a prison only to those who think it so. What must the convent appear to a discontented nun? "To be forced against the inclinations of nature to do the will of others, to be distrusted, despised, reproved and chastised by those with whom we live, to be shut up in a place of confinement, from which it is impossible to escape, in a word, to be in continual torture without a moment's peace", and in all this "to be separated from God" by the disgruntlements of self-will, there's nothing lacking for this life to be "an anticipation of the torments of hell". Then, again, life in the convent may be, if looked at differently, "an exemption from the cares and afflictions of the world", "a part in the conversations of the saints", "a continual peace in God". This life, he repeats, is "a foretaste of Paradise".[56]

Making his assessment of the witness of contemporary women, Alphonsus has brought together his personal knowledge of the drudgery of their lives, their "traditional" place in society, with his appreciation of the value of martyrs, their place in the Tradition of the ecclesial community. There can be no higher evaluation of any individual human being than that which Alphonsus intends by his use of "martyrdom". However undervalued they may feel themselves to be as their brothers, husbands, and sons stride about the village, their woman's share in the Passion is being given ecclesial acknowledgement now.

A matter of temperament?

What Alphonsus says about martyrs and martyrdom, about the significance of individuals and their responses to circumstances, about the people with whom he worked, derives from his sense of the present as a participation in eternity. He does not suppose that this is at all an idiosyncratic sense. It seems to him that whatever there were in his present tense usage which might be reckoned a peculiar response to life, the liturgy, and the Cross, becomes, at the great cry of Jesus, "It is accomplished", the primary truth which is to be announced in every Christian's theology and practice. In this moment, Alphonsus knows by temperament what others may have to learn, and learn from him. Time is rolled away. He hears the eternal and the present coinciding. "'It is accomplished', Jesus says, turning to his Eternal Father; 'It is accomplished', he says, turning at the same time to us."[57] All at once, human beings, whatever their temperaments, are made aware of themselves as inhabitants of an atemporal order with the Eternal Father. Jesus' cry is, all at once, directed towards us as it is directed towards the Father.

Reading the Passion narrative, Alphonsus is thoroughly persuaded that it is "the end of the ages" for us now. "Let us therefore thank the goodness of God for not having sent us into the world until the great work of redemption had been accomplished."[58] All there is, is ours. Not Alphonsus only, it seems to him, not those who share his temperament only, but all of us live now with the possibility of discovering the mystery of things.

We all live, too, with the responsibility for the disclosure of this mystery. And here again individual temperament and circumstance come into play. Christ, as Alphonsus reads *Hebrews* again, has presented himself in the sanctuary "once for all" securing our "eternal redemption". What is once for all is remembered in the eucharistic celebration of the community. This eternal redemption is not to be contained within the theology of any single member of the community or expressed through any one Christian life, any single martyrdom, any single death. Each woman and man has to find out a personal way of apprehending that death of the Lord which is for all. "Yes, all grown-ups who are saved are either martyrs in blood or martyrs in suffering."[59]

Alphonsus' theology suggests how it is that to become aware of what is accomplished on Calvary is to be called to die a like death. So he reports that Peter Sukegiro was crucified "on a hill" and "outside the city".[60] That St Januarius awaited the executioner's stroke while "repeating the words 'Into thy hands I commend my Spirit'."[61] To have a share in the eucharist is already, for all of us, to have a share in the Passion of Christ. Any one of us may discover the final demand upon us in "the offering of this sacrifice".

Standing round the altar, amid angels and saints and their praying dead, Alphonsus would have his congregation realize that there is more than one way of offering this sacrifice; more than one way of dying; more than one martyrdom. In 1758 about twenty-five of the younger Redemptorists volunteered to go off to the Orient. They would risk their lives there. Alphonsus himself, as a young man, had felt the tug of these foreign missions. It is at such enthusiastic moments that the endurance of the mothers may be significant for the rest of the Church. "I must first be certain of the spirit and the perseverance of each one", Alphonsus wrote back to the novices, "I therefore beg you to apply yourselves for the present to your studies".[62] The excitable students, and all of us, have to be ready to recognize, like those mothers, whatever gracious opportunities there are not only in temperament, but in up-bringing and professional occupation and domestic circumstances, for us to respond to the call to be persevering witnesses.

On 3 October, 1731, Celeste Crostarosa (1696-1755), in the Scala convent, saw the Lord talking with St Francis of Assisi on the vigil of his feast and with Father Alphonsus de Liguori. She heard him say, "This soul has been chosen as the head of this my Institute; he shall be the first Superior of the Congregation of men". Alphonsus and his fellows in this Institute were to be pulpit and confessional witnesses to the good news, preaching "to every creature" that "the kingdom of heaven is at hand". Being thus chosen, he must now, by God's grace, make the best of his natural gifts. To the ways in which Alphonsus himself discovered the enduring uses of his education and experience as a young man in structuring his particular missioner's vocation, I shall now turn.

NOTES

1 The catholicity of Alphonsus' mind is nicely evidenced by this small group of favourites: a greek Father, a mediaeval scholastic, and two modern women.

2 31 December, 1758; it was, indeed, he says next, "more theological than ascetical", 5 April, 1759.

3 *Reflections on the Passion of Jesus Christ*, 1773, (hereafter cited as *On the Passion*,) I, iii.

4 29, October, 1730.

5 *Meditations for all Times of the Year*, LXVIII: *Eight Meditations*, IV.

6 *Meditations for all Times of the Year*, LX.

7 *Divine Office*, on Psalm CX.

8 *Practice of the Love of Jesus Christ*, Introduction, III.

9 *Preparation for Mass*, Introduction: Aquinas: *In Jo.6, lect. 8.*

10 *Treasury*, Pt. II, Instr. I.1.

11 *Loving Aspirations*, XXVI.

12 cf. "Early Formulations", Carl Hoegerl, *Founding Texts of Redemptorists* p.100.

13 *Exercises of the Missions*, IV.

14 *Pious Reflections on Divers Matters of the Spirit*, 1773, (hereafter cited as *Pious Reflections*), XXXVIII

15 cf. "Those who love Jesus Christ do not know how to wish for any other Paradise on this earth than to be in the presence of their Lord", *Choice of a State of Life*, Consideration XI; cf. also *True Bride*, XVIII, iii and *Visits to the Blessed Sacrament*, Introduction, I and Visit IV.

16 *True Bride*, XVIII, iii.

17 *Della Vita, ed Instituto del Venerabile Servo di Dio Alfonso Ma. Liguori*, Naples, 1798, p 31; cf. also Tannoia's account of Alphonsus' way of life, even in his father's house, as *"un Paradiso anticipato"*, p.23.

18 *Maxims*, Tuesday.

19 *Pious Reflections*, XXXIII.

20 *Brief Dissertation*, I, v; Marietti, 463b.

21 *Ibid.*, I, I; I, ii; II, v; Marietti 443b, 447ff, 469b' and *Truth of the Faith*, I, ii and iv; Marietti, 545a-548b and 552b-554a.

22 *Meditations for all Times of the Year*, VI; *Pious Reflections* I; *Prayer*, Pt II, IV, iii.

23 Letter to a nun, 1782, (?), cf. *On the Passion*, VIII, iii.

24 *Divine Office*, Dedication.

25 *Rubrics of the Mass*, VIII, 2.

26 *On the Passion*, VII, ii.

27 *Truth of the Faith*, III, vi; Marietti 701a.

28 *True Bride*, XVII.

29 *Reply to Abbate Rolli*, II.

30 *True Bride*, XVI, iii.

31 *Truth of the Faith*, I, ii; Marietti 547a.

32 8 August, 1754.

33 *Meditations for all Times of the Year*, LXVIII.

34 Alphonsus is always a little uneasy when Christians go looking for the liveliness of the Lord at some historical site: "Many pilgrims make long journeys to visit the holy house in Loreto, where Jesus Christ once dwelt, or to venerate the places in the holy land in which he was born, in which he suffered and died", but they should remember that in a chapel now "Jesus Christ has not only once dwelt and suffered but truly lives". *True Bride*, XVIII, iii, 9.

35 cf. *True Bride*, IV, iv, VIII, I, XVII; "Works on Moral Theology are ordinarily useless and sometimes injurious to a religious…", "To some the reading of books on Mystical Theology may be pernicious…", "but in the Lives of saints we read what so many holy men and women, who were flesh as we are, have done; their example, if it has no other effect, will at least humble us", *True Bride*, XVII. But there were, too, for him as for others, moments of fine fun in reading such biographies. Besides the solemn record of Frigenius' *Vita* of Aquinas, *Novena on the Litany of Loreto*, II,ii, Alphonsus skipped through Surius' *De probatis Sanctorum historiis* and found the anecdote of the corpulent Thomas huffing and puffing as he trotted after an impatient Brother, *True Bride*, VII,vi, "The Second Degree".

36 *Victories of the Martyrs*, Pt I, LXV.

37 *True Bride*, I, iv.

38 *Victories of the Martyrs*, Pt I, LXI, Pt II, XXVII, Pt I, XIV, Pt II, III.

39 *Ibid.*, Pt II, XXXII.

40 *Truth of the Faith*, III, I; Marietti, 682ff.

41 *Meditations for Advent*, IV.

42 *Divine Office*, Friday Lauds; *On the Passion*, I, ii and X, ii; *Glories of Mary*, I, ix and Pt I, I, i, and *On the Passion*, X, i and ii.

43 So, in the Introduction to his *Explanation of the Psalms and Canticles,* he puts aside what he takes to be the historical sequence of their composition in order to concentrate attention on their present recitation in the Church: "I have resolved to follow not the order of the psalms but that of the breviary".

44 *Reflections and Affections on the Passion of Jesus Christ*, 1751, (hereafter cited as *Affections)*, X,i, and *On the Passion*, III, v.

45 *Truth of the Faith*, II, xix; Marietti, 671a.

46 *Ibid.*, III, vi; Marietti, 705b.

47 cf. Austin Berthe, *Vie de Saint Alfonse*, trans. Castle, II, p. 370.

48 *True Bride*, I, 2, *Meditations for all Times of the Year*, LXX.

49 'Discourse to Pious Maidens' in *Exercises of the Missions*, 8.3.

50 In 1707 Bishop Falcoia gave Alphonsus a copy of his little prayer that the Lord 'might graciously grant that he should die and be killed as a martyr'; cf. Hoegerl, *op.cit.*, p 113, note 18.

51 *Glories of Mary*, Pt II, 'Dolours of Mary', 1.

52 *Ibid.*, and *True Bride*, I, 2.

53 *Glories of Mary*, Pt II, 'Dolours of Mary', 1.

54 *Lib.* VI, *Tract.* III, *de Eucharistia, dubium* v, 391.

55 *True Bride*, II, ii.

56. *Ibid.*

57 *Simple Exposition of the Passion*, XVI. Alphonsus receives from S Maria Maddalena de Pazzi the idea of a reciprocal "*Consummatum est*" after Holy Communion: "*Consummatum*

est, that is to say 'My Lord, having given himself to me, has nothing more to give me'". cf. *On the Passion,* V, I.

58 *Meditations for Advent,* IV.

59 *On the Passion,* XI, I.

60 *Victories of the Martyrs,* Pt II, II.

61 *Ibid.,* Pt I, LXV.

62 27 July, 1758.

PART TWO
Converting Experiences

A theology is not to be defined simply in terms of "talk about God", it is the talk of a particular human being. Leisure is enjoyed differently by St Augustine and Benjamin Jowett. School is endured differently by Luke and Caterina Benincasa. Revelation is received differently by Moses and Julian of Norwich. Theologies, in their prevailing tones, in the topics which occupy greatest attention, in their assumptions and often enough in their conclusions, are autobiographical. Some more openly than others. Luther's "justification" and Newman's "development" are, most evidently, ways of talking about themselves in the universities of Wittenberg and Oxford: "I feel myself to be a sinner, I know that I am saved" and "I have changed a great deal but I am still the same person". Others, having a less directly autobiographical tone and structure, still declare the theologian's experience. The Christology of the anonymous poet of "The Dream of the Rood" is shaped by the anglo-saxon horseman's experience of warfare. The Christology of *Why did God become man?* expresses Anselm's experience of the demands of honour among feudal barons. Another Christology entirely comes out of the present-day Philippino experience. The most remotely-phrased structure may be informed by the personal passion of the theologian. There were tears in Garrigou-Lagrange's eyes at his retirement dinner as he affirmed to the company that he had devoted his life to defending the beautiful distinction of essence from existence.

It is to be expected that Alphonsus' rejection of our usual temporal categories, his recognizing a coincidence of the Passion of Christ and the Eucharist and the Paradise, should have a beginning in what had happened to him and how he had learnt, as a youngster and as an adult, to cope with what had happened. It may be hoped that an exploration of what is known, after the labours of half-a-dozen early and recent biographers, about Alphonsus from his boyhood to his throwing over of a quite established career in the law courts, will suggest answers to a couple of connected questions. What brought Alphonsus to think about human experience in this way? What prompted his particular mode of expressing these thoughts?

50

This is not simply a matter of noting what books he took down from the shelves of his father's den or his tutor's apartment or the university library. These original haphazard encounters were, of course, of great significance for Alphonsus' coming to some self-understanding. But it was not that on reading William Whiston's *Longitude and Latitude* or Virgil's *Aeneid* or Paul Lucas' *Journey in the Levant* or, a little later, Quintilian *On Oratory*, that the configurations of Alphonsus' mind were fixed for life. Nor that when, more methodically, he read the works of Chrysostom, Aquinas, Teresa of Avila, or other of his favourites, Alphonsus patiently accepted even these authors estimate of life. His great Neapolitan contemporary, Giambattista Vico (1688-1744), marked out in an intellectual autobiography the four writers who, one after another, had shaped his thinking. But Alphonsus was not that sort of reader.

Alphonsus returning to the shelves to take down the works of the same authors, along with his returning to the same ways of dealing with his clutch of theological ideas, and especially his enthusiasm for what is "always the same", point to his neither reading nor thinking progressively. His intellectual work does not fall into any "beginning, middle, and end" categorization. His general comportment as an author suggests that it is not anywhere near so important, as it is in the cases of Luther and Newman, for an appreciation of intellectual scope and style, for a reader to take up Alphonsus' books in the chronological order of his writing them. He certainly would not have put together anything like that "history of my religious opinions" with which Newman sought to justify himself against Kingsley's charges. If, for example, there is any alteration in what Alphonsus says of "eternity" in the course of his career, it would certainly not be discovered by a critical comparison of his late *Theological-Moral Dissertation* and his early *Maxims*. I have, at any rate, on occasion assumed the freedom of his writings, and made connections between them which, in their ignoring "before" and "after", could not be allowed anyone who wanted to comment faithfully on the work of most other theologians.

Alphonsus' attitude towards authors is repeated in his reactions to those who had successive charge of his education: the modest, civilizing, Don Domenico Bonaccia, the easily-distracted Don Carminiello Rocca, the precise musician, Gaetano Greco, the sadly deteriorated lawyer, Luigi Perrone, and the rigorous theologian, Canon Giulio Torno.

Alphonsus was careful both to retain what they had told him, and to go on sifting it, sometimes for thirty years or more, to get just what he needed for his own enterprise.

With his picking up books and his taking classes with teachers, there are likely to have been particular personal experiences which, whether he ever stopped to recognize them or not, influenced his later sense of what might be done by a missioner Congregation. In the old hagiography, it was accepted that either a saint had been as nearly innocent as a human being may be from lily-white youth to gentle old age, or as horribly bad at first and then had a changing experience and become as good as the one who was always innocent. Alphonsus was brought up to appreciate both sorts of saint. He talks of both equally. Of St Stanislaus, and how "this holy youth was wholly dedicated to the love of Mary", and of St Augustine, St Pelagia and St Mary of Egypt, who had none of them exhibited holiness in youth. Alphonsus has one nice instance of a saint who had things both ways. "St Margaret of Cortona was for many years in a state of damnation but even then cherished a desire of sanctity."[1] Tannoia writes of Alphonsus himself keeping 29th August, the anniversary of his refusal in 1723 to attend the Vice-regal court with his father, as the day of his conversion. But Don Giuseppe took Alphonsus' stubborn tone that day as quite in character, quite as he always was. Even if the importance that Freud and the Jesuits are rumoured to allot to early childhood experiences and responses is not wholly to be accepted, Alphonsus' conversion at the age of twenty-seven was the conversion of someone who had already settled into ways of imagining, feeling, and thinking.

If Alphonsus himself was unsympathetic to the work of the historian, it is not possible, in the effort to understand something of his mind, to avoid some reference to his history. I mean here to suggest ways in which some early incidents in Alphonsus' life seem to be shaping his theology. The selection between incidents, which shall count as significant and which shall not, as accounts of Alphonsus through the nineteenth and twentieth centuries demonstrate, may be a tell-tale indicator of a commentator's own character and interests. I hope that the references here to Alphonsus' planisphere, to his experience of music in the Naples theatre, to his studying in a Law School whose most eminent professor is even now to be reckoned the first authority on the uses of myth, and to the frustrating of his career in the law courts, may reveal more about Alphonsus than they do about me.

The boy's own Planisphere

Alphonsus realizes that his understanding of their share in the eternal present may be altogether too rare an idea for the larger part of his hearers and readers to accept easily. He had heard too many sermons about the northern Reformers disregard for Catholic "traditions", too many sermons about the four "Last Things", to be unaware of the importance of the past as past and the future as future in the popular mind, clerical and lay. To deal with this pastoral difficulty, Alphonsus recovered something from his boyhood enthusiasm for cosmology.

It is quite usual with us to connect eternity and the gods with the vastness of space and the stars. The ziggurats of ancient Mesopotamia were built so that astrologers might read the divine writing in the night and learn the will of the gods. What seemed in the night a strange country to these magi, was recognized by Christians as their homeland. "We have", Paul wrote in his further letter to the Corinthian community, "a house not made with hands, eternal in the heavens." We are called to live in the Church there. The stars are signals of the fore-running saints to Gerard Manley Hopkins:

> Look at the stars! Look, look up at the stars!
> O look at all the fire-folk sitting in the air!

Looking up, we should see

> Christ and his mother and all his hallows

Alphonsus' own most popular verses make the same identification of the starry skies and Christ's home:

> You came down from the stars, O King of Heaven.

In that Heaven, where star differs from star, Alphonsus has distinguished those fire-folk: "apostles differ from martyrs, confessors from virgins, innocents from penitents".[2] But while Alphonsus, in employing this spatial, astronomical, figure in his poem for Christmas, was latching onto a generally acceptable mode of imagining, fitting with the Church's celebrations of the Ascension and the Assumption as well as those for Christmas, he was making especial use of his own knowledge.

His interest in the stars in their courses may have had a very early start as his father told him about the problems of navigating the galley-ship across the sea to Spain. Or maybe, conversation in the cosmology lessons Alphonsus took with Don Carminiello Rocca had drifted from the philosophic problems they were professedly investigating together towards the pleasures of amateur astronomy. At any rate, it was in the apparatus of contemporary cosmography that Alphonsus found the figure which should render his sense of contemporaneous eternity more readily understood, and, as importantly, more readily imaginable.

Don Giuseppe de Liguori (1670-1745), had seen to it that his eldest son be taught, along with the four foreign languages required for a young man to feel at his ease in the city's reception rooms and a little history and geography, the elements of "dialling", that measuring of the heights of celestial bodies which interested navigators and astrologers and lovers anxious not to miss their assignations with the tall stranger or the dark lady. Alphonsus knew quite a lot about the garden sun-dial, about the armillary sphere by which a seaman might calculate the ascensions and declinations of the stars, and the more recent mechanical orrery which represented on metal hoops the motions of the planets and their moons around the sun. These intricate models were both the instruments of contemporary science, enabling a lecturer to demonstrate the intersections of the planes in which the planets moved in regular orbit about the sun, and the toys of the aristocracy. The Medici, whom Galileo had encouraged to think that they owned the satellites of Jupiter, had a particularly fine collection of these little universes. Alphonsus had one, too. He had, Tannoia says, in another flash of hero-worshipping delight, built this grand sphere himself.[3] The model made a pleasing "visual aid" when, later, Alphonsus set about teaching cosmology to Redemptorist students.

Alphonsus' constructing this sphere, which probably does not survive, and also a careful drawing of an armillary, which does, may be for us simply pointers to a charming, even quaint, aspect of his gentlemanly education. But at the start of the eighteenth century, such a sphere might be a figure of theological significance. What was a scientific instrument or a toy for those who had differing sorts of interest in the physical universe, was for others a painful model of the effects of sin. It was commonly believed that as the heavenly bodies moved in their divinely ordered orbits, they made together a most harmonious noise. Our human ears had, originally, been sensitive to what John Milton (1608-1674), in his second *Prolusion*, called "that exquisite music of the stars". But, after the Fall, only Pythagoras, the patron philosopher of Magna

Graecia, who, Alphonsus says, in his *Brief Dissertation Against the Errors of Modern Unbelievers*, knew something about "eternal", had heard this music. The rest of human kind remained deaf. Milton allowed himself to wonder if, "on the morning of Christ's nativity", the sound made by the rotating spheres might just once more "bless our human ears"; he bade the crystal spheres, on which the planets were carried, to move in melodious time:

> And with your ninefold harmony
> Make up full consort to the angelic symphony.

In contrast, Alphonsus, writing his poem about the Madonna's contemplation of her sleeping son, suggested that the stars, hearing her lullaby, would cease their coarser musics:

> Heaven's harmony falls
> Silent at the cradle song
> That Mary sings.

Contrastingly again, Alphonsus confidently employs the planisphere as a model of redemption.

The "admirable order of the heavens and the planets" was of continual interest to him. Though, in *The Treasury*, he expresses surprise that there were priests who could find the time "to study mathematics, geometry, and astronomy", there is perhaps a hint in *The Truth of the Faith* that he had been re-reading the *Elements of Astronomy*, 1684, of Giovanni Domenico Cassini (1625-1712). Even if it be doubted that Alphonsus had the energy for such recreation in 1767, he must, then, have been returning in memory to some enjoyed episode in his lessons with Don Rocca. That interest in the plotting of the heavens had certainly stayed with him for life. It is, he says in *The Truth of the Faith*, one of the particular happinesses of being human, "that we can penetrate the mysteries of the skies", "map out the courses of the planets", "predict the eclipses and the equinoxes", making our observations of these events with exact mathematical instruments.[4] The very possibility of that astronomical exactitude is a convincing indicator of the universe's being the work of a mind. Our star-gazing and our measuring are affirmations of a divine creativity.

That human delight in cosmology and that Christian appraisal of the movements of heavenly bodies shows itself at diverse moments of his theological work. It surfaces, for example, when, in his reflections *On the Passion*, Alphonsus is discussing the various theories put forward to account for the darkening of the earth at the time of Christ's dying. He has consulted books of ancient, mediaeval, and modern astronomers in the expectation of getting a satisfactory answer on this question. "It could not have happened as an eclipse of the sun, by the interposition of the moon between the earth and the sun" because, as Alphonsus remembers well enough, Don Rocca had taught him that "this eclipse always occurs at the new moon and not at the full moon". And Passover is a full moon festival. Further, "as the sun is much larger than the moon, the moon could not hide all the sun's light". There would have been a contemporary record of a penumbra. Further yet, even if the moon could have darkened all the light of the sun, the course of the sun is, "we know", so swift that a total eclipse which began at the sixth hour would have been ended long before the ninth hour. The darkening must have been miraculous.[5] Anyone can see that, if the three heavenly bodies are put into position in the orrery model.

While in these reflections he is referring to astrophysics to support the witness of scripture, it is more usual for Alphonsus to make such references as an element in his exposition of doctrine. Resonances of the Copernican system are to be found, for example, in his discourse on the Assumption of Mary and in his discussion of what might be meant by her title "Mediatrix of all Graces". Most often, the orrery model of the solar system functioned for him as an image of the Church circling round Christ. "The sun is", he says plainly in The *Glories of Mary*, "a figure of Jesus Christ."[6]

In employing the machinery of a contemporary cosmography to make his theological appreciations clearer to others, Alphonsus would know that he had plenty of precedents. He can take example of his looking to such a science for a theological language in the psalmist's celebration of the Lord as the sun shining upon the just man, in the lover's praise of the lady of the *Song of Songs* who is fair as the moon, and in Job's bridling at the rebuke of Eliphaz the Temanite: "See the highest stars, how lofty they are!" He can take example, too, from the writings, as he supposes, of both Paul and John, for with the celebration of the *Hebrews* cosmological liturgy which was so important to his apprehension of the Christian condition, Alphonsus can allege the vision in *Revelations* of the woman with the crown of twelve stars. And then, he was encouraged by the cosmological ventures to be found in the grand

Scripture commentaries of St Athanasius, St Basil, and St. Ambrose, and the familiar excitements of St John Chrysostom's homilies on *Genesis*. These were enough, as Alphonsus grinned happily when making his commentary on the *Psalms and Canticles*, to deal with even "the greatest number of those modern commentators" who were producing such cloudy expositions of Scripture. But, should he require further authority for this Christian exercise of heavenward imagination, Alphonsus can point to the cosmographical exegesis of Pope Innocent III (1160-1216). Alphonsus always read that pontiff's work with real pleasure.[7] And then there were, if he cared to employ them, the writings of some authors who were "modern, but learned and pious". Alphonsus was, at any rate, ready to revive the astronomical conceits of seventeenth century devotional literature, the *True Devotion to the Holy Virgin*, by Jean le Crasset, which the Jansenist, Antoine Arnauld, had tried to get condemned at Rome; the *Client of the Virgin*, of Paolo Segneri the elder, and *Paradise Opened* of Paul de Barry. Whatever Alphonsus took from his readings among Christian authors, he adapted and reconstructed, even what he took from Pope Innocent, until it should fit with his use of the orrery.

The golden orrery displayed in the Palazzo Pitti might seem rather too aristocratic a figure for our common life in the universal Church. Certainly, such a figure complemented the conventional self-image of the nobility in the Kingdom of Naples. There were social circles in which, in the early eighteenth century, men of Alphonsus' class supposed themselves to be fixed as the stars in their courses. That human beings move in circles round a lordly centre like the heavenly bodies round the orrery sun would have been one of the first lessons that Alphonsus would have learnt from his class-conscious father. Though it was only at Versailles that women and men spoke of their moving in a courtly dance around a sun-king, Don Giuseppe might well have used an orrery when he was explaining the significance of the five circles of Neapolitan nobility around the Viceroy. Upon the enjoyment of a place in one of these circles, and upon the circle to which one belonged, depended the quality of a gentleman's life. It was relevant, for example, to the management's decision at the San Bartolomeo opera house on which one of the house's five tiers would be available when a gentleman wished to hire a box for the season. But Alphonsus' employment of the cosmographical circle had nothing about it of class privilege. Though he approved the religious policies of Louis XIV, even naming him, in the *Fidelity of Vassals*, 1777, one of six exemplars of princely virtue,[8] Alphonsus did not have that Sun-King in mind when he turned his sphere for the students at d'Iliceto.

The sphere bore, in Alphonsus' recurrent employment, a psychological challenge to each hearer and reader. Who does the hearer think she is? What place does the reader think he occupies? In what sort of universe? There was, at any rate, precedent for this last question. In Alphonsus' time, such spheres were generally used in the classroom to demonstrate the difference between the old, Ptolemaic, view of the universe and what were still felt to be new notions of the sun's being at the centre and the earth's moving round it just like any other planet. Most women and men understood that the Ptolemaic construction had been thrown sufficiently into doubt by the Copernican scientists, but many found it difficult to imagine the universe as anything but earth-centred. They did not cease from talking of "sun-rise" and "sun-set". There was, in this common usage, a hint of a very real problem for Alphonsus' contemporaries. They were no more ready than any of us for the psychological displacement of human being from the centre of things. The Medici Grand Duke habitually spoke of the satellites of Jupiter as "my stars". Lesser persons were as apt to talk of "our universe". And there was a movement among the "moderns" at Naples university to put the individual human being back at the centre of academic attention. The mathematician, Tommaso Cornelio (1614-1684), and the jurist, Francesco d'Andrea (1625-1698), had been regaling the *Investigatori* at their club with the "new philosophy" of Descartes and its defining proposition that "I think" and its comfortable conclusion "I am". Alphonsus' uncle, Emilio Cavalieri (1663-1726), had, as Inquisitor of the city, been much alarmed by that sort of supper-table discussion. These troubling arguments were sustained into Alphonsus' time by the literary critic, Gregorio Caloprese (1650-1715), and the great book-collector, Giuseppe Valetta (1636-1714), at the Palatine Academy, and the debate had been powerfully re-stoked by Paolo Mattia Doria (1662-1746), in his *Critical Discourses*, 1724, and his *Against Signor Locke*, 1732. Whatever pleasure Alphonsus got from reading Doria's attack on John Locke (1632-1704), and on that even tougher Briton, Thomas Hobbes (1588-1679), his dogmatic treatises witness to his dislike of the new as much as of the old self-centredness. And to his dislike of it, whether this new self-centredness were phrased in the original stark Cartesian language, or put about in the decently veiled expressions employed by Gilbert Burnet (1643-1715), Bishop of Salisbury, when he stopped on his Grand Tour to visit the Naples academies. Burnet was delighted to discover men of "freer thoughts" in Naples than elsewhere in Italy, and was not much disturbed that these academicians were generally "ill looked on by the clergy" as mere atheists.

While it seemed to most of the "moderns" that Descartes went along with Copernicus and Galileo, Alphonsus could make a distinction in his estimate of their enterprises. Contrastingly with the philosopher's demonstration that "I am", the astronomers' hypotheses suggested that women and men, being displaced from the centre of the planetary system, should practise some humility. Alphonsus' omitting, in his exploration of the uses of the orrery figure, all reference to those scriptural texts which had provided material for the curial cosmologists in their discussions with Galileo, is likely to have been quite deliberate. He was always careful in his management of examples and quotations, and reminders of those controversialists would not have been to his purpose. Thus, he says nothing in his comments on Psalm 19:7 that would renew old arguments about the sun's taking a circuit about the heavens. Alphonsus' imaginings would always be "Copernican" in their arrangement of the universe. His devotions point away from himself towards Christ, "the centre of every good". The system he proclaims is held together by the gravitational pull of love. "Thou lovest me, and I love thee, and love thee more than myself."[9] Alphonsus remained in love even when it offered no emotional satisfaction, protesting in the midst of a terrible loneliness, when he had no sense at all of Christ's presence, "If thou wilt that I continue thus afflicted and desolate even unto death and through all eternity, I am content". Whether he felt it or not, he always knew that the love of Christ was at the meaningful centre of all existence and experience. He could, therefore, more readily than most, appreciate that the heliocentric system, with the psychological re-arrangements it required, was expressing what had always been the case. Humanity had never been at its own centre. The orrery showed how the heavenly bodies always have been, will be, and are. As a figure, it might show how human beings always are. And, further, how wondrous it is to be in orbit round the loving Christ, "the Sun of Justice".

Once he has brought his hearer and reader to appreciate that the heliocentric system may be taken as figuring the centrality of Christ, Alphonsus can proceed to make figurative sense of other members of the machinery. He can point to Mary as the moon. A mariological relation of space and grace had already been suggested by St Albert the Great (1200-1280), who wrote of Mary's being "in incomparably closer proximity" to the Lord "than all other creatures". And with this, Alphonsus cites, from Part III of Aquinas' *Summa Theologiae*, a passage in which Mary, because "she is the most near" to Christ, is said to enjoy "a greater fullness of grace than others".[10] He found St Bonaventure (1221-1274), helpful here, and repeated his careful comparison which showed that "as the moon, which stands between the sun and the earth, transmits to this latter whatever she receives from the former, so does Mary pour out on us who are on earth the heavenly graces which she receives".[11] "Mary", Cardinal Hugo de S. Charo (d.1623), reading Psalm 136, delights to proclaim, "is the moon by whose means those who are in the midst of the night of sin are enlightened."[12] A turn of the orrery model may evidently be the occasion for taking thought about that doctrine of Mary as "Mediatrix of all Graces" for which Alphonsus is, later, to make his particular argument.

It is easy now to appear a little too definite in alleging Alphonsus' engagement with such an interplay of cosmography and theology. He does not pause in his writing to explain how he came by the orrery model or how he is using it. It would be odd if he did. He and his readers would take such a model as part of the ordinary library furniture. What seems somewhat out-of-the-way to us, he and they take for granted.[13] We and they do, however, share the understanding that the model does not correspond to the actuality of the planetary system. Milton thought that God had made the courses of the planets not quite circular so that he might have a quiet laugh at the quaint shifts which astronomers would adopt to explain the deviations "when they come to model Heaven, and calculate the stars". The orrery-maker had to ignore such niceties. Alphonsus uses this discrepancy between model and system to make his comforting affirmation of a congruence between model and Church. As the aristocratic owner turned the machinery, the circling hoops would suggest that at any one time a planet is as near to the central sun as it is at any other time. This would be the case of our earth. Yesterday as today. All the year and every year. Those who stood on the circling earth in antiquity, in Elizabethan times, and now, in Rome and Nagasaki and here, would stand at an equal radius from the sun. Holding in imagination the motions of the orrery model, Alphonsus' contemporaries might be able to see themselves standing on the earth's hoop with all human beings of all times of the race, having their assured places in a circle moving about Christ. At whatever point on the circumference they were standing, Christians of each time would be as near Christ at the centre of their circle as Christians of every other time. The figure offered in the hoop of the cosmographic machine should persuade them to attend to what in their relation with Christ is "always the same".

Alphonsus' hearers and readers should, by imagining these hoops, be better able to apprehend what he was saying about the eucharistic liturgy as a cosmic celebration. They should be able to recognize that angels are moving with women and men, atemporally, about the Lord. His dear master, St John Chrysostom, had suggested that "the angels wait for the time for Mass to intercede with greater efficacy in our favour".[14] Alphonsus liked this idea. But he would rather put his emphasis on what angels are always doing, and what, at the intersecting moment of the liturgy, angels and human beings do together. This is precisely what his "planisphere" would illustrate. Those gracious beings whom Isaiah could hear crying from heaven, "Holy, holy, holy", and whom Paul's communities had recognized in the starry Thrones, Dominions, and Principalities of the gentile astrologers, are present with us at the *Sanctus* of the liturgy. And what we do on earth, they do in heaven. "They also give thanks for all the gifts which they have received."[15] At this moment, all things, on earth or in the heavens, enjoy the same eucharistic relation with their Lord. Angels on their hoop. We on ours. The orrery is proving to be a figure of that liturgical enjoyment of the eternal which is the recurring subject of Alphonsus' theological work.

The cosmological machinery and its hold on contemporary imagination are being used by Alphonsus in something very like the way in which a creatively intelligent writer today may be using the conventions of modern science in a piece of science fiction. There is a like excitement of the reader's imagination and like provocation to self-scrutiny as Alphonsus suggests that we contemplate ourselves wheeling round Christ, each of us in an orbit equally near to "the centre of every good", each of us being enlightened "as the planets are illumined by the sun". Looking at the metal hoops, imagining the circling bands of angels and saints, of Christians from the first, second, thirteenth, eighteenth, and our own century, from ancient Rome, and Nagasaki, and our own circumstance, we may better recognize ourselves as members of one universal community which has been given a gracious vocation, we may recognize ourselves as the Church.[16]

There is a pleasant indication of the ease with which Alphonsus steps among the intangibles and tangibles of the universe, among metaphysical and astrophysical beings, in his comment on Psalm 148:6, "He hath established them for ever". "This 'them' refers", he says with no sense at all of saying anything remarkable, "to the angels and the heavenly bodies." There is a perfect likeness of the planets going round the sun to the angels going round Christ. The one pronoun serves for both. So does the one verb. They praise the Lord together. Alphonsus almost seems to be reconstructing the Pythagorean cosmology in which those spheres which bore the planets moved, and made their music, because they were being moved by kindly spirits.

The Demon at the keyboard

St John Chrysostom has supposed that on hearing "the best music" a human being might for that instant be caught up to heaven. Milton, too, knew that there is a music of the spheres to which human beings, if they could only hear it, would be compelled to attend "as all their souls" were "in blissful rapture captivated". He had not held out much hope of our hearing such music. Conversely, Samuel Wesley (1766-1800), had, on his return "to my father's faith" after a temporary conversion to Catholicism, lamented that "if the Roman doctrines were like the Roman music we should have heaven on earth". But, taking doctrine and music together, "heaven on earth" was precisely what Alphonsus enjoyed. And what he knew about harmony would seem to him to fit very well with what he knew about planispheres. Astronomy remained a required study for any eighteenth century music student.[17] It must have been cheering to all musicians that it was the organist of the Octagon Chapel in Bath, William Herschel (1738-1822), who in March, 1781, discovered Uranus. Reconsidering doctrine, turning the planets of the orrery, practising at the harpsichord, Alphonsus was working on the language for that "blissful rapture".

Certainly, the Christian working on such a language might find encouragements in contemporary music-making. "Let all the saints terrestrial sing", wrote Charles Wesley (1707-1788), and Alphonsus might have been happy to sing his song of the real presence of the Eucharistic Christ:

> *Freely let me take of Thee,*
> *Spring Thou up within my heart,*
> *Rise to all eternity.*

Saints were, indeed, singing everywhere. This is the time when Israel Baal Shem-Tob (c.1700-1760), was leading the first Hasidim into their celebration of the melody at the heart of creation, and affirming the faithful response to the divine message in community songs. It is the time when the great Lutheran Pietist, August Hermann Francke (1663-1727), was making Halle a place of singing lay-people. As Johann Anastasius Freylinghausen (1670-1739), wrote in the preface of their *Kingdom's Song-book,* 1705, Francke was convinced that God "has placed a new song in the hearts and mouths of his children". They had collected godly songs for the kitchen, the picnic ground, and the hay field, as well as for the choir loft. Graun's *Death of Jesus,* Telemann's *Day of Judgement,* C.P.E. Bach's *Israelites in the Desert,* and Leopold Mozart's famous hunt for another Lenten text, "it does not have to be a Passion", after all, "this year the penitent David will be done", witness to a popular scriptural music-making through eighteenth century German music. This German story-telling was part of a European-wide activity. Telemann had been the most international of composers, taking what pleased him from Corelli and Rameau as well as the older tunes of Lully, that Italian at the court of King Louis. Frenchmen were borrowers, too. In Alphonsus' time, Marc-Antoine Charpentier (1634-1704), came to Rome to study with Carissimi, and on his return to Paris, his *Judgement of Solomon,* and *Denial of Peter,* and *Cecilia, Virgin and Martyr,* and *Dialogue of Christ and the Sinner,* demonstrated the diverse sorts of Christian story-telling that his Italian master had taught him to manage. The Germans were as ready to learn from Naples musicians. The young Johann Adolf Hasse (1699-1783), wrote for the *Incurabili* hospital, in which Alphonsus worked as a volunteer auxiliary, a couple of Latin oratorios on *Moses* in the desert and *Mary Magdalene* at the tomb of Jesus. He went back, after ten years study with Nicola Porpora (1686-1768), and Alessandro Scarlatti (1660-1725), equipped to be Dresden's leading composer. Hasse earned many commendations for his series of Italianate oratorios, from *Daniel* in 1731 to the climactic *Conversion of St Augustine,* 1750. This rococo piece was composed to the Italian text of the daughter of the Elector of Bavaria, and confirmed the court fashion for all things Neapolitan.[18] Alphonsus may not have noticed what these Frenchmen and Germans were taking home, but it was part of his profession as a gentleman to stay awake to what was happening in the music of his city. "I am fond of music", he acknowledged years after he had ceased to attend concerts or operas, "and, when a layman, I devoted a fair amount of time to it."[19]

The Neapolitan composers' exploration of a relation between Christian story and music-making was given encouragement when, after the Austrian "restoration" in 1708, the Hapsburg's Viceroy, Cardinal Vincenzo Grimani, brought Alessandro Scarlatti back to his post at the Chapel Royal. During his exile in Rome, Scarlatti had been writing oratorios. He had produced music to fit distinctly Christian subjects, *St Philip Neri, The Most Holy Virgin of the Rosary,* and, as his part in a Holy Week double-event with Handel's *Resurrection* in 1708, a *Passion* oratorio. Returning to his Naples organ-bench, the old gentleman hurriedly refurbished a Roman oratorio he had written for the Feast of the Assumption, using precisely those biblical texts for this *Spouse of the Song of Songs* which, forty years on, Alphonsus would employ in the structuring of the *Glories of Mary.* Scarlatti's traditionalist oratorios were entirely suited to a restoration of the old ways of doing things at court, and there was nothing new, except the libretto written by the Viceroy himself, about Scarlatti's opera *Theodosius,* given at the San Bartolomeo opera house in January, 1709. Fifty years on, Alphonsus remembered the incident of Theodosius' being entertained unawares by a solitary monk when he was looking for an improving example for the *True Bride of Jesus Christ* in 1760. Grimani was also encouraging younger local men to find their own ways of composing, and, as generously, commissioning music from foreign composers who, in ever-increasing numbers, were making their ways to Naples.

Don Giuseppe insisted that his son should enjoy more than a gentlemanly knowledge of the history and theory of music and more than a gentlemanly skill at the keyboard. He arranged that the boy be sent to study with Gaetano Greco (c.1657-c.1728), the head of the Conservatorio dei Poveri di Gesu. Greco was not a distinguished composer but he was a most competent instructor. In the course of his career, he counted Domenico Scarlatti (1685-1757), Leonardo Vinci (1696-1730), and Giovanni Battista Pergolesi (1710-1736), among his pupils. And he was known for bringing less gifted Conservatorio boys to play violin or harpsichord with brilliant effect. Greco relished more the hours he spent with his better-educated private pupils and in his last years at the Conservatorio paid out of his own salary for an assistant to look after the general training of the boys in his stead. The sons of gentlemen were readier to be taught something of the history and theory of the art. They could be told about the classical proportions of Pythagorean music and the renascence experiments of Vincenzo Galilei, father of the Medici's astronomer, what was happening after Bach in German courts and the general direction of Rameau's *Treatise on Harmony*. Greco's private pupil would be equipped, if he had had the wit to pay attention, to bear a distinguished part in the civilized conversation of the opera house box and the Viceroy's salon as well as to accompany a trilling young lady at a family party.

"Music is an art which, if not perfectly learned", Alphonsus observed, "not only does not delight, it positively displeases."[20] It is not clear, even from an inspection of his own compositions, how much he learned of music theory during his lessons with Greco. All, it seems, that he read afterwards on such topics was the famous essay of the Benedictine, Augustin Calmet, identifying the musical instruments mentioned by the Psalmist.[21] But his not keeping up his reading is surely to be explained, like his not keeping up in astronomy, by a careful husbanding of time and energy. At any rate, Alphonsus learned enough in these Conservatorio sessions to take a constant delight at the keyboard for the rest of his long life. And to fit some more religious words to the popular tunes of the street. Even to venture upon the composition of a number of spiritual songs himself. These were immensely successful with his mission congregations. People liked singing these new songs between sermons. They went on singing them after the missioners had gone on to another village. They were still being sung a hundred years later. Verdi, not a Christian, remarked that "Christmas would not be Christmas" without one of Alphonsus' little carols, *You came down from the Stars*. Everyone enjoyed singing this on the way home from Midnight Mass. With this management of a singable tune, Alphonsus' compositions exhibit sometimes a quite sophisticated command of harmony, and an intenser emotional power than the popular song usually contains. His *Duet between the Soul and Jesus Christ* is justly admired by historians of music. And may, equally, be admired by catechists. Both should be pleased, for example, at the delicate balance of content and form at the end of this *Duet*. As the Christian soul is enabled to share "life with Thee", the music of the two voices comes together for the first time in the piece as a true duet.

With the elegancies of keyboard fingering and the rudiments of harmony and counterpoint, Alphonsus learned what was happening in contemporary music. Especially in the theatrical music favoured at Viceregal lodge. Anyone turning over the score of that *Duet* in the British Library will be immediately aware of the influence of contemporary operatic conventions. This music tells a story. Characteristically, it is a story of the Passion, and of the present Christian's being present at the Passion as it happens. The Christian's question, "O my Jesus, where are you going?" receiving the immediate response, "I go to die for love of you". This story is told most dramatically. The sudden entry of the trumpet at the moment of Jesus' being condemned to death is, indeed, melodramatic, and is set in fine contrast with the slow march tune as Jesus makes his way up the hill of Calvary. The *Duet* made its proper stir in Naples on its first performance before Alphonsus' retreat sermon in the grand church of the Trinita de Pellegrini. His congregation recognized both what he was attempting in competition with the San Bartolomeo composers and what he had achieved. And they were the more ready to accept the echoing demand in the sermon that they give their hearts to the Lord. Village congregations got an even greater sense of the dramatic and evangelical powers of music as they were allotted the chorus part in a lengthy dialogue song. The missioner began by placing them all in the presence of the tortured Christ:

> *My Jesus, say what wretch has dared*
> *Thy sacred hands to bind,*

then the congregation sings out a response which at once makes personal sense of what is going on:

> *'Tis I have thus ungrateful been.*

Such immediate, dramatic, and participatory, music must have its effect. "These hymns, as graceful as they are moving", Tannoia observed in his biography, "created as much enthusiasm as his preaching." At their singing of these graceful hymns, Alphonsus was making the same suggestion about all their lives together as he made when he turned the orrery. Nothing could be left of any self-centredness after they had sung the soaring line *"All that I am I give"*.

There might, even then, have been a danger of some clapping in the church. When a student, Alphonsus had learnt something of the excitements of the long-held high note and of *"Brava!"* and *"Bravo!"* at the opera house, and the young men shouting at the tops of their voices to applaud the soprano and the castrato.[22] Théodule Rey-Mermet, in the first volume of the new *History of the Redemptorist Congregation,* 1993, says that going to the opera at the San Bartolomeo was a passion with Alphonsus as a young man about town. Alphonsus could be mightily severe about such time-consuming things in the *True Bride,* but at the time he was himself enthusiastic enough to sit down at the keyboard on returning from a performance and write out the catchy tunes he had heard that evening. These all came in handy later when he wanted to put a melody to his own verses. He experienced, too, that obliviousness of the performer to all else but the world of rehearsal, performance, and deluding recollection of personal triumph. He took the Demon's part in a *Sant' Alessio* opera sponsored by the Oratorian community, and enjoyed a friendly clap from his audience. But the thought of this little success came back to disturb him. "If you are invited to take part in any little opera", he warned, "avoid it as much as possible, for it will distract you for a month or two at least."[23] The Oratorians may have staged the *Sant'Alessio* of Stefano Landi (1590-1655), which had a libretto written by Pope Clement IX, Giulio Rospigliosi (1667-1669). When he had been nuncio in Madrid, he had amused himself and the court by writing more than a dozen such pieces in decent, dignified, measures, laced with more vulgar verses for comic demons and farcical servants. Landi's tunes for the below-stairs characters were almost scandalously catchy. Then again, the Oratorians may have put on another *Sant'Alessio* piece by Bernardo Pasquini (1637-1710), which, though not making many dramatic demands, required that, on his sitting down at the keyboard, the Demon should display the technical skill of the virtuoso. The Pasquini piece would have demanded hours of practice. Perhaps the result, however kind the applause, did not quite justify the effort. Perhaps the excitements of the figured bass that the Demon played on the harpsichord in this Oratorian entertainment were enough to show Alphonsus that he should resist further invitations to perform. Looking back on his life in his father's house, Alphonsus could recollect only one occasion on which he had disobeyed Don Giuseppe. Some time after the *Sant'Alessio,* he refused to take another part in a private performance of such an opera. That the captain had made this a matter of obedience and that Alphonsus long remembered this refusal indicate the importance of such musical evenings in the lives of the Neapolitan gentry. Not everyone could make this grand refusal. It was against another such "figured music" in their convent chapel that Alphonsus warned the nuns at Foggia in 1746, "on account of the amount of care to be taken, the vanity, the distractions, the expense involved", and the next year, he organized a petition to the Cardinal Prefect of the Congregation of Bishops and Regulars against this music.

Of course, what might be mere vanity in a convent chapel, and just permissible in a meeting of the Brothers at the Oratory, might be decently applauded in the public theatre. Alphonsus went on getting seats at the opera until the collapse of the Amatrice law-suit in 1723. And he went on singing all his life, solo singing at intervals between his preaching the mission sermons. There is a pleasant story of his forgetting the words of his own Christmas carol when he sang it first to the congregation.

At the opera house, the palace, and the little evening parties of his father's friends, Alphonsus was being made aware, along with the tunes he was copying down, of a great range of musical story-tellings. A movement was just starting in which composers would review the memories of pagan myth and mediaeval romance with those of Hebrew and Christian scriptures and local hagiography.

A most sensitive visitor recognized more quickly, perhaps, than many Neapolitans what was happening in their music. In 1708, when the twelve years old Alphonsus was just being brought by his ambitious father to take an interest in the ways of the Naples court, the Duke of Alvito had commissioned George Frideric Handel (1685-1759), to compose an entertainment for a princely wedding party. Coming straight from the triumph of his *Resurrection* oratorio in Rome, Handel proposed a little opera of *Acis, Galatea and Poliphemus.* It did not seem odd to anyone in Naples, that, after the gospel saint, an homeric cyclops would present Handel's version of human being. Cardinal Grimani and the other wedding guests might want to identify with the lively boy and the pretty miss, but they are held by Handel until they acknowledge that it is the rough, ugly, Poliphemus who has remained constant in his loving. Where shall such a lonely, weary, despised, creature find rest? The myth is being pointed towards gospel. Handel appreciates very well what local composers were suggesting about the interaction of a variety of story-tellings. This recourse to myth to express the human condition in ways which fit with scriptural story-telling was something for Alphonsus to consider as he took a place in the musical life of his city. If he had not been at the wedding performance, he would have at least heard about it. Everyone had heard about it, for at the end of the evening, Cardinal Grimani had declared his intention of writing Handel's next libretto.

Though he might resist suggestions that he take any further part in private performances, Alphonsus found himself in the midst of public musical events — on Sundays as well as high holidays. The library cupboards of the Oratorian community contained the largest collection ever made of Neapolitan scores and song-books, and the community was justly famous for its patronage of young composers. Alphonsus would have encountered all the notable composers of the city in the pillared courtyard of the Girolamini after the High Mass. And then, in 1710, the young Alphonsus was introduced by his father to the *sedile* of Portanova. For the next dozen years or so he went regularly to the meetings of this little magistracy. The members of the bench were not allowed to run anything that the vice-regal bureaucrats thought important, but they had some local status, and exercised some local patronage. It was in their organizing the civic processions on great feasts and in their choosing the composer who would supply the festival music that they touched the lives of the borough residents most nearly. In their considerations of these matters, Alphonsus was as informed, assuredly, as any of the older members of the bench about the individual gifts of the men teaching at the local music schools. Greco had returned to teaching at the Conservatorio dei Poveri in 1709, and in several of the next years Alphonsus' old instructor suplied the *flottole,* the songs and dances to accompany the floats of the procession that the *sedile* commisioned for the celebration of the feast of St Januarius. In Alphonsus' time on the bench, the great Pergolesi began his career as one of the youths running, singing, and at the same time playing their violins at the head of this procession. From 1710 onward, Alphonsus' *sedile* had dealings, too, with the Conservatorio della Pieta dei Turchini where Leonardo Leo (1694-1744), was then a paying pupil. This Conservatorio provided singers for the borough's festivities on St Gajetan Day. In 1713, Leo produced his own little music drama of *Sant'Alessio* for the entertainment of the Conservatorio's benefactors.

The position of Alphonsus' father in the borough, his well-known interest in all things musical, and his son's personal acquaintance with the local musicians, would have ensured that the two of them had respected voices in the discussions about these commissions by the benchers. Ensured, too, that they were invited, in 1714, to the performance at the Turchini of an oratorio by the young Francesco Feo (1691-1761), which celebrated *The Martyrdom of St Catherine* and was, appropriately, concluded by a grand firework display. Alphonsus' father would, indeed, have been quite unable to bear the disgrace of not receiving an invitation to such a performance. Even in his mid-seventies, Alphonsus could bring back, as an image of hell, the pain a member of the nobility must feel if he were excluded from the singing and the ballet dancing of the private theatre: "How bitter would be his anguish and disappointment when, from without, he would hear the shouts of joy and applause within!"[24]

Feo, along with Pergolesi, Leo, Vinci, who "first traced the circle of periodic song", and an advancing squadron of composers of the Naples School, was discovering stories in a variety of source books. For more than a quarter of a century he went on writing music drama for the San Bartolomeo management, the Oratorian community, the parish carnival organizers, the university authorities, and the Court, with the widest range of subjects: *St Francis of Sales, Don Quixote,* and *The Magi,* tumbled out with *Andromache* and *Orestes.* Leo grew to be equally appreciative of these different story-tellings. His career began with a music drama about St Clare for the Turchini contributions to the festivities of 1712, reached a fashionable climax with the grecian *L'Olimpiade* he composed for the opening of the San Carlo opera house in 1737, and finished in 1744, when he was organist of the Chapel Royal, with a series of *Introits* for Lent and a revision of *"That is to say...",* his comic opera of the Neapolitan street-people. Leo found the range of his employments an occasion of delicious fun. He made unlikeness into likeness. The most popular song of his demotic comedy was a parody of the Chapel chanting. Such diversity was generally expected of composers. Pergolesi, in the very last weeks of his short life, was working on a *Flaminio* romance, a *Stabat Mater* for the Confraternity of St Luigi di Palazzo, and an *Orpheus* opera. And the Naples public was always ready for more of the mix of styles that Leo had achieved in *"That is to say...".* They were quite ready to accept that diverse stories and story-telling techniques belonged together in a representation of the complexity, the muddle, of ordinary life. Even the old-fashioned Alessandro Scarlatti thought it proper to shift out of the ecclesiastical mannerisms of his setting of the first verses of his *Salve Regina* into something very like Calabrian folk music at the end.[25]

At the process of canonization, the devil's advocate took it that Alphonsus' frequenting musical evenings and theatrical entertainments had been the ordinary round of a young squire in that society. But Alphonsus was no ordinary cavalier. His latest biographer noting that Alphonsus "frequented the San Bartolomeo", supposes that "his interest centred on the music, not on the plot or the acting".[26] I think, rather, that Alphonsus recognized that music and plot and libretto and acting have to be appreciated together in the theatre. What he says, later, of nuns' singing suggests that he could not at any time have been a mere "canary fancier". His admiration for almost everything written by Lodovico Antonio Muratori (1672-1750), would have led him, if indeed he were not already aware of these things, to take notice of that most learned man's insistence, in his *Best Italian Poetry*, 1706, of the importance of an opera composer's getting the right libretto. Alphonsus would have recognized that it was through their government of plot and verse, through their direction of character and story, that these Neapolitan composers were making statements about contemporary life in the Kingdom. It would be apparent to Alphonsus, as to anyone listening in a San Bartolomeo box or on a chair at the Conservatory, that these composers were taking the mythic stories and the scriptural stories to be equally communicative of human possibility. The musically sensitive and sophisticated Alphonsus would be prompted at *Andromache* and *Orestes* and *Orpheus* to ask what there was in such myths to suggest that they should be heard alongside the gospel stories of the adoration of the Magi, of Peter in the High Priest's house, and Mary at the foot of the Cross. These matters, as Alphonsus' references to Pietro Metastasio (1698-1782), demonstrate, became more interesting to Neapolitan intellectuals in 1720, when the great librettist took up residence in Naples.

Metastasio had visited Naples in 1718, when he was admitted to the Accademia Aletina, and, liking the cultural liveliness of the city, decided to stay. He found himself a place in a Naples law firm and set about establishing a reputation as a maker of theatrical verses. If Alphonsus had not got himself invited to the private performances of *Endymion*,

1720, the Hercules opera, *Gardens of Hesperides*, 1721, and the *Galatea*, 1722, he would certainly have been aware, later, of the way in which Metastasio's versions of these and other Grecian story-tellings were exciting fashionable Naples. The ladies and gentlemen were right to be excited. The operas that Feo and Vinci and the rest composed to Metastasio's verses dealt with great human questions of frustrated love, the perilous search for truth, and the vitality of art. The intelligent opera-goer was being brought to assess the claims of the myths to treat the most important aspects of modern life. Alphonsus himself observed that there was nothing left in the Metastasian response to myth of that old Neapolitan nonsense of Marini's *Adonis*, 1623. Metastasio had always avoided the "obscenities" which sullied "the impious works" of that baroque poet.[27] Talented and respectable, Metastasio got, in 1727, on the recommendation of Muratori's friend, Apostolo Zeno, an invitation to become Caesarian court poet and left Naples for Vienna forthwith, but his librettos continued to hold the Naples stage.

Alphonsus could not but be very much aware of Metastasio, "the applause of worldlings" which he excited, and the influence he had in Naples on "many young persons who seek to acquire a great reputation by similar compositions on profane love".[28] He would recognize that these little-poetasters had no real hope of rivalling Metastasio. Composers would rather set and re-set and re-set again the librettos of Metastasio. Between 1737 and 1776, two thirds of all the operas performed at the San Carlo had Metastasio texts. In 1773, the year that Alphonsus was, in the course of putting together his *Pious Reflections*, reflecting again on the verses of Metastasio, a dozen composers within the Hapsburg sphere of cultural influence were working on new settings of Metastasio's old librettos, including, for the San Carlo management, the *Alexander in India* of Niccolo Piccinni (1728-1800), who was re-using the libretto used by Vinci in 1729. Whoever was composing the music, Alphonsus was chiefly concerned, then, with the moral tone of the libretto.

Metastasio's operas were generally concerned with the start, process, and resolution in a happy finish, of the political and emotional entanglements of a royal household, mostly a royal household of pagan antiquity. In the exploration of the relations of dignified class-conscious, self-important, persons, Metastasio shows himself to be the master of what Muratori called *corporeal* beauty, the pleasing style, and of *incorporeal* beauty, the instructive meaning. The writing of librettos was for him the poet's way , as Alphonsus was most reluctant to allow, of '"inducing, by way of pleasure, the love of virtue so necessary for general happiness". Alphonsus remembered that Metastasio had once admitted that he had "wasted his entire life in order to instruct mankind in a pleasing way". But in less despondent moments, Metastasio thought his dramas nicely exhibited that clash of passions which necessarily leads to the triumph of virtue. He backed his dramatic practice with informed appeals to classical poetics, producing a translation of Horace's *Art of Poetry*, 1749, and a commentary on Aristotle's *Poetics*, 1772. But Alphonsus was still appalled, in 1773, at the influence of the fashionable libretto.

He had, while writing his *Pious Reflections*, been preparing his commentary on the Psalms which came out in 1774. Quietly going through Xavier Mattei's notes to his translation of the Psalms, which was, he judged, a work "worthy of general approbation", Alphonsus came upon "the eulogies that he lavishes upon the poetical compositions of his celebrated friend, Signor Pietro Metastasio".[29] Alphonsus acknowledged that Metastasio's "sacred verses'", the *Passion*, 1730, *Joseph*, 1733, *Isaac* and *Abel*, 1740, and the *St Helena on Calvary*, 1746, were "excellent and deserving all praise". The opera librettos, however, seemed to Alphonsus to be "as noxious as they are beautiful" because "those which treat of profane love" must, by the tenderness of Mestastasio's verse, "kindle in the breasts of young persons the pernicious flames of impure affections".

Perhaps Alphonsus would not have got so angry with Metastasio if he had not connected him with *The Faithful Shepherd* of Battista Guarini from which Giacomo Rossi made a libretto for Handel in 1712.[30] The tender little comedy which Rossi fashioned, in which a muddle of lovers is resolved and the villainous is forgiven, would scarcely seem to deserve Alphonsus' particular stricture. He is surprisingly wide-sweeping in his sallies against "this pestilential work" which, if not already condemned by the Church, deserves, he thinks, to be so. Alphonsus, by one of those slips of human memory, was confusing *The Faithful Shepherd* with the quite different Metastasio libretto, *The Royal Shepherd*, which was set by twenty-five composers between 1750 and 1800, including Maria Agnesi, Gluck and Mozart. Still, in making his criticisms, Alphonsus is thinking quite generally of the high-flown heroics of a noble woman pursued by a tyrant, who declares her anguish as she falls into his clutches, or the nobleman condemned to languish in a dungeon to satisfy the jealous tyrant. And of their all being ready to give "all for love". Such things may seem, in our opera houses, more derisible than romantic, but Alphonsus understood their power in the contemporary theatre. "It is true," he allows, "that in the poetry of Metastasio there is nothing immodest." But the catastrophic plot, the noble sentiment, the castrato thrill, come together in opera to proclaim an all-importance of a single human being's emotions, most especially that human being's eagerness for social honours and the satisfaction of individual sexual desire. The opera performance itself, not simply the tiers of boxes round the auditorium, placed the members of the audience in social circles with a human centre. Alphonsus is combatting, in his attack on Metastasio's beautiful but noxious verses, just that self-centring delusion which he is combating when he turns the Copernican orrery around "the centre of every good".

He had, certainly, long before he was confronted in the confessional with the anguish of the betrayed woman and the languishing of the infatuated man, discovered the lifelikeness of opera plot for himself. The *Sant' Alessio* operas re-told the story of a young fifth century patrician of Italy who renounced his birthright, left his father's home, his betrothed, and his aristocratic companions to nurse the poor in an Edessa hospital. By some nice turns of event and character, Alphonsus seems to be making choices in the next few years which reflect the story-line of these little operas. From 1715, when he joined the Oratorian sodality for lay graduates, until his tonsuring in 1723, he took his turn working among the patients of the *Incurabili* hospital; "Here", Tannoia wrote, "God waited for him" and Alphonsus heard an inward call to "leave the world and give yourself to me". That "leaving the world" and "getting mixed up with the world" were not everywhere easily distinguishable must have been borne upon Alphonsus' mind when he learnt something of the hospital's finances. The *Incurabili* trustees owned the Teatro San Bartolomeo and raised the greatest part of the hospital's income by leasing the opera house to the Febiarmonici company. The *Incurabili* trustees also exercised, up to 1737, a right to tax anyone who planned to stage operas in any other theatre in the capital. During the vice-reign of the Duke of Medinaceli (1696-1702), the theatre was enlarged and with the extra income the hospital brought the number of its beds to just over a thousand. What comfort could be secured for the dying was always clearly related to the amount of money to be raised from the opera company, and so, ultimately, to the popularity of the season's operas. At the hospital, as at the Conservatories and the meetings of the magistrates of Portanova, the young lawyer was confronted by what was happening in the Naples theatres. There was for him both a musician's and an hospitaler's interest in the San Bartolomeo operas from Feo's *Tyranny of Love*, 1713, and Leo's *Pisistrato*, 1714, at least until Feo's *Siface* and Vinci's *Silla the Dictator* in 1723.

Such comings together of theatre and life for the young man, especially his Alessio-like experience in the hospital, cannot but have had a repeated influence on the ways in which the maturing Alphonsus would see the world. The opera characters would return to him in the city square, along the farm track, and in the confessional. The self-absorbed bully-boy of Leo's *Achilles* would return as the sulking loser, withdrawn into his own honour, after some Neapolitan law-suit; "I'll never take his hand, Father". The lamenting queen of Vinci's *Dido* would return as the abandoned village girl; "But he promised to marry me. What is left for me now?" The menace of Poliphemus and the helpless protests of the youngsters of Handel's *Acis and Galatea* would return on the estates of the new landlord with new notions; "Do I, or do I not, own this town?" In a 1758 meditation, the *Admetus* of Ziani 1660, Lully 1674, Strungk 1693, and Handel 1727, returns as Alphonsus himself. "The divine Apollo out of love for Admetus, kept his flocks for him." Thinking on this popular opera plot prompts Alphonsus first to state a young man's belief that "the lover does not consider his own dignity when it is a question of gaining his beloved". Then he brings his meditation to the maturer expression of the self-careless love of the divine Lord, the good shepherd of the flock, who "humbled himself so far as to make himself nothing, that mankind might know how much he loved them". Such divine abandonment of all dignity must prompt in him a reciprocal self-forgetfulness. Apollo having shown him what sort of divine Lord the Christ is, Christ is showing him, the Admetus of the event, what sort of human being he is to be, and what sort of lover. "I did not know how to bear affronts patiently, because I did not know how to love thee." The theatre, its re-telling of such wondrously self-disclosing stories, and his own responses, contrasted terribly with what was happening at the ordinary celebration of the liturgy in the

Kingdom. All about him, Alphonsus saw priests, "even priests of a reformed Order", who performed the liturgy with far less attention than those who performed on stage, and women and men in their congregations looking as bored with the liturgy as if they were sitting at a concert which was lasting hours too long. No wonder that, in a 1771 sermon, acknowledging the effectiveness of the theatre in his own experience, Alphonsus revived the sixteenth century devotional language of the *Theatre of Paradise* of Mattia Bellintani (1535-1611), and the *Great Theatre of Humanity* of the Fleming, Lorenz Beyerlinck (1578-1627). He would open his own "theatre for the display of divine love".[31] There, along with the strange vitality of the Metastasian opera characters, Alphonsus would acknowledge the structuring skill of the poet. In accordance with the three act structure of contemporary opera, he would bring his congregation with him to "the first theatre" of Gethsemane, then to "the second theatre" of Pilate's judgement hall, where the lord is a "player king" for the soldiery, and at last to "the third theatre" which is "the horrible theatre of Calvary".[32] That Alphonsus did not find it at all odd, at a time when he was very suspicious of contemporary theatre, to use this libretto structure to present the most heart-stirring moments of the Church's memory of Christ, suggests how important his youthful opera-going had been in shaping his sense of what was significant for him, and how that significance should be expressed.

The Law Professor's 'New Science'

Alphonsus' acquaintance with the Greek gods and heroes had not, of course, begun when he first took his stand in the back of a box at the opera. From 1702, even earlier perhaps, until Alphonsus went off to University, the good priest Don Dominico Bonaccia had taken learned care of Alphonsus' classical studies. He had been taught to read with precise attention to the text. The literature demanded such attention. "Who", Alphonsus asks rhetorically sixty years later, "reading the *Aeneid* of Virgil, or an *Oration* of Cicero, would say that such a composition could fall out accidentally?"[33] But a precise care for the text would not, of itself, have led him to look for anything in Virgil or Cicero of significance for Christians, anything that touched on the questions treated in the theology tutorial. It is in large part because of his experience of the opera-house alignment of classical with scriptural narratives that Alphonsus can place Greek and Roman authors in such easy companionship with patristic and modern writers throughout his writing.

Alphonsus proves to be never at a loss in his dogmatic treatises for a useful classical reference or comparison. Lucretius and Epicurus mix in a short passage of *Truth of the Faith* with Eusebius and Clement of Alexandria, as well as with Hobbes and Locke, as Alphonsus struggles to make sense of the relation of Adam and Abraham and Moses to the Trojan heroes of Homer.[34] Virgil, St Cyril of Jerusalem, and the essay *On the Origin of the Franks*, 1714, of Nicolas Fréret (1688-1749), come together in Alphonsus' further discussion of Sodom. A question about divine justice in the 1756 *Brief Dissertation* which is stated in the terms proposed by Hobbes and Spinoza is given an answer beginning from a verse in Jeremiah and going on, without any suggestion of discontinuity, with citations of Homer and Hesiod, Virgil and Horace, until Alphonsus is able to make a nicely conclusive coupling of evidences from Moses and Orpheus. His lengthy contrast of the German jurist, Samuel von Pufendorf (1632-1694), and the French dictionary-maker, Pierre Bayle (1647-1706), in the 1773 *Reflections on the Truth of Divine Revelation* is sustained by references to Plato, Democritus, and Grotius, *Ecclesiastes, Ezekiel,* and Rousseau's *Emile*.[35] Alphonsus is as easy in his placing of classical references with scriptural evidences in his ascetical writing. In the *Preparation for Death*, 1758, for example, Diogenes, Seneca, and Horace, mingle with James as well as with Saladin and St Basil in a short section about our going empty-handed into the grave.[36] In one of the discourses for his *Christmas Novena* that same year, Plato, ably seconded by St John Chrysostom, ushers in Luke and Isaiah.[37] Classical references scatter through Alphonsus' analyses of ecclesial life, too. At a mention of the death of the anti-Pope and martyr, St Hippolytus, Alphonsus at once makes space to relate the death of Theseus' son, Hippolytus, "that fabled personage", who "falling from his chariot, became entangled in the harness, and being dragged along by the horses, was torn to pieces".[38] He has been reading Euripides' play. Perhaps he has been looking again at Seneca. Or renewing his recollection of the greatest of Racine's re-working of classical myth. And if he were more familiar with the philosophic and poetic achievements of the classical world, he knew something of the art of Greece. The myth of Daedalus and his work for the terrible King Minos of Crete puts him, for a moment of *The Truth of the Faith*, in mind of the splendid Parthenon frieze of Phidias and the Farnese Hercules of Lysippus displayed at Naples.[39]

In some part his easy couplings of myth and scripture are simply particular examples of his habit of holding material from different cultures together as members of a universal witness to "the truth of our holy faith". They may be reckoned with his reading the essay of Nicholas Fréret (1688-1749), on "the Chinese chronology" in the expectation of its fitting with what Archbishop Ussher had calculated from the Hebrew histories. Or with his culling from the *Geographica Sacra*, 1646, of the great Protestant scholar, Samuel Bochart (1599-1667), evidences of the first Sicilians and Cretans for a paragraph in *Truth of the Faith* about the dating of Lamech. Or his entering the philological maze of the *Origines Sacrae*, 1662, of Edward Stillingfleet (1635-1699), and coming thence with the pleasing information that the Egyptians' "Ammon" is a derivative of "Ham". Or his listing Zoroaster as the original law-giver among the Persians alongside Moses and the Jews. But although he can put the Egyptian god in parallel with the memory that "the Greeks, Romans, and other Europeans" have kept in the name of "Ion" the son of Apollo, and put Zoroaster in parallel with Pythagoras, the law-giver of Graecia Magna, there is a real difference in his use of comparisons with what had been happening in Egypt or Persia from his enjoyment of analogies founded upon elements of the glory that was Greece. He readily identifies the particular conjunction of a Greek myth with a Hebrew narrative as having peculiar interest for a Christian. He regularly puts them together. That argument, for example, in *The Truth of the Faith* about the world's not being eternal, which is so important to him, is shaped as a commentary on the first verse of *Genesis* whose apparatus includes references to both Homer and Orpheus. Alphonsus' position is sustained there by a pairing of examples of worldly things having had a beginning, one classical, one Hebrew. In 1409 BC, "as a marble tablet in Oxford records", Ceres first gave wheat to the Greeks. In Noah's time, "as Moses writes", grapes were first pressed into wine. As a side-argument to this pairing, Alphonsus confirms what some might now think a Hebrew myth by reference to a clutch of classical authors; the giants who built the tower of Babel were, his school-room reading has shown him, well known to Ovid and were at least mentioned by Virgil.[40]

His way of combining references to Greek and Hebrew cultures distinguishes Alphonsus from the run of contemporary theologians in two ways. It was distinguishing to be interested in the scriptural stories, and, equally, to be interested in considering these stories along with those of pagan culture. Joseph Butler (1692-1752), for example, the most noteworthy of those contemporary theologians, while attempting to make sense of "analogy" in terms of "likeness", dismissed the narrative forms of the Bible as irrelevant to his investigation of their doctrinal content. Nor could he, though he was the great explorer of what was meant by "Conscience", make much use of those narratives in his discussions of Christian conduct. He gave up, without regret, after he had made a moralizing mess of the lively story of Balaam and his talking ass. Lesser theologians, Catholic and Protestant alike, did not make even Butler's modest effort. Whatever energy was left after the Reformation and Counter-Reformation debates, was not employed in the exploration of the gospels as narratives. The biblical stories were put out for the philologists to pick over. Nor were gospel stories being re-told by the fashionable preachers in Lisbon, Geneva, or Uppsala. Congregations in Catholic, Calvinist, and Lutheran churches were, like those in St George's, Hanover Square, having to accustom themselves to sitting under muddled parades of controversialist learning which led into recommendations of social propriety with, perhaps, a final phrase of conventional piety. John Wesley (1703-1791), is the British exception. He proved a popular renewer of scriptural story-telling. Significantly, Wesley was like Alphonsus not only in belonging to a family that secured a musical education for the children, in enjoying a game of cards when a young man, and in preaching effective story-telling sermons when older, but in being an enthusiast for classical antiquity, though rather more careful than Alphonsus in the matter of exact and footnoted quotations.

Alphonsus took it that his readers were as well acquainted with the Greek stories and as enthusiastic for them as himself. He is quite ready in a city sermon or an ascetical tract to tell his Christian stories in ways that lend them a peculiarly classical resonance. Some contemporary readers might have noticed a hint of Aeschylus' *Agamemnon* or another of Apuleius' *Golden Ass* in the way in which Alphonsus told an anecdote of the Venerable Serafina of Capri. Many more would have recognized a pleasant memory of Prince Paris, the apple, and the three goddesses vying for his approval, as they read further in those 1758 Christmas discourses. Alphonsus adapts a story from the *Flowery Meadow* of the infant Jesus standing on the altar in front of the tabernacle and with him three young women waiting for his approving smile. With a neat demonstration of reversal of all that the world teaches us, in Alphonsus' story it is the one to whom he gives no smile at all that will receive the prize in the judgement of Jesus. The third young woman proves to be a figure of those courageous Christians who, although constantly desolate, and deprived of spiritual consolations, do not cease doing all they can to please their Lord. In a recollection of Paris and Venus, Alphonsus has been reaching for a meaning to our present loneliness. These desolate ones are, Jesus explains to the lady, "the souls in which he takes greatest delight". They are sharers in the moment of his own cry "Why hast thou forsaken me?" In the characteristic sweep of Alphonsus' theology, the Trojan princeling, the desolate young woman, the watching visionary, are brought into eucharistic coherence with the suffering Lord. Jesus makes his choice between the young women "at the moment of the elevation of the sacred Host".[41]

Alphonsus is entirely at his ease as he makes such incidental allusions to the classical story-tellings. But Christians, from patristic times, have had difficulty in defining the proper relation of pagan story and gospel. The question was certainly not resting quietly in Alphonsus' own time and city. The young man's opera-going afforded him an informal, imaginative, appreciation of the ways in which individual myths could work. But there is a theory as well as a practice of myth. He would need still to be shown how a mythology might serve the purposes of a community. How myth might be related to ritual. Most particularly, he would have to make a start on resolving questions which arose from his characteristic understanding of truth.

As far as Christian truth is distinguished from the historical, so far it may seem to be indistinguishable from the mythical. The myth is always happening. Always true. Always alive in memory and present action. Balder is always being slain by those who are driven by jealousy and blinded by ignorance. The Hopi chief's son is always unable to bring his people out of the slothful city. Demeter is always weeping for Persephone. And, to keep with the myths that Alphonsus knew from boyhood, Freud has shown us that Oedipus is always the boy next door. Medea is always living with Jason at next door but one.

It must be a question for Alphonsus how the "always" of myth is related to the "always" of the promise of Christ's mysterious presence, "I am with you always". And Alphonsus would be prompted to think more carefully of the capacity of Greek myth to bear meaning for him and his contemporaries as soon as he started to attend lectures at Naples university. Admission to the Law School was supervised by the foremost European authority on myth.

Naples, at the start of the eighteenth century, was a city of distinguished intellectuals, and among them Giovanni Battista Vico (1668-1744), was the most distinguished. A supper-table crony of Giulio Torno, a regular member of the Sunday congregation at the Girolamini church, well acquainted with Alphonsus' confessor, Tommaso Pagano (1671-1755), for whose Oratorian community he had negotiated the purchase of the library of Giuseppe Valletta, and a familiar correspondent with Ludovico Muratori, Vico, as Professor of Latin Eloquence at the University, admitted Alphonsus to the Law School in 1708.[42] It is possible that they had already met in the bookshop in the Via San Biagio dei Librai run by the professor's father, Antonio de Vico, but he died the year that Alphonsus matriculated.

These were times when social re-organization was being forced upon "the ancients" by "the moderns". The re-organization affected Neapolitan practice in some curious ways. The putting of seats at the San Bartolomeo on public sale in 1654 had effected what seemed to members of the minor nobility a most regrettable shift in the composition of the audience. Lawyers, Doctors, and even the better sort of University Professors, with their wives, were crowding the stalls. At the same time, the nobility was finding it more difficult to sustain the expense of modern life. It became a matter of some importance to Alphonsus' widower brother, Ercole, that he should find some rich princess to be his second wife if he were to keep himself in accustomed style. These nervous aristocrats were always quarrelling among themselves, chiefly about property and rents. At a time when the Naples courts were taken up with these disputes about fiefdoms, Vico thought it the lawyer's responsibility to ensure that the courts exercised a practical wisdom which took account of changes in society. In his judgement, the attorney should be the active colleague of those among the King's administrators who were then struggling to wrest power from the landed gentry and those "nobles of the bench" whose status was so important to Alphonsus' father and brother. The civil servants were also determined to subvert the powers of the ecclesiastics, especially the Inquisitors, like Alphonsus' uncle, but Vico was careful not to offend such dangerous clergymen. He concentrated in his lecture course on clearing away the mediaeval clutter of the civil law and on suggesting ways in which the law of the Kingdom might be brought into coherence with the tidier equity of Justinian.

There was some donnish clucking at Vico's concern with equity as an instrument of social justice and, therefore, of social change. He was too loud in his proposing that the law treat commoners and nobles and professors as equal in civil rights as they are equal in human nature. These things had to be discussed more delicately. So, when, in 1708, Grimani, newly-installed as Viceroy, announced that he would attend Vico's lecture inaugurating the academic year, the lecturer was persuaded to approach the topic of social change and human nature through some general remarks about the history of the world and the way in which an academic study of changing history should be conducted. Vico put himself to work with a will. He came to regard this lecture "On the Method of Studies in our Time" as indicating the whole course of his later work on the *One Principle of Universal Law,* 1720, and the even more ambitious *New Science,* 1725.

Alphonsus, as a first year student, would not yet have discovered the general unhelpfulness of university lectures. He must, like the Viceroy, have heard Vico's inaugural. After this, Vico and Alphonsus would, as Frederick Jones says, "have met each other regularly" in the course of their university business. There's no guessing how interested the great professor was in any freshman. It is evident that Alphonsus took especial note of Vico and his enquiry into the origins of contemporary social structures and the significances of myth at those origins.

Vico suggested in his 1708 lecture that there is an "eternal history" of cultures. Each passes through a course of ages, first, adoring gods, secondly, admiring heroes and thirdly, coming to rely on ordinary folk to work out the necessary conditions for a civilized life. Though Vico's *storia ideale eterna* was not quite Alphonsus' scheme, there was something in all this to encourage him in his re-examination of beginning, middle, and collapsing end. Vico concentrated attention not on inevitable collapse but on the civil lawyer's responsibility for the meantime restraint of rough, competing, forces within a modern society. So far as he allowed himself to comment on ecclesiastical matters, Vico would have the clergy as the lawyers' collaborators in this restraining project. He was, as his reference in his 1727 funeral oration for Angela Cimini evidences, especially an admirer of Antonio Torres (1636-1713), as just the sort of mystic his fellow-citizen should be, wise, well-read, conversational, and, as Vico's, "a man of holy civility, habitually courteous". The mystic was, on these same counts, greatly venerated by Alphonsus. There's no record, however, of his engaging in polite conversations with Vico about Torres and his Pious Workers, or anything else. Alphonsus makes no mention of Vico in any of his letters, books, or pamphlets. Perhaps Alphonsus is simply being as well-mannered as Torres. Perhaps it is in gentlemanly recognition that Vico had himself avoided stepping onto theological ground that Alphonsus never brings his greatest contemporary into a controversy. Such courtesy might be the nicer in the conduct of a man of the minor nobility towards a poor book-seller's son.

Vico came to speak of jurisprudence as the study of the historical stages by which each nation comes to acknowledge "a natural law of the peoples". In the first age of nature, human beings had supposed that their laws were given them by a divine authority. The "law of Jove" was exercised through significant natural events. The descent of a thunderbolt, for example. Divination was then the only appropriate jurisprudence. But such a theological state of nature never lasted. It was always followed by an age which acknowledged a "law of Achilles", the brute hero who simply referred every question to the tip of his spear. Under this law, derived from the nature of the bully-boy, the jurisprudent could only maintain fairness in men's dealing with one another by that plausible oratory and special pleading exampled in the speeches of Ulysses in the *Illiad*. This heroic law must in turn be substituted by a law which human beings had agreed to observe among themselves. This third age of nature, which is the age of "human nature", would, because it is humane and intelligently ordered, be the time of a law expressive of conscience, reason, and a sense of duty. The complementary jurisprudence, applying the third natural law to events and persons, will "look to the truth of facts themselves" and "benignly bend the rule of law to all the requirements of equity". This will be the age of complaints being taken to law courts and justly settled. There would continue to be law suits under this humane regime because there would still be men around like Achilles, and these would be employing men like Ulysses to talk for them, perverting if they could the course of justice, even, it might be, in the courts. And even in the name of the gods.[43]

At the time of Alphonsus' matriculation, Vico's influence in the university seemed to the more intelligent law students to be all for the good. Vico had vastly enlarged the scope of legal studies not only with his explanations of jurisprudence as the exercise of practical wisdom, but with complementary considerations of philosophy and philology and social theory. This, of course, made less distinguished academic specialists in the faculty very nervous. And when Vico produced his *Universal Law*, its very title seemed proof of his being a mere generalist. Vico had written in hope of being promoted to a professorship of Civil Law left vacant after the election of Nicola Capasso (1671-1745), to a chair whose lectures were time-tabled at more convenient hours. Everyone knew everyone else in the Naples Law School, and jobs were passed around an old-boy network. Alphonsus knew at least enough of Capasso to be wary of him, and that quick-witted professor proved, a few years later, to entertain a decent respect for Alphonsus. Vico's experience of the appointing committee led him to esteem Capasso a mean-spirited fellow. This was, indeed, the general opinion. At any rate, Vico's career in the university juddered to a halt when in 1723, the year of Alphonsus' own disillusionment with those charged to promote equity in Naples, it became clear that things had been fixed to secure the appointment of Domenico Gentile, a most unpleasant fool. Domenico Caravita (1670 (?)-1770), who did much to encourage Alphonsus in his legal studies, had been out-manoeuvred on the committee by Capasso. He could only counsel Vico to retire from competition.

Despite his being denied academic promotion, Vico went on widening his enquiry into the changing relation of law and the institutions of our common life. He undertook a scientific study of the history hidden in story-telling, reckoning that story-telling revealed not simply the personal traits of the story-teller but the general character of the society within which a story was being told. The careful examination of evidences in Homer's epics allows a reader, even now, to reach back to the age of "the heroic poets", and then even further back to the age of "the theological poets" and the shared beliefs of their fellows which find expression in the myths.

Late seventeenth century intellectuals, the members of the Royal Society, the gossips of Voltaire, the curial researchers of Bossuet, were generally of the opinion that other people's myths were of little or no value. As Bernard Fontenelle, 1657-1757, remarked in his essay *On the*

Origins of the Fables, 1724, "let us not look for anything in the fables but the history of the errors of the human mind". This was the opinion, too, of the Neopolitan *Investigatori*, their rivals the *Oziosi* and the members of the Viceroy's club, the *Medinaceli*. Vico belonged to all these academic societies but, contrastedly, he recognized that the Greek myths had "raised the human minds of the gentiles from earth to heaven". The myths had also carried the moral directives of heaven down to the gentiles, indicating most especially the ways in which marriage and burial of the dead should be solemnized. The myths offered the peoples of the most ancient world a "true narrative" of their society, explaining themselves to themselves.[44] Domenico Ausilio (1649-1717), the great polymath among the Naples professors of Law, had already pointed out that the first self-expressive laws of the people of Israel were set out in narrative verse. With rather greater ideological thrust, and with greater regard for the inquisitors, Vico brought philology to bear on pagan verse. His archaeological study of Greek and Roman language and literature enabled him to reconstruct the process of Greek and Roman history. Thus, he derived law, *Ius*, from Jove, *Ious*.[45] This Jove, the thunder-bearing king of Roman gods who in myth made the original landgrants to men, was a figure of all law-giving. Further myths had encouraged the primitive Greek communities to shift from hunting into agriculture. Thus, Hercules' descent into the underworld and his return in happy triumph gave them a way of understanding the seed's dying and returning. That hero's struggles against the Hydra and the Nemean lion, and his hardy pilgrimage to the garden of Hesperides, showed his people that they were to dig and delve and earn the fruits of their labours.[46]

Not everyone was pleased to discover that the myths, which they had been told by cultured tutors and which they had applauded from a box at the opera, were relics of a bestial age. It is noticeable that after *Garden of Hesperides* in 1721, the very year he began to read Vico's writings for himself, Metastasio wrote no more Herculean librettos. He did not care to think that he might be employing rough camp-fire yarns as the bases for his formal verses and elegant plots. There seems, indeed, to have been only one publicly performed Hercules opera in Naples in the years between the 1725 publication of Vico's *New Science* and the little revival of mythical subjects, after Alphonsus' death, represented by the 1793 *Hercules* of Niccolo Piccinni (1728-1800), and the 1794 *Penelope* of Domenico Cimarosa (1749-1801).

It might well seem to Vico's disgruntled colleagues in the Law School that he was conducting something very like Ludovico Muratori's Modena critique of *The defects of Jurisprudence*, 1741. Perhaps, as a young law student, Alphonsus first took notice of this element in the Professor's much-discussed project. But he came, within a very few years, to recognize that Vico's questions about narrative pressed as keenly as his questions about justice on those who preached the gospel and celebrated the eucharist. It was well enough, perhaps, for Vico to develop the contention of Phaedrus that it was by story-telling that the poor kept alive an alternate version of human life to that contained in the proclamations of the rich and powerful. Alphonsus' own missioner preaching might be heard as a complementary appraisal of that value system. And Alphonsus might have accepted, as offering parallels with his own appraisal of practice, Vico's three-fold account of the myth-maker's reasons for telling stories, "to fit popular understanding", "to disturb popular prejudices", and "to teach the vulgar to act virtuously".[47] And having been alerted first in the most positive way to some musical complementarity of myth and gospel, of *Orpheus* and the *Stabat Mater*, Alphonsus might, even as a student, have appreciated what Vico was saying about myth as both a memory of what had created a particular society and as a continuing representation of what was always true for all human beings. Vico was seconding the challenge to the theologians' conduct of their discipline which arose in the foyer and conservatory talk of contemporary music theatre.

The question of the relation obtaining between that poetic theology of the Greeks, which afforded him so much pleasure, and the gospel, seems to have been raised particularly for Alphonsus, in the midst of the general questioning prompted by the opera composers and the lawyer, when he came suddenly upon a group of Christian texts which placed a Greek god in immediate association with the crucified Lord. Preparing a sermon, he commonly found some serviceable material in the erudite *Commentary on the Bible*, 1614-1642, of Cornelius a Lapide (1567-1637), and gathering together material for his considerations *On the Passion*, Alphonsus came again upon a story that the great exegete told of Denis the Areopagite who, being then in Egypt, exclaimed as darkness covered the earth at Christ's death: "Either the God of Nature is suffering or the fabric of this world is being dissolved". The God of Nature is the arcadian Pan, whose name was commonly supposed to be connected with the *all* of pantechnicon and pantheism. Aphonsus knows that Syngelos, who wrote the *Praise of the Blessed Denis*, tells the story somewhat differently. In this version, Denis understands that "an unknown god" is suffering in the flesh. He is, in this story, evidently being readied for Paul's announcement of the identity of that "unknown god" honoured at the Athenian agora shrine. Alphonsus knows, too, the further story, lovingly preserved by Eusebius, of another pagan's hearing, on the isle of Praxos, at this same moment, a voice call out "Great Pan is dead". Eusebius, telling this story in his review of *Preparations for the Gospel*, had retreated from the identification of the Greek god with Christ. He suggested that "Great Pan" must be the Devil whose reign was ended at the saving death of Christ. But then, again, Alphonsus has been impressed too, by the suggestion of the learned Jesuit, Sebastian Barradas, (1543-1615), in his *Concordant Commentary on the Four Gospels*, 1599, that the dying Pan is the "All" that is, the Lord of All, and a figure of the "All" that is dying on the cross. Alphonsus starts this little discussion, which is supported by his reference to a number of other scholarly works, quite expecting that those who make the meditation with him will be as interested as he in such a puzzlement. He cannot, there and then, decide between the contrary opinions held by such impressive authorities. For the moment, he must leave the question hanging. He returns the meditator to the original text from which all this discussion has depended: "What we have in the gospels is that, on the day of the death of the Saviour, the whole earth was covered with darkness."[48] But the particular puzzle having been side-stepped, there remains the larger general problem of the relation of the talk of Pan and other gods in the myths to what is being announced in the gospel and in the liturgy. And it was precisely in his reading of story and ritual together that Vico's thesis must strike Alphonsus as relevant to his own enterprise.

Vico, like Wittgenstein, believed that man is a ceremonial animal. He supposed that those rites of religion, of marrying and burying, define what it is to be an human society. He argued for the persistence of a ritual principle from the most primitive times. He asserted the working of such a principle in the social arrangements of those who lived long before the reflective arguers of Grotius. They had, quite unreflectively, discerned a demand for ritual as they were telling their stories of divine power and care. But while affirming the persistence of a ritual principle from tribal times into later societies, Vico had to distinguish his meaning from that of Pierre Bayle (1647-1706), who had turned that persistence against Christian religion.

If there were continuities, these were, Bayle warned, continuities of "the dark side". In his *Historical and Critical Dictionary*, 1697, Bayle presented Jupiter as an adulterous, debauched, and vindictive mis-ruler of the pagan universe. He gave roughly the same account of King David and his government of Israel. And he noted that Christians had accepted David as a type of Christ. Bayle's subjection of Greek myth to "the principles of natural light", and this "new kind of commentary" on the scriptural record, resulted quite naturally in his proposing the thesis that the very first societies, not yet contaminated by the story-tellings of Greek or Hebrew theologians, would have been atheistic. Alphonsus was as alarmed as Vico by the style and content of Bayle's argument. The *Dictionary* became for him an exemplar of all that was wrong with modern writing. Vico showed how its influence might be countered.

The old orthodox view of these matters had been most recently expressed by Bishop Jacques Bénigne Bossuet (1627-1704). His *Universal History* , 1681, showed that the pagan decadence and its mythologies occurred once the race had abandoned that one true revelation given to Adam and preserved among the Chosen People of God. Bossuet could not be bothered by Bayle's satiric account of Israel. He was, on occasion, happy to propose David's son as a model for the son of Louis XIV. Similar notions of pagan myth were maintained by Edward Stillingfleet in his *Origines Sacrae*, 1662, and he was relying on the researches of the great German Calvinist scholar, Gerhard Johann Voss, "Vossius" (1577-1649), and the Frenchmen, Samual Bochart (1577-1667), and his pupil Pierre-Daniel Huet (1630-1721). There was some comfort in notions of pagan decadence for all sorts of Christians, evidently. Bossuet took the same model of history in *The Variations of the Protestant Churches*, 1688. He showed that the Protestant revolt and its heresies constituted a falling-off, while the one true faith, given by the Apostles, was preserved in the Catholic Church. Myth represented an early form of heretical teaching. Bossuet doubted whether there was anything more to be said about men and myth and error.

Vico read Voss and Bochart and Bossuet and recognized how old-fashioned their way of putting the argument was. But Bayle seemed worse than old-fashioned. The nastiness of Bayle's thesis was its expression of his total lack of sympathy with other human beings.

Vico knew as much as Bayle about the perverted horrors of human rituals, but he was much more sensitive than Bayle to the creative energy, the lively beauty, the forwarding idealism, which was articulated in the myths of the race. Everything that Vico said in his lectures about the recollection of the hero's story, about the function of story-telling in shaping a society, and about the society's ritual self-expression, would come together in Alphonsus' deepening appreciation of the eucharistic celebration. And it would seem that Alphonsus recognized the particular reference of Vico's favourite hero-story to Christian story-telling.

Countering Bayle, Vico declared that if Jove were so often merely an authoritarian thunderer, Hercules was a wondrous imaginative personalization of our shared appreciation of our human condition. The story of the hero which begins with "the child Hercules slaying the serpents while yet in his cradle" is, in Vico's striking phrase, "a true narrative", and the remembering and re-telling of the story is a remembering and re-telling of the truth about ourselves. His myth is always telling us that we need divine aid if we are to survive, that we can live together only if we labour for one another, and that the good human being undertakes such labour. This is universally our case. Hercules is "an imaginative universal". This demi-god manifests both a divine care for all of us and our individual human care for each other in society. The members of every viable society will have discovered their need for that divine care which is announced at the several crises of the Hercules myth. Their tellings and re-tellings of the myth will make them aware of a divine response to their need. They will, in gratitude, maintain the ritual celebration of such a signifying hero. In this ritual, they will discover the call upon them to care for each other in community. It did not at all surprise Vico that Varro had identified forty or so variants of Hercules figure among the tribes.[49] And it is not at all surprising that it is precisely in a meditation upon the imaginative universal of Hercules that Alphonsus should find his way to formulating his view of the relation of myth and revealed mystery. Or that he should have been making this meditation while kneeling at the Christmas crib.

"Behold him already come, and born in a little cave"

"It is a custom with many Christians to anticipate the arrival of Christmas", Alphonsus wrote rememberingly in 1750 or so, thinking of what they had all done to please the little Ercole, "and put up in their homes a crib for the birth of Jesus Christ". Gathered at the family crib, he and the other children heard, each year, their mother repeat the story of the baby "in a manger, unknown, and abandoned, with none around him save a few poor shepherds and a couple of animals". Such story-tellings were going on at cribs all over the city, all over the Kingdom.

Alphonsus is very aware of the distinctive local culture within which he first heard the story of Christmas. Whatever would have been the Neapolitans' case "if we had been born in Asia, or in Africa, or in America", among the savage peoples of those climes, we cannot very well make out now. As it is, "we who have been born in these regions" must attempt to appreciate the story of Jesus in the cultural terms of these regions. "All our ancestors were gentiles."[50] His view of other civilizations may be gathered from his describing the boy Jesus in Egypt as "a stranger in the midst of a barbarous people", and from his astonishment that so many admirable martyrs should have come out of "the barbarous nation" in Japan.[51] He is content that the Neapolitans are *by nature* inheritors of a particular classical culture which they are to put into relation with all that *by grace* is received by the race. The infant Jesus in the crib is described in the language of that well-known story of the infant Hercules and the serpents.

This is the way that the classic story was re-fashioned in Giraldi's great Counter-Reformation epic, *Ercole*, 1554, in d'Aubigne's *L'Hercule Chrestien*, c.1600, and Ross' *Mystagogus Poeticus*, 1648. Milton makes just this identification in his hymn *On the Morning of Christ's Nativity*, 1645:

> Our babe to show his Godhead true
> Can in his swaddling bands control the damned crew.

Alphonsus shares an education and a habit of imagination with the civilized readers and civilizing poets of contemporary Europe. It would not at all surprise those for whom he was writing this meditation that, kneeling at the crib, looking at the baby, recollecting his great labouring future, Alphonsus' imagination should carry him to the cot of baby Hercules. And then, as is the way with memory and imagination, on to the life and adventures of this baby when he grew to manhood.

"It is related in the stories of pagans", Alphonsus declares, and this opening line has precisely the form of the opening lines of his re-tellings of what is related in the *Chronicles of the Cistercians* about the Brabant monk, in the Bollandists' history of the Blessed Coletta, and in the Dominican *Diary's* entry for the seventh day of October about the beautiful but naughty Catherine.[52] There would be for Alphonsus something vulgar in stopping to put one animating story into a different category from any of these others, especially if this categorizing would leave the impression that chronicle and history and diary are somehow in a higher category. "It is related", he says, that Hercules, the son of the great god Jove, "because of the love that he bore King Augeas" undertook to tame the horses in his stable.

In Alphonsus' memory of a son of a god who for love of human beings came into a stable and undertook a life of labours, there is a confluence of mythic and christian imaginings and, perhaps, of peculiarly Catholic imaginings. When, in his poem on *"The Passion"*, Milton describes "our dearest Lord" as "the most perfect hero" who undertook "labours huge and hard", and, in the very next line, as the "sovereign priest" who enters the heavenly tabernacle of *Hebrews*. Louis Martz, one of the keenest of modern literary critics, at once suggests that Milton is attempting, not wholly successfully, to manage the imagery of Catholic post-Tridentine devotion.[53] Alphonsus, of course, moves as a native in this imaginative territory. Perhaps Don Giuseppe had told him the tale of the manly exertions of Hercules while he was on leave from the fleet when Alphonsus was a small boy. Perhaps Don Bonaccia had introduced the bright youngster to the hero in hopes of making his explanations of Greek grammar more exciting. Perhaps, again, he overheard a helpful visitor explain to his brother, Ercole, something of the grand significance of his name. Certainly, Don Giuseppe and Donna Anna, in having this last child christened Ercole Maria in 1706, had shown the ten years old Alphonsus, if he still needed to be shown, that classical and christian cultures came together for noble Neapolitans at the celebrations of a baby son.

These meditations for Christmas were published at the very lowest point of Hercules' popularity as a hero in the local theatres. But the myth of Hercules clearly delighted Alphonsus by its present truthfulness, its expression of what is always the same: divine love is always expressed in a stable. He has yet, of course, to specify the relation of the "always" of myth to the "always" of the gospel, but only after the affirmation of likeness, is Alphonsus ready to speak of some unlikeness. This pagan story is, he says, "of the imagination" while the Christian story of Jesus from manger to cross is "of faith".[54]

Alphonsus makes the same distinction of imagination and faith in *The Truth of the Faith* and in the *Meditations* which he excerpted and revised from his 1773 reflections *On the Passion* and in the *True Bride of Jesus Christ*. There is, he says there, more than one way of coming into the divine presence. The first is by imagining. We can re-present the Redeemer at one time in one mystery and at another in another. "Now as an infant lying in the manger of Bethlehem", for example, or "as a criminal in his Passion in Jerusalem."[55] It is a guarantee of the Christian uses of such imagining that St Teresa praises this practice. The second method consists in seeing with the eye of faith that the Lord is ever-present and that we are ever in his presence. To realize this divine presence, we have only to make an affectionate act of faith. From this, we may readily go on to fuller acts of love. There is not an opposition but a complementarity of entries upon the presence of Christ. In saying that the first method is good but not so secure as the second, Alphonsus is making a careful assessment of what is available to the Christian. He was making this assessment of imagination and its Christian uses within a local debate. In the years just before Alphonsus was born, Cardinal Innico Caracciolo of Naples was complaining that his city was full of madcap "Quietists" who had set themselves to rid religion of every work of imagination. They were liable, as they walked to the altar-rail for Communion, to give a physical shake of the head to rid themselves of any distracting image. Among such images, they included that of the Lord on the cross. There was nothing in any of this to attract Alphonsus. Contrariwise, a theology which starts from the sight of Calvary that Paul sees at the celebration of the liturgy is a theology which suggests that Christians take the risk of exercising that faculty of imagination themselves. By that power Christians may make their fullest response to the Lord. It is Alphonsus' oft-repeated theme that "by imagining" as he says in the *True Bride of Jesus Christ*, that we know "our Redeemer is present in our company", and "by imagining" that we remain in his company.[56] More particularly, it is by imagining that we come into the theatre of Christ's Passion.

"Imagine thyself", Alphonsus suggests in his *Considerations and Affections on the Passion*, at the scourging of Jesus by the Roman soldiers of Pilate's barracks, "present at this horrible tearing of the flesh."[57] Alphonsus had seen the marked backs of galley slaves among the rowers of his father's fleet. There is a realism in his language which might make its terrible appeal to the sadist hiding in each of us, but here again Alphonsus effects a shift from the imagining of physical torture to the imagining of psychological torture. This shift does not bring about any lessening of horror. "Imagine", he says, Jesus at the post, "blushing all over for shame."[58] There is an immediate rush of sympathy. He feels with Jesus at this moment. He shudders. In his final years of illness, it was a climactic humiliation for Alphonsus to be undressed by others. "I cannot explain myself fully on this subject", he said when describing how, even in his last agony, St Peter of Alcantara would not allow any of his brethren to touch any part of his body.[59] But, however obscurely, Alphonsus knew that there was some dreadful, immediate, connection of what was thrust upon his imagination when he was touched by others and the suffering of Christ among the soldiery which he was imagining in his meditation. Imaginative sympathy makes real demands. However ashamed of his own nakedness, however distressed by the thought of others touching his body, however horrible his phantasms, he must, on imagining the nakedness of his Lord, "my Jesus, wounded and torn for me", cry out to the executioners to halt their scourging and to strip him, "would that I might be torn myself for thee".[60] The silent bounds of Alphonsus' meditation are burst open by his cry; "It is I myself who have offended!"

Such imagining is not an instrument for time travel, merely making the past, things as they were, emotionally powerful, rather it is an operation of the faculty by which we may come to accept the present truth about ourselves. Any imaginer on the Way of the Cross, "meeting Jesus as he passes along this sorrowful journey" will be prompted to ask, feelingly, "Have you not yet had your fill of suffering?",[61] but imagining Christians are to be brought further along the way than human sympathy would take them. Further than the terrible imaginings which drove Alphonsus to dab great gouts of painted blood across his picture of the crucified Lord. Alphonsus is offering not only "affections" but "considerations". He has, as ever in the most impassioned of his ascetical writing, the theological end in view. His imagining the Passion is towards an intensification of the Christian's faithful understanding. He has made his own Vico's estimate of "imagining" as a way of "comprehending" experience. He has seen the possibilities of such imaginative comprehension at the originating centre of christian experience. The Christian may, by imagination, come into the very Trinitarian life of God. Others, even the young Michelangelo, may pause in compassionate imagination at the Pietà, at the sight of Jesus dead in the arms of Mary; Alphonsus brings the Christian into the further dimension of this moment: "Imagine yourself, then, to behold the Eternal Father with Jesus dead in his arms".[62] The Eternal Father looks to the Christian imaginer across the body of his Son: "See how I have condemned him to die upon this cross, afflicted, abandoned even by myself who love him so much". And the imaginer will be told the cause of this awful reality: "This is what I have done that you may love me". By imagining, the eternal, present, significance of the torture and death of Christ is made apparent. Imagination may be propaedeutic to faith.

He cannot bear even to imagine the horrid idols of pagan liturgies.[63] But in categorizing the ancient myths of his own culture as a work of imagination, Alphonsus is not suggesting any simple lessening of the significance of the stories that his ancestors told of Hercules or any other of the culture's figures of divine presence. Rather he was putting a more precise value on these gods and the stories told of them, just when most Neapolitans were interpreting Vico's thesis as encouraging them to put a distance between themselves and their ancestors.

If, getting up from the prie-dieu at the crib, or closing the meditation book which has made the scourging of Christ "so real", we suppose that imagination will yield to faith at the eucharistic celebration or as the Christian kneels before the Blessed Sacrament in the tabernacle, we are still dealing in our own sense of every distinguishing implying some devaluation. But for Alphonsus the most intense moment of imagining can be the most intense moment of faith. "Imagine, when you celebrate", he tells the priest, in *The Sacrifice of Christ*, 1776, "that you are on Calvary." And the best way to keep from distraction at the priest's communion is that he hold "the wounds of the Saviour" in imagination, and then "let us imagine to ourselves that Jesus is saying to us what he once said to his servant Margaret of Ypres, 'Behold, the beautiful union between me and thee'".[64]

The exact relation of what is "of imagination" with what is "of faith" in his theological procedures, is made clearer by what Alphonsus does not do with the Hercules cycle as much as by what he does do with it. The classically aware meditator, once the imagination has been stimulated to recognize Herculean resonances in the infancy narratives, might well expect to be brought on to another famous incident in the hero's adventures and its relation to the resurrection narratives of the gospel.

"It is related" that Hercules, like the god Apollo, was the friend of Admetus and his wife Alcestis.[65] Whether Don Bonaccia gave him Euripides' *Alkestis* to read or not, Alphonsus would certainly have known the tale of Hercules' return to Admetus' court after some fight, and his discovering that Alcestis had willingly given her life for her husband. The gods had demanded that either Admetus die or some other die in his place. Alcestis had sacrificed herself for him. She had been buried. So Hercules went down to the land of the dead to find her. And, after three days, she had been brought back by the triumphant hero. This splendid story had its place in the conversation of all civilized people. The widower Milton, in *Sonnet xix*, had been able to celebrate a dream of resurrection happiness in the assurance that this Herculean resonance would be immediately heard by his audience:

> *Methought I saw my late espoused saint*
> *Brought to me like Alcestis from the grave,*
> *When Jove's great Son to her glad husband gave*
> *Rescu'd from death.*

Lully's *Herakles* ballet, 1658, and his *Herakles the Lover*, 1662, had led into the *Alceste* or *The Triumph of Herakles* opera of 1674 with just such a resurrection climax. In the years when Alphonsus was putting together these Christmas mediations, there was a Gluck *Alceste* at Weimar. More nearly, Aurelio Aureli (c.1652-1708) had produced a dramatic version of this episode, almost wholly taken from Euripides' play, which had been vastly popular among Neapolitan audiences since the end of the seventeenth century, and which Pietro Andrea Ziani (c.1616-1684), master of the Chapel Royal at Naples, had made into an equally popular opera *L'Antigona delusa da Alceste*, 1660. After a visit to Naples, Handel made his own version of the story in his *Admeto* opera of 1727. That same year, Andrew Ramsay (1686-1743) had, in his *Travels of Cyrus*, made a lengthy parade, quite in Vico's manner, of the likenesses of Hercules and every Son of Jupiter who rescues his people from death and every enemy, leading to a likening of them all to Christ. Even when other elements of the Hercules myth cycle had ceased to hold the

Neopolitan stage, Gaetano Latilla (1711-88), could put on an *Alceste* in 1740 which played alongside the still popular Ziani opera.

Whatever the source of Alphonsus' acquaintance with the Hercules cycle, his meditating in 1758 upon Jesus, the "true Son of God" who "for love of men" had humbled himself and been born in a stable, had led a contemptible life, and had been put to death on an infamous gibbet, he would seem immediately positioned to make the Herculean connection with the tomb and the risen Lord. Almost any other eighteenth century gentleman would have proceeded into something of the sort. But what almost any other gentleman may achieve will not necessarily be Alphonsus' aim. He does not take up the opportunity provided by the Alcestis incident to present a little resurrection paradigm. That element of the Greek myth did not fit his characteristic exposition of Christian faith. Not at Christmas. And not even at Easter. The infant Hercules is not allowed to grow into the hero who comes back victorious from the underworld.

The hero of poetry and opera is converted, in the very next meditation, not into a figure in a resurrection drama but into an usher for a Corpus Christi mystery: "Happy was that grotto, that crib, that straw; but still happier are those souls who love this lovable Lord with fervour and tenderness, and who receive him in the Holy Communion into hearts burning with love. Oh! with what desire and pleasure does Jesus Christ enter into and repose in the heart that loves him!"

Alphonsus' early enthusiasm for cosmology had equipped him with a language in which he might say what he wanted to say about a shareable presence of Christ and a cosmic liturgy. His opera-going had enabled him to reach a generous view of the interaction of revelation and his classical culture. Kneeling at the crib, he is recapitulating what Vico had been saying about the relation of the figure of Hercules, that "imaginative universal" to what is always true of human beings. Alphonsus would effect a similar conversion of what he next learned of the world. After Law School, Alphonsus was placed by his father in the Law Office of Don Luigi Perrone, and then, gradually, he built up his own thriving practice. His experience in the courts proved decisive for his understanding of another element in his theology. He came there to appreciate the dangerous irrelevance of temporal categories in any consideration of our significant life before God.

Alphonsus' theology declares itself on different occasions to be the theology of an educated and cultured man, interested in planets, enthusiastic for music, theatre, and at home in the classical mythology. It is also, most evidently a lawyer's theology.[66] It takes its illustrations from the world of the accused's guessing that there is not enough evidence to convict him, of the claimant's calculating the portion of a property that is his rightful inheritance, and of the criminal's being condemned to throw the dice with his life as the stake.[67] These are his common examples. As with Luther in his Türm and Newman in his Littlemore rooms, a vital, differentiating, element of Alphonsus' theology was laid down at a moment of his being taken by surprise in the midst of his professional occupations. The pattern of his theology bears the mark of the Amatrice law-suit.

Amatrice is a small town in the Abruzzo Altiore, seventy kilometres east of Rieti, the officially-recognized geographical centre of the country, *umbilicus Italiae*.[68] The main street of Amatrice is just long enough to accommodate a town-hall, two small palaces, and three churches. Around this rather ordinary hill-settlement circles, as the modern guide-book says, a chain of mountains; these heights are more impressive than beautiful, bare-cliffed at their tops, and it is a good way down their slopes before the hardiest ever-green trees get a hold on soil. At their very bases are some few poor fields walled against winter snows, and a splendid, shining, lake. I do not suppose that Alphonsus travelled so far north to get a feel of the place, but he had acquainted himself enough with the geography of the area to supplement with a reference to Mount Colombo the list he found in Baronius' *Ecclesiastical Annals* of places where rocks had split at the *Consummatum est* cry of Christ.[69]

A "little patch of ground", then, but like Hamlet's sledded Polack and Norweyan Fortinbras, the Hapsburgs and the Grand Duke of Tuscany were, in 1716, prepared to try their whole force to "debate the question of this straw". They both made loud claims to the ownership of the fiefdom. The resulting law-suit was conducted in the Naples courts because Amatrice had, since the accession of Carlo I in 1268, been a Northern outpost of the Kingdom of the Two Sicilies, and was, indeed, distinguished as *Fidelis Amatrix* on account of the little university town's having remained loyal to King Ferdinando during the Barons' Conspiracy of 1485.

There has been a generally-accepted story of the linkage of this court-case with Alphonsus' turning from the worldliness of lawyers and litigants. Newman repeated this version of events in his *Apologia*, remarking that on this occasion Alphonsus was "betrayed into the commission of what seemed like a deceit, though it was an accident", and that Alphonsus thereupon left the profession, repeating to himself the disappointed moan, "O world, I know you now!" Newman was relying on Tannoia's account, published very soon after Alphonsus' death, and already expressive of the Congregation's settled view of the Founder. In Tannoia's story, Alphonsus, having misread a document in the brief, wasted his considerable oratorical gifts in defence of the indefensible, and was quashed, humiliatingly, by the opposing lawyer's indicating the correct reading of the text. Benefitting from the researches of Oreste Gregorio in 1953 and André Sampers in 1980, we may reconstruct events rather differently.[70] The indefatigable Théodule Rey-Mermet was, in his 1987 biography, *Le Saint du Siècle des Lumières*, able to present a view of this "accident" and its concluding cry which makes much better sense. As he observes, the older biographers should, under the circumstances have expected Alphonsus to exclaim: "Alfonso, I know you! You are unpardonably absent-minded!" But a note set down on 29 August, 1758, by Pasquale Bonassisa, recording Alphonsus' recreation room conversation that evening, when put into place, gives the incident a wholly new aspect. That the Amatrice case and its result should have prompted Alphonsus' reconsideration of his plan for a life in the law courts is now quite understandable. And a re-reading of other documents in the case suggested by the Bonassisa note makes clearer the effect of these proceedings on Alphonsus' subsequent thinking about a range of matters. Neither Rey-Mermet nor Alphonsus' most recent and most stimulating biographer, Frederick Jones, had reason to look at all closely at the arguments that the opposing litigants were employing but they seem to me most significant for an understanding of Alphonsus' theological enterprise.

In 1723, when Alphonsus was twenty-seven years old, he was retained by Filippo Orsini, Duke of Gravina, in a claim upon Amatrice against Prince Gian Gastone, the second son of the Grand Duke Cosimo III de Medici. He was more fortunate than Vico in the workings of the old boy network among the Naples lawyers. His friend Domenico Caravita, the son of Nicola Caravita (1647-1717), at whose house he had attended informal seminars on a wide range of legal topics, was now president of the Sacro Regio Consiglio which was to oversee the case. Alphonsus had, too, an ambivalent connection with the Orsini of Gravina. In 1715, Don Giuseppe, presuming as one nobleman on another, had confidently presented his fourteen years old son Cajetan, not yet ordained but destined that way, as a candidate for the benefice of the Abbey of San Martino de Ferrilli which was in the Orsini's gift.

Filippo Orsini's claim upon Amatrice derived from a murderous relative. Alessandro Orsini of Bracciano had been put under preventive detention in 1648 to await trial for killing his duchess, Anna Maria Caffarelli, upon suspicion of her unfaithfulness. On his release from the Castel San Angelo, still untried, in 1677, the accused nobleman found that among his huge debts there was one owed to his cousin, Domenico Orsini of Gravina, which had been accumulating interest all the time he had been in jail. Alessandro Orsini, therefore, mortgaged his property at Amatrice to the Duke of Gravina as surety for the eventual repayment of the thousands of ducats. The wretched man died in 1692 and, without any reference to the Orsini of Gravina, the Regia Camera della Sommaria, the tax office in Naples, sequestered Amatrice in lieu of the deceased's unpaid taxes. Alessandro Orsini's heir, Duke Flavio Orsini of Bracciano, seems not to have wanted to have anything to do with the debt-laden fiefdom. The tax-men, to recover something of their losses, sold a grant of the fiefdom to the Grand Duchess of Tuscany, Vittoria della Rovere, who had a family connection with the barony and entertained a notion that it might be pleasant to sit by the shining lake. The Orsini of Gravina may have despaired of ever getting the killer's debt repaid, but they never surrendered their right in the mortgaged Amatrice. It was this right which Filippo Orsini hired Alphonsus to promote in 1723.

The Duke of Gravina had been stirred to renew his family's claim at the noise made by a related case begun in the Naples law courts in 1716. The Holy Roman Emperor, Charles VI, appeared at the Tribunal to claim Amatrice from its present occupier, the Prince of Tuscany. The Emperor's claim to the barony derived from the son of the killer. Francesco Felice Orsini, upon his father's being detained by the Roman authorities, had instituted a suit against him, intending to vindicate his mother's honour by bankrupting his father. Winning this case, Francesco Felice Orsini retired to the court of Vienna. There he died, childless. He bequeathed his property to the Emperor, Leopold I. This history could be represented as vindicating a Hapsburg claim on the barony. There was, said the imperial lawyers in 1716, a line of inheritance from father to son, Francesco Felice had been heir to his father Alessandro Orsini, and Emperor Charles is the heir to his father, Emperor Leopold. So Francesco Felice Orsini's fief of Amatrice should have been inherited by Charles VI. This Hapsburg claim was, however, vitiated by the Orsini son's having died before his father. Amatrice had not been his to bequeath to the Emperor.

The Imperial claim was rendered shakey, too, by the Emperor's not being descended from Alessandro Vitelli of Cita di Castello. This gallant captain had been granted Amatrice in 1538 by the Emperor Charles V, the present Emperor's great-great-great-grandfather's brother, "on account of his prudence and his courageous service in the wars". The grant was to the captain "and to his successors legitimately descended from his body in perpetuity". Alessandro Orsini had been the grandson of Vitelli's elder daughter, Beatrice. The Grand Duke of Tuscany's mother, Vittoria della Rovere, was the great-grand-daughter of Vitelli's younger daughter, Isabella. So Prince Gian Gastone might have been expected to rest his case on this direct lineage. But the Medici family had always hesitated to state their case in this historical way. Their lawyers had told them that to do so would have left them heirs not only to Amatrice but also to the debt owed to the Orsini of Gravina which would come with it. The approach of the Grand Duchess Vittoria to the Camera della Sommaria in 1693, if it had begun with some quick flourishment of her Vitelli ancestry, had gone on rather more quietly to suggest that they could get some of their money back by off-loading the estate for cash. The revenue men would grant Amatrice to the Grand Duchess as a new fiefdom, *in feudum novum*, to which, in accord with the law governing new fiefdoms, *iuxta feudum novum*, no debts would be attached. Everyone kept a knowing silence about the more than five hundred thousand ducats now owed to the Orsini of Gravina. Shortly thereafter, the Grand Duchess died. Her second son, Cardinal Francesco Maria de Medici, possessed the township in unjust peace until his death in 1711. Amatrice then passed to his nephew, Prince Gian Gastone. But, rather belatedly, in 1716, the Hapsburg lawyers began proceedings to enforce the will of Francesco Felice Orsini. Three years before this, the Austrian Hapsburgs had been confirmed at the Treaty of Utrecht as the rulers of Naples, and they now had time and energy and the necessary influence to pursue their interests through their own Neapolitan courts. Francesco Felice Orsini had died, they asserted, owing moneys to their master's ancestor and, in settlement of his estate' debts, the Medici would have to turn over the barony to the Hapsburgs. In 1719, as this suit was moving slowly through the Naples courts, and the lawyer's clerks were fetching all the old documents out of the archives in the Uffizi, the Kanzleigericht, and the Tribunal, the Duke of Gravina woke up to the possibility of his being paid the vast sum to which the mortgage now amounted. He, too, hurried into court. The Sommaria dealt quite quickly with the Orsini side-show, refusing to entertain a Gravina claim on the fiefdom's revenue. The Duke, however, having scented the possibility of some extra cash, became enthusiastic for litigation, and appealed to the Sacro Regio Consiglio. He recruited a couple of young lawyers to retrieve all that was being unjustly with-held from the Gravina Orsini.

It was on the Orsini case that the Medici possession of the township was wrongly based. The Camera della Sommaria had had no authority to dispose of Amatrice to the Grand Duchess as a new fiefdom. They should have withheld it from her, as the rightful inheritor of an old fief, only until they had obtained their just returns from the estate. Then the Grand Duchess, as the Vitelli heir, should have paid the Orsini their just dues. The Orsini added that the tax-men had no right to make a grant of Amatrice, or any other fief, new or old, to anyone. The granting of fiefdoms was not the business of the tax-collectors. On his looking over the papers in the case, Alphonsus seems to have concluded that the courts would have very little sympathy for any suggestion that their fellows in the bureaucracy had done anything improper by their disposing of a fiefdom. But there did seem to be a good hope of the judges listening to an argument that the tax-men had not been empowered to make this particular grant of Amatrice as a "new" fiefdom.

A precedent, established by Giovanni de Rosa in a case before the same court had, Alphonsus and the Hapsburg lawyers thought, made it possible to argue in their cases that a new quality does not by itself make a fief new and that being free from debt was merely such a quality. So it was Alphonsus' plea that being declared "free from debt" could not have converted Amatrice into a new fiefdom in 1693. The Grand Duchess Vittoria had entered into an old fiefdom. The Prince Gian

Gastone now owed old debts. If it were, contrarily, argued that while being declared free of debt did not "by itself" render the fiefdom new, that declaration, being taken with an explicit grant by the Camera della Sommaria of a new fief, added up to enough to settle the matter in law, Alphonsus was convinced that his client had a claim in equity. Every just debt should be honoured in a court of justice. Whatever the rival claims of the Hapsburgs and Medici to baronial rights, the Orsini had a right to the redemption of the original bond.

Neither the linear argument of historical inheritance from father to son, nor the assertion of a wholly new situation, could, Alphonsus thought, suppress the plain justice of his case. But, in July, 1723, both together, they managed to do just this. The judges knew what was required of them by the greater men concerned in the main case. They pointed to the specific words of the grant to the Grand Duchess. They accepted as given, not open to argument, that the fiefdom, being granted *in novum feudum* was free of debt. They might have read things differently if they had delayed a little. In less than a year, Filippo Orsini's uncle, Cardinal Pietro Francesco Orsini, would be enthroned as Pope Benedict XIII. But on the judges' yielding to the unjust pressure of the Emperor and the Grand Duke, neither of them wanting a fief with debts attached, and their refusing to ensure the equity of the proceedings, Alphonsus realized, for the first time it seems, what the world is like, *"O Mondo...."*

The law-suit as a paradigm of the ways of the world presented a warning against his continuing in the Tribunal. "Courts of law", Alphonsus observes in *The Treasury* of preaching materials, 1760, "are dangerous places." He would be an advocate only in "the causes of poor sinners" before God. Only in the heavenly courts could the disregard of equity be witnessed with equanimity. There, he could, as he says, rely on Mary to suppress evidence, call off the debt collectors, and quietly press her hand on the scales to outweigh the sinner's guilt.[71] Alphonsus, in contrast to his later reference in all his petitions to "Mary, my great advocate" expresses the disappointment he felt at the proceedings of Domenico Caravita, of Giuseppe Sorge, the procurator of the Hapsburgs, and of Antonio Maggiochi, the Medici agent. He would not live with such men.

Alphonsus would not wait for the judges' second move in the game, which was to propose that, since there might, if it were looked at, be some plausibility in the suggestion that the Grand Duchess had inherited the fief as an old fief before she bought it as a new fief, the Medici should pay off some of the outstanding debts, those owed to the Hapsburgs, for example. Thereupon, the court decreed, all contention would be at an end. The case dragged on for forty years. The lawyers were still arguing in 1766 when Maurice de Landes, on a tour of Italy, observed that the Naples barristers "dispute so loudly and threaten one another so fiercely that you tremble for their lives; but usually nothing happens".

This warning paradigm remained with Alphonsus. There are reminiscences of the Amatrice proceedings as late as the 1766 *Way of Salvation* and the 1773 reflections *On the Passion*. "The kings of the earth, after a victory over their enemies", as everyone knows, "confer a share of the spoils on their soldiers", from this resorting to warfare and this rewarding of warriors with title-deeds the rest follows. "Men esteem it a great affair to gain a law-suit, to obtain a title, or to acquire an estate."[72] Thus it is that lawyers flourish.

It might seem fanciful, even mischievous, to suggest that there is some connection between his experience with the Medici lawyers and Alphonsus' enthusiasm for St Maria Maddalena de Pazzi, who was a member of the Florentine family which had so famously opposed the government of Lorenzo de Medici and his brother.[73] Or his attributing to a Medici pope, Leo XI, 1-27 April, 1605, rather than to St Leo IX (1049-1054), the dying regret: "It would have been better for me to have been the porter of my house than to be pope". It is as unproveable that his experience of the imperial procurator prompted Alphonsus' distaste for the Hapsburg courts of Maximilian II and Rudolf II at Vienna and Philip II and Philip III at Madrid.[74] But as often as he tells unflattering stories of these Hapsburgs, they suggest some reminiscence of the powerful men who perverted the course of justice in the Amatrice case. And he tells them often: in *Preparing for Death*, 1758, *Prayer The Great Means of Salvation*, 1759, *The Way of Salvation*, 1766, *The Practice of the Love of Christ*, 1768, and *On the Passion*, 1773. And if the reader is reminded of the Amatrice lawyers and their clients, then it is likely that Alphonsus was reminded of them too. Making an estimate of what Alphonsus says about the Hapsburg princes is perhaps complicated by his writing, after 1734, as the subject of the adulation-demanding and Hapsburg-envying Bourbons, but there are other, simpler, reminders of the litigants in Alphonsus' works. The story that he tells, for example of the companion of Giovanni Vitelli who ignored the good advice of that Servant of God and ended up being murdered by another member of the family. Or the more cheerful memory of Maddalena Orsini, who made such a spirited reply to Christ when he appeared to her, and who urged the sisters to laugh in the cloister, "for you have every reason to be happy". Or, his quick reference to the great Servant of God, Lucrezia Orsini, and that excitable visionary's shout on her being shown "the sublime dignity to which consecrated virgins are raised in heaven".[75] And there is a resonance of Alphonsus' indignation at the behaviour of Caravita and of Mauleone, the President of the Regia Camera della Sommaria, in the impassioned apostrophe of Alphonsus' 1760 *Duet* to the "unjust and unfair judge", and in his denouncing, during his reflections *On the Passion*, "that miserable judge"who perverts justice because he is "blinded by fear of losing imperial favour".[76] The Naples judges showed what Pontius Pilate is always like. Alphonsus can even take a mature look at his own melodramatic response to this court-room defeat. He knows better now what injustice really is. It is only at Pilate's condemnation of Jesus that a decent man should exclaim "O injustice" and "Injustice such as the world has never known!"[77]

Beyond these anecdotal reminiscences, there are hints of this miserable suit in Alphonsus' use of the lawyer's terms which theologians generally have taken to express their soteriologies. His meeting with injustice, with the withdrawal of surety, and the refusal to redeem a debt, may have given an urgency to Alphonsus' use of justice and surety and pledge, and led him into shaping his Christological arguments by reference to written security and to the possibility of your entire property being lost and to the need to keep an exact account of all your goods for your heirs.[78] But it is in his consistent and distinguishing distaste for what is new and what is historical that the resonances of this old Amatrice case can be most clearly discerned in Alphonsus' theological writing. That insistence on the Christian's living in the present, and, in this present, enjoying the eternal, which is so striking in Alphonsus' mature theology has a prompting in the 1723 case.

Coming to the court-room with total trust in the due process of equity, Alphonsus was compelled to endure the success of iniquity. The litigants presented themselves to him as figures of opposite but equally negative forces. The Medici rejection of anything in the past which they did not relish, and their self-serving adoption of something novel, showed him what underlay the errors of contemporary heretics. The falsifying repetition of "new fiefdom", "new fiefdom", by the Grand Duchess, the Prince, and the Medici agent, warned him against every innovator, every "modern unbeliever". Equally, that deceitfulness in the management of history which had characterized the proceedings of the Hapsburg lawyers as they alleged the Vitelli and Orsini connections of their Imperial masters, warned him against another heretics' trick. The truth-seeking Christian should not look for satisfaction from those who cited history for their purpose. He never forgot that pile of dusty documents on the table in front of Giuseppe Sorge who later, quite in character, composed a foot-noted and appendixed history of the Hapsburg claim.

Alphonsus did not, in 1723, have to make the connection of unfairness, a dispute about property, and breaking away from the harmful company of his fellows, and religion. That had been made for him fifteen years before. One of the very few stories recorded of his boyhood has just the shape of the Amatrice story. On an outing with other twelve-year-olds, Alphonsus had been accused of cheating at a game of rolling oranges, his beaten opponent had been loath to honour his bet, and had sworn in frustration. "So you are prepared to offend God for a few carlins", said Alphonsus with the same sense of a conjoint dishonouring of equity and the divine order which sound in "O world, I know you". And he had taken in 1708 the way he took in 1723. He had left the picnicking boys as fast and completely as he left the lawyers. He had gone off to pray. This story was told, years later, by Don Domenico Villani as suggesting that Alphonsus was "a saint from his youth". Re-telling it recently, Frederick Jones suggests that another story of Alphonsus' scrumping for lemons in the Caravita orchard shows Alphonsus in a more normal light. Alphonsus, however, is neither typical as a saint nor normal, he is particularly distinguishable among the saints as among the rest. The story of the orange game, taken with the Amatrice case, evidences Alphonsus' having just his sort of distinction from his youth.

Alphonsus was, too, when he was hired by Filippo Orsini, already the man to distrust the claims of the old-fashioned and the new-fangled. An event is received differently by persons of different temperament.

105

If God were waiting for him in the *Incurabili* sick ward, he was waiting for him in every sort of experience, and, assuredly, in the conduct of this case. Alphonsus' cry *"O Mondo!"* suggests a sudden realization of how things are in this world, but Alphonsus was taking the outcome of the Amatrice law-suit as confirming what he had always known deep-down. Temperament will always find out occasions for its expression. The Amatrice litigation and its outcome re-convinced Alphonsus of his own rightness in concentrating on whatever is always true for him, irrespective of the historical or future circumstances of his experience.

"From whom all fatherhood comes", and all motherhood

In 1723, Alphonsus was still living at home and the immediate effect of his resolution to quit the courts was a violent estrangement of the Captain from his son. Don Giuseppe was furiously uncomprehending that a single set-back should have so confirmed Alphonsus against a career in the law courts. But it was not his rage that Alphonsus found most difficult to resist. There is a fine story of his responding with equal ferocity when his father lost his temper with a servant. He found it much more difficult to deal with Don Giuseppe's sulks. His father would not attend the ceremony in 1724 when Alphonsus received the clerical tonsure. He looked away when he met Alphonsus wearing the cassock in the house. For a whole year, he avoided, so far as he might, talking to his son. Much later, Alphonsus' brother, Ercole, a grown man, married, with a house of his own, was reduced to tears by their father's emotional tyranny. Alphonsus, writing to his father then, remembered as if it were today, what it had been like for him: "For heaven's sake, put an end to your black humours....he is your son, not a dog".[79] But in 1723, Muzio di Maio, the senior advocate of the Naples bar, had ceased to invite the bright young man to supper, expecting him to show a proper respect, and to agree with Don Giuseppe's view of the matter. Caravita urged him not to make so much of the affair, to be sensible, to come back into court. Such continuing estrangement from his father, and those whom he had been trained to honour, would prompt any decent youngster to ask himself over and again whether he were not in some way guilty for this terrible situation's arising, even if he were assured, when he thought about it clearly, that he had done nothing wrong. That pain could not be forgotten. Alphonsus returns many times to that angry situation with fascinated horror. "When one's leaving the world is in question, there are no worse enemies than parents, who, either through considerations of their own interest or through emotion, prefer to set themselves against God, by turning their children away from their vocation, rather than give their consent to it." Alphonsus waited until after Don Giuseppe's death in 1745 to liken him and other fathers to "the princes of the Jews" to whom the apostle said "Judge whether it is right to obey you rather than God". But, alive or dead, it may have been the worst insult that Don Giuseppe was ever offered by a member of his own class when Alphonsus put such an opposing parent into the same category as the German, bourgeois, heretical, Luther, "who taught that a person sins by entering religion without the consent of his parents". He has a range of saints to back him. "Let us, with St Bernard, call them not parents, but murderers!" But he really does not need them. "St Thomas expressly teaches that in the choice of a state of life children are not obliged to obey their parents." That should settle the matter.[80]

Don Giuseppe's anger was, however, sustained by his sense that his eldest son had gone against the divinely established rights of a father over his children. Don Giuseppe identified with the possessive and punishing divinity of Israelite story. On his cabin shelf stood four lurid statues of Jesus, showing the Son of God agonizing in the Garden, lashed at the post, crowned with thorns, and receiving the Cross. There was a likeness, evidently, of the world ordered by God and the ship commanded by the Captain. Everywhere men, innocent and guilty alike were to be stripped, and tied down, and whipped. The chained ranks of condemned oarsmen were quickly made to realize what had to be endured. Obedience was the only virtue which the Captain required aboard his ship and everywhere else, in the home as on the bridge. "A man should chastise his children", Alphonsus remarked ruefully more than fifty years later, "with the tenderness of a parent, and not with the harshness of a galley-sergeant."[81]

Don Giuseppe would not have been the only father, then or later, to impress upon his family the divine sanction for his fault-finding authority. Not at all reflectingly, perhaps, they might be persuaded to find in him the image of God. And then to find in God the image of Don Giuseppe. The Father, like his father, would note, judge, and punish each jot and tittle, dram and scruple of his fault-filled life. Alphonsus might be the more awfully convinced of the truth of this image by the *Hebrews* account of the oppressed life. "God is treating you like sons." But not Alphonsus alone in the house, his sisters, too, Marianna and Teresa, were plagued by a fearful awareness of the minute demands of God, and it was only days before her death that Donna Anna obtained peaceful release from her scruples.

A scruple is a matter of small weight. To be "scrupulous" is to be concerned with small things. It is to be precise, exact. Like a lawyer reading a document. In this sense of exact care about small things, Alphonsus was scrupulous in his dealings with his Venetian publisher, Giambattista Remondini and his son Giuseppe, maddening them with his minute instructions about the printing of his works. But to be "scrupulous" is to be both exact and exacting in one's self-estimate. And such exacting self-scrutiny opens the way for a dread of a yet more exacting divine scrutiny. If one can see these faults oneself, then, assuredly, the all-seeing God will note these and more offences. It may be, though it does not always seem so, that human law does not care about the smallest things, but the gospel demands that Jesus' followers be perfect. And mistresses and masters of the spiritual life have agreed on the possibility of a Christian's getting rid of the slightest impeding imperfection. Women and men of truly good will see this more clearly than others and may be the more disturbed by what they see. It was just such a nervous sensitivity to the demanding righteousness of God that Luther endured until the release of his Turm experience. Only after acute distress did Luther realize that the righteousness of God was, in its effectiveness in his own life, the power of God to bring him into righteousness. He was relieved by grace. But perfection is hardly to be appreciated in terms of grace by those who live in a society which has obscured the distinction of order from law, of authority from tyranny. Rather it is likely to be figured, in the imagination of the scrupulous, as an attainable, total obedience to each jot of an enacted and promulgated code. Such a figure of perfection may be accompanied by terrifying visions of God as Judge and of Eternity as torment, and these may generate a self-preserving subservience in some and a self-ruining rebelliousness in others. But, usually, for the scrupulous it is not a phantasm of the wrath of God which fills the foreground of the imagination. The scrupulous are much more immediately concerned with themselves, with the state of their own souls, with their own most extraordinary and fascinating sinfulness. A consuming self-interest prevents their appreciating the offer of grace. It was this indulgent self-awareness, this putting of God from the centre of their attention, which Alphonsus fixed upon as the besetting fault of the scrupulous. Their terrors are real enough. But they had allowed themselves to be terrorized by looking so long and so often in the glass.

These destructive habits of maddening self-scrutiny seem to have been quite common among Alphonsus' contemporaries. More common, certainly, in the Kingdom of Naples than elsewhere in the Catholic world. But more common everywhere then, than in our present society anywhere. It may have been that only the gentry and the bourgeoisie had leisure enough and energy to entertain these fears. Rather in the way that Freud's later Viennese patients were usually not from the labouring classes. And that they were commoner among religious than they were in those sections of society where women and men have to get on with their worldly business. But something more socially widespread is suggested by the treatment of scruples by Giuseppe Jorio, the Pavone Father, who was a good friend to Alphonsus from his early days as a missioner, and who influenced the shaping of Alphonsus' moral theology. In his works for country and town pastors, *Instructions for Village Confessors*, 1740, and *The Town Parish*, 1748, Jorio made equally strenuous efforts to find something useful to say to confessors who had to deal with scrupulous persons of all classes. Alphonsus himself, writing from his experience of the peasantry of the remoter mountain settlements and the urban poor as well as the comfortable and time-wasting citizenry of Naples, seems in his *Moral Theology* and *The Apostolic Man* and *The Work of the Confessor*, to assume that there is a shared risk of such self-interest and its terrorizing effects at every corner of the Christian community.[82]

Alphonsus found himself time and again in the grip of such scruples. They came suddenly, unbidden, and remained with him, as if with horrid wills of their own, just when he might have hoped to be free to say his prayers. Even when he was celebrating the sacraments, they loomed large and maddeningly. And this intermittently throughout his life. He was continually beset by fears that he had skimped the service of God, fears that he had encouraged unchaste imaginings, fears that his writings might by some carelessness lead readers into error. It was difficult for him, sometimes, even to be sure that he had obtained his doctorate quite innocently. Seventy years on from graduation, in

1785, in the ninth edition of his *Moral Theology*, Alphonsus is still asking, "Is it permissible to take an oath on receiving the degree when one has not fulfilled the conditions for the doctorate?", when, for example the candidate has not completed the required number of terms of study. As well as being three years under the regulation age for the conferring of a doctorate, for which he had in 1713 obtained the necessary dispensation from the university registrar, Alphonsus had been short of a term of the regulation five year course when he entered the examination room, but he had still signed the form which began "I affirm with an oath..." and so had sworn that he was a qualified candidate. In the *Moral Theology*, Alphonsus was ready to tell others what Pagano had told him, "those who are doctoral candidates in Naples do not seem to me to be perjured by a once-only signing of the matriculation form", even if they are aware that they are officially under age, because an oath is only an oath if it is proposed as an oath. In Naples university no one was doing anything of the sort. No one took such signing to be the taking of an oath. This, Alphonsus assured those who were asking him, is demonstrable from "common usage". But was there still a question about that missing term?[83]

Pagano warned him: "These things must not be thought on after these ways. So it will make us mad". There is, indeed, an entry in Alphonsus' personal note-book terrifiedly admitting how close he had come to unbalancing his mind by such unending re-considerations. He would for a while be comforted and hold himself still. But even in the last five years of his life, Andrea Villani (1706-1792), who was his spiritual director at Pagani, had to issue the very same warning against the same danger. Brother Romito (1722-1807), repeated the warning at an inopportune moment. Alphonsus had by then his own way of accepting that horror: "And if God wants me to die mad, why should I object?" He had overcome any temptation to look in the glass.

It was not a quick, easy, business for Alphonsus to come to the confident point at which he could preach, heart-feelingly, of the love of God. In part this was an effect of the common use of the language of "Judge". There remains always a nervousness in Alphonsus' accounts of the justice of the Father. The dreadful coincidence expressed as "Pilate says on earth 'Let Jesus die' and the Eternal Father, in like manner, says from heaven 'Let my Son die' "[84]is not rendered immediately receivable by Alphonsus' careful statements that Pilate is reading "the unjust sentence" while, as Jesus knows, "The Father himself justly condemns thee".[85] Alphonsus feels this as keenly as any of his readers. After "I love thee, O Eternal Father, who dost condemn thine innocent Son to liberate me", it is manifestly a relief for him to exclaim next "I love thee, O Eternal Son, who dost accept the death which I, a sinner, have deserved".[86] He was generally better content when he could realize a title of the divine in a eucharistic context. The dread reverberations of "King" for example, were controlled, with the help of St Teresa, by the observation that while it is impossible for poor subjects to obtain an audience with their king, "everyone that wishes can find thee in the Most Holy Sacrament".[87] King Ferdinand I thought the making of this distinction tantamount to treason. But there was more; in his *Visits to the Blessed Sacrament*, Alphonsus says, in greatest amazement, that "He, the King of Heaven, comes down from heaven in obedience to men".[88] So with all the language of power, the affirmation "God is omnipotent" in Alphonsus' meditation for Corpus Christi at once prompts its happy antithesis, "but after he has given himself in this Sacrament of Love, he has nothing more to give".[89]

Not every one of Alphonsus' images of the divine fitted the conventions of that Neapolitan piety encouraged by Pagano. It was not on account of some modern sense of gender and correctness, but from an experienced need for divine love that Alphonsus supported his reference of God as Father with another of divine motherhood. However nervous her piety, however contagious her scruples, Donna Anna had been a listener, an encourager, when the children ran to her. She had been a comforter. "The Lord", Alphonsus says at the start of *Conversing familiarly with God*, "delights that you should use towards him that confidence, that freedom and tenderness, which children use towards their mothers", and "as a mother delights to place her little child upon her knees and so to feed and caress him, with like tenderness does our gracious God delight to treat those whom he loves."[90] His experience[91] readied him to receive Falcoia's powerful language as truly reporting what Christ was saying to them from the Cross: "I am also your mother, who gave you birth to a life of grace, and I do not desire anything else but to give this to my children".[92] To some readers, Alphonsus may seem, in this section of the *Great Rule*, drawn up after the first General Congregation in 1743, to be simply sanctioning one of those little baroque flourishes which pleased Falcoia and their friend Cesare Sportelli (1701-1750). Or he may seem to others to be deliberately echoing the Christological language of Augustine and Anselm, of William of St Thierry and Hugh of St Victor, of Mechtild of Hackeborn and William Flete. He certainly had read Raymond of Capua's *Life* of St Catherine of Siena, and found there that the saint had told her confessor that she panted "to suck the divine milk" at Holy Communion, just as "an infant presses anxiously to suck milk from its mother's breast". [93]

He knows that some of the sacred commentators, frightened by the language of sucking and milk, have brought forward the manly handsomeness of the breast of the Beloved of the *Songs of Songs* as a figure for the graciousness of the eucharistic Lord. But Alphonsus does not feel at all nervous. He allows that Jesus may well be imaged by St Catherine as a nursing mother. That he does not himself find this an adequate image is simply because his appreciation of the significance of motherhood is not limited to the physicalities of the baby at the breast. "Some mothers give their children to nurses to be fed."[94] They are not less mothers. There is more to being a mother than that. More to a mother's martyrdom than that. Children, as he had told the *True Bride*, when they are small, cry and scream, growing up, they make their mother anxious for their future, and when they are older, they are yet a worry on account of their getting mixed up with bad companions. She is even "disturbed by a fondness for them at the hour of her death".[95] That natural care of human mothers may, like all else natural and human, be misdirected. Many mothers, Alphonsus read in a homily of St John Chrysostom, put their minds to the merely temporal settlement of their children. "To see them happy here is all that they desire." But Donna Anna had not been that sort of mother. Her worrying, as Tannoia noted, had been lest any of her children should inflict that sorrow which even minor faults cause to the heart of Jesus. So Alphonsus supposed that most mothers were "disturbed by a thousand scruples of conscience" like his own mother.[96] He had heard of the whale in Philostratus' life of Apollonius of Tyana that "seeing its young in danger, either from tempests or pursuers, opens its mouth to swallow them",[97] and he had read in Paciucchelli's *Excitationes* that "tigers, on hearing the cry of their cubs taken by hunters, will dive into the sea and swim to the boat in which they are being carried away".[98] These could very well be received as partial figures of the anxious human mother. But there is a more than natural care. He had been kept from worse dangers by his mother. "Any good I did as a child as well as any avoidance of the bad, I owe to my mother."

There was a torment for him in those imaginings of lapses from true obedience to a Father like his father. But the imagination which thrust him towards such madness could draw him back again. However difficult he found it to put his father's authority into relation with the fatherhood of God, Alphonsus had no trouble translating his mother's scrupulous care of him into a comforting representation of divine providence. He could make an image from Isaiah's question, "Can a woman forget her child?" and the divine promise, "if she should forget, yet I will not forget thee". And there was for him the greatest confidence to be had in that image of the mother's care at the hour of her death. Alphonsus, as he takes thought about a divine motherhood, will only imagine Jesus dying for him on the Cross. Loving him still. Alphonsus brings those images of the mother's breast, the mother's care, and the mother's death, to a eucharistic resolution more immediately than those of the father, the king, and the omnipotent ruler. The spear-pierced Jesus invites him to do so. In his *Loving Aspirations* he effects this resolution in mid-sentence: "Come and suck my divine milk which I give you in this Sacrament wherein I offer you my blood to drink". He manages it, indeed, in mid-phrase: "the milk of this Sacrament".[99]

There is an intimate relation between this image of divine motherhood and Alphonsus' steadfastness in the face of the offers of his father. "O my beloved Jesus, since thou wilt feed me this morning with thine own blood in the Holy Communion, it is but reasonable that I should willingly renounce all that the world might give me."[100] But, however helpful he finds this idea of divine motherhood for the resolution of his personal difficulty, he is not going to pause here. He is, as ever, concerned to direct attention to the loveable Lord presenting himself in the wondrous relation of Calvary to Communion. From "He shall abide between my breasts", throughout Jesus' determination "to pour out his divine blood from his wounds", Alphonsus is able to make his way to the declaration that "I will always belong to Jesus and Jesus will always belong to me". The image of breast-feeding, amplifying his appreciation of the stream of blood from Christ's side, and this imaginative appreciation informing his understanding of the eucharistic celebration, "this morning", compels the Corinthian response: "I wish to love thee — always, always, always!"[101]

NOTES

1 *Glories of Mary*, Pt II, Disc. VII; *True Bride*, IV, iv.

2 *Glories of Mary*, Pt II, Disc. VIII, ii.

3. Tannoia, *Lib.* I, p9.

4 *Truth of the Faith*, I, iii; Marietti, 550b.

5 *On the Passion*, VII, I.

6 *Glories of Mary* Pt I, III, ii, and IV, ii, and *Meditations for Seven Feasts*, VI, the Feast of Mary's Nativity, 1; Christ is "the greater light to rule the just", "the resplendent sun itself", appearing to Sr Domenica as "the child resplendent with beauty like the sun", and to the rest of us now as "the sun behind the clouds", cf. *Glories of Mary*, Pt I, III, ii, Pt II, Disc. III, ii, and *Pious Reflections*, Pt II, xxv.

7 Meditations on Litany of Loreto, VI.

8 *Fidelity of Vassals*, 5. 1-2.

9 *Meditations for all Times of the Year*, XXXVI, cf. XVIII abd XXXIV.

10 *Glories of Mary*, Pt II, VIII and IV.

11 *Reply to an Anonymous Writer*.

12 *Glories of Mary*, Pt I, III, ii

13 There may well have been a to and fro of such imaginings in Alphonsus' conversation with the Venerable Celeste Crostarosa. She was equally ready to use such a language: "At another time it was granted to her to understand how Jesus Christ is the Divine Sun in the brightness of eternal glory and how he is equally the Interior Sun of the just soul", cf. unedited MSS, Postulator General's archives, Rome, cited by Domenico Capone in his Preface to Sebatino Majorano, *L'Imitazione per la Memoria del Salvatore*, p. 1.

14 *Novena for Christmas*, IX.

15 *Short Explanation of the Prayers of the Mass*, Pt III.

16 There was an appropriateness in the affirmation of the Sacred Congregation of Rites, 21 December, 1815, during the beatification process, that 'the omnipotent Word of God who bids the stars to shine in the firmament has called this Venerable servant Alphonsus Liguori to shine also'.

17 Alphonsus himself was well aware of the relevance of a study of Babylonian and Greek astronomy to considerations of the origin of western music. cf. *Truth of the Faith*, I, ii; Marietti, 547a.

18 For the history of oratorio writing and performance at this time, see Howard E. Smither, *A History of Oratorio*, Vol. 2 and 3.

19 *True Bride*, XXIII, I.

20 *Ibid.*

21 *Divine Office*, commentary on Psalm CLV.

22 cf. *True Bride*, XXXIII, I.

23 *Ibid.*, XXIV, vii.

24 Sermon XLVIII for the Nineteenth Sunday after Pentecost. Contrariwise, "our hearing harmonious sounds" allows us a hint of 'eternal delights', *True Bride*, XVI, iii, 3.

25 Eighteenth century operatic excitements have lately been subjects of renewed research and comment; for what was happening in Italian theatres, *vide*, for examples, William C. Holmes, *Opera Observed*, 1993, Peter le Huray and James Day, *Music and Aesthetics in the Eighteenth and Early-Nineteenth Centures*, 1988, Richard Strohm, *Essays on Handel and Italian*

Opera, 1985, my own *Handel*, 1990, in the Outstanding Christian Thinkers series, and, of course, the articles on individual composers, singers, and directors, in the *New Grove Dictionary of Opera*, 1992.

26 Jones, *Alphonsus de Liguori*, p27.

27 *Pious Reflections*, note to XVII.

28 *Ibid.*, note to VII.

29 *Ibid.*, note to XVII. Alphonsus had been reading Xavier Mattei's *Memorie per servire alla vita di Metastasio e di Jomelli*, 1785. Their generally approving each other's enterprise is evident in the correspondence of November, 1774, and Alphonsus was particularly pleased at Mattei's pointing out the novelty of the Protestant opinions about Psalm XXXIV.

30 *Ibid.*, note to XVII.

31 *Preparation for Death*, XXV, 2; *Treasury*, Pt II, Instruction I; *Preparation*, XXVII, 1.

32 *Simple Exposition of the Passion*, Introduction; *Meditation on the Passion*, Wednesday.

33 *Truth of the Faith*, I, iii, 9; Marietti, 550b.

34 *Ibid.*, I, ii, 12; Marietti, 547b.

35 *Brief Dissertation*, II, iv; *Reflections on the Truth*, I, 5; Marietti 460b and 471b.

36 *Preparation*, II, 1.

37 *Novena for Christmas*, Disc. II, Introduction.

38 *Victories of the Martyrs*, Pt I, LXVIII.

39 *Truth of the Faith*, I, II, 10; Marietti, 547a.

40 *Ibid.*, II, II, 7, I, II, 11, I, II, 10, and I, II, 8; Marietti, 582b, 547b, 547a, 546a.

41 *Examples of the Infant Jesus*, I.

42 *vide*, A. Freda, "S Alfonso universitario" in *S Alfonso De Liguori, Contributi Bio-Bibliografici*, 1940, 81-110, p108.

43 cf. *New Science*, 915, 937ff.

44 *New Science*, 401, 808, 814.

45 *Ibid.*, 433.

46 *Ibid.*, 540.

47 *Ibid.*, 376.

48 *On the Passion*, VII, I, Eusebius, *Praeparations evangelicae*, V, xvii, Migne, Gk 21, 358.

49 *New Science*, 196.

50 *Novena for Christmas*, VIII.

51 *On the Passion*, I, I; *Victories of the Martyrs*, Pt II, Notice.

52 *Examples of the Infant Jesus*, III, IV and X.

53 Milton, *The Passion*, 1630(?), stanzo II, cf. Louis Martz, *The Poetry of Meditation*, 1954, 167ff.

54 *Discourses for the Novena of Christmas*, IX, 2.

55 *True Bride*, XVI, iii.

56 *Ibid.* All that Alphonsus says of "image" and "imagining" is evidently related to the intensity of his appreciation of the visual arts, see *S Fundatoris vita illustratur duabus imaginibnus Marianis*, in *Analecta Congregationis Ss Redemptionis*, XVIII, 139, 96ff. For some preliminary analysis of Alphonsus' own painterly skills see *De Christi Crucifixi imaginibus Alphonsianis, Analecta*, VIII, 1929, 218ff and *Il Pittore*, in Marcelli and Rapone, *Un Umanista de '700 Italiano*, 1993.

57 *Affections* VII, ii.

58 *Ibid.*

59 *True Bride*, VIII, iv.

60 *Affections* VII, ii.

61 *Ibid.*, XI, v.

62 *Ibid.*, XV, ii.

63 cf. *Treasury*, Pt I, VIII.

64 *Preparation for Mass*, II, Monday, *Meditations for Corpus Christi*, V.

65 *Discourses for Novena of Christmas*, IX, 2.

66 "I have been a lawyer", "*Sono stato avvocato*", he wrote with some self-assurance to Francesco de Paola, 19 February, 1779. cf Freda, A., *art.cit.*, and Vereecke, L, *Sant'Alfonso giurista, La formazione giuridica e l'influsso sulla morale, Studia Moralia*, XXX1/2, December 1993, 265-282.

67 *Meditations for all Times of the Year*, XXXV and XLV.

68 Andrea Massimi, *Itinerari Amatriciani*, 1971.

69 *On the Passion*, Vii, iii.

70 cf. Andre Sampers, '*Quelques details communiques par S Alphonse en 1758*', *Spicilegium Historicum*, 28, 1980, 469-476; Oreste Gregorio, *Richerche intorno alla causa feudale perduta nel 1723 do Alfonso de Liguori, Archivio storico per le Province Napoletane*, N.s. 34, 1953-1954, 181-203; Antonio e Giuseppe Cantalamessa, *Dissertazione sul "Denaro"*, Amatrice, 1987.

71 *Glories of Mary*, Pt I, II, iii, *Practices of Devotion*, VII, *Glories of Mary*, Pt I, III, ii.

72 *On the Passion*, IX, ii, *Meditations for all Times of the Year*, I.

73 cf. egr. *Affections* XI, iii. Another old family opposed to the Medici in Florentine politics is represented by Sr Maria Strozzi who spoke so well of the perfection of the religious life, *Glories of Mary*, VI, I and *Eight Day Retreat*, IVth Day, 2.

74 cf. *Practice of the Love of Christ*, X, ii, *Pious Reflections*, VIII, *Eight Day Retreat*, II, I, *Preparation*, XIII, I and II.ii, *Pious Reflections*, XXX, *Eight Day Retreat*, II, I, *Preparation*, XIII, ii and XIX, ii, and *Considerations for those called to the Religious State*, II.

75 *Instruction for the People*, Pt I, VI, *True Bride*, II, 2, *Glories of Mary*, Dolours, I, *Discourses for the Novena of Christmas*, VIII, and *True Bride*, I, 3.

76 *Affections* XI, I.

77 *Simple Exposition of the Passion*, XII, I, *On the Passion*, VII, v, *Lenten Meditations*, VII, ii.

78 *Meditations for Novena of Christmas*, VI, *Darts of Fire*, XXXVI, *Preparation*, V,2.

79 End of October, 1737(?).

80 *Concerning a Religious Vocation*, IV, 2 and III, 1, *Treasury*, Pt I, X. Alphonsus' "uncle", Emilio Cavalieri, had been pursued through the ecclesiastical courts by his furious father, the President of the Real Camera della Sommaria, in order to winkle him out of the Pious Workers. Even the *Arbor genealogica matris S Alphonsi, Analecta*, X, 1931, 45ff, derived from Giovanni Rossi's *Vita* of Emilio Cavalieri, 1741, does not make entirely plain how "cousin" and "uncle" are being used in the family's talk of Bishop Cavalieri and Canon Gizzio.

81 *Instructions for the People*, I, iv, II, ii. It is not surprising that whatever Alphonsus knew of captains and ships did not often inform his imaginings of things divine. There are very few references to such matters in his great body of work: an impersonal reference to "one bark, one pilot", in a controversial passage of *Truth of the Faith*, III, vii, 3, Marietti, 713b, a carrying-over from Aquinas of talk about tempests and safe harbours in the *Meditations*

for the Novena of the Blessed Virgin, VIII, a re-telling of S Maria Maddalena de Pazzi's story of a lady steering her boat between rocks and wrecks, *Glories of Mary,* Pt I, VIII, iii, a likening of nuns in a convent to the crew of a ship in danger of being wrecked, *True Bride,* XII, iii, and, more immediately personal in its language, a comparing, in a 1767 meditation, of the terrified passenger on a vessel sinking in rough seas and 'the confused sinner who at his death finds himself in bad conscience', *Meditations for all Times of the Year,* LXXXVIIII. The conjunction of fault and ship and terror evidently came home to him. Even when Mary is the pilot of the ship, Alphonsus thinks at once of a condemned criminal, *Glories of Mary,* Pt I, V, ii, 2.

82 Jorio's book for the village confessor had, Alphonsus wrote to Remondini, 3 June, 1764, "an immense sale" but "now mine certainly surpasses it in abundance of doctrines and thoroughness". He concluded that "my book serves the country confessor, his doesn't".

83 After Pagano, Tommaso Falcoia encouraged him to restrain his natural urge towards a too fearful self-examination. Alphonsus relied on such spiritual direction. "Obey your director and do not depart from his directions, even when what you wish to do so in opposition to his advice seem better to you", and "I repeat and I lay it down, obey in all things your spiritual father and have confidence in obedience, for by the practice of obedience you will always be secure", *True Bride,* XVIII, i and iii.

84 *Simple Exposition of the Passion,* XII, ii, *Meditations for the Last Fifteen Days of Lent,* VIII, iii.

85 *Meditations of the Last Fifteen Days of Lent,* VIII, i. cf. *Affections,* X, ii and *Meditations on the Passion,* Friday, II.

86 *Meditations for the Last Fifteen Days of Lent,* VIII, i.

87 *Meditations for Octave of Corpus Christi,* II, *Visits,* X and XVIII.

88 *Visits,* XXV.

89 *Meditations for Octave of Corpus Christi,* III.

90 *Manner of Conversing Familiarly with God,* I, cf. *True Bride,* VII, i.

91 There may be something in Tannoia's reconstructions of Alphonsus' early years, and in Frederick Jones' account too, that derives from the hagiographers' convention of a saint having an unsympathetic father and a holy mother. Eadmer fitted Anselm's experiences into that shape. Augustine fitted his own. But certainly Alphonsus' experiences seem to fit this pattern very well.

92 Hoegerl, *op.cit.,* 119.

93 *Loving Aspirations,* VII. cf *Visits,* IX. It was a matter of town gossip that "that great Sicilian", Luigi la Nusa, "in tearing himself away from the bosom of Jesus Christ" in the Blessed Sacrament, "had to do himself just such violence as a child that has to detach itself from its mother's breast at the very moment when it is filling itself with greatest eagerness", *Visits,* Introduction, I. For the high estimate that Alphonsus and others made of the Venerable Luigi see also *Treasury,* Pt I, ix.

94 *Preparation,* XXXIV 2.

95 *True Bride,* I, ii, *Meditations for all Times of the Year,* LXX, *True Bride,* II, ii, *Loving Aspirations,* VII. cf. also *Preparation,* XXXV, iii: "As a mother whose breasts are full of milk goes in search of infants to give them suck in order to be relieved of the burden, so our Lord from this sacrament of love cries out, and says to us all: 'You shall be carried at the breast…As one whom the mother caresses, so I will comfort you'".

96 *True Bride,* II, ii.

97 *Glories of Mary,* Pt I, I, ii. Alphonsus found this piece of pleasant lore in *Umbra virginea,* 1632, by the prolific Luigi Novarini (1594-1650).

98 *Glories of Mary*, Pt I, I, iii. Alphonsus had met such tigers in the *Excitationes dorminantis animae* of Angelo Paciucchelli, O.P., d.1660.

99 *Loving Aspirations*, VII.

100 *Ibid.*, cf. *Visits*, V.

101 *Loving Aspirations*, II.

PART THREE
Towards an Imitation of Christ

Alphonsus' sense of what it would mean for him to stay among the lawyers in 1723, and follow a career at the Naples bar, reflects our ordinary estimate of experiencing. So does his coming to a decision, in June, 1729, to quit his father's house, and take a room with the Congregation of the Holy Family at the Chinese College which Matteo Ripa (1682-1746), had just set up to train missionaries for the Orient. We very well understand that 'living with' becomes, for wives and husbands, owners and dogs, oftentimes, the occasion of 'being like'. And children, living at home, are, as Alphonsus says, like monkeys in their quickness to pick up bad habits, doing what they see their parents do.[1] Only a very self-unaware parent could be surprised at this. "It is related in fables", that a crab one day rebuked its young for walking crookedly. "Father, let us see you walk", they replied. The children had learnt, and, in Alphonsus' telling of their story, were cheekily aware that they had learnt to be crooked by living with the crooked walker.[2] Alphonsus' experience of women and men and children in the next fifty years did nothing to lessen his conviction of the relation between 'living with' and 'being like'. In 1750, he was warning a girl that she must be careful to enter a convent of strict observance, otherwise, among naughty nuns, she would 'live as they live' and quite quickly come to 'do as they do'. In 1760, he set out a warning for those who conducted the *Exercises of the Mission* that the women who lived in a man's house would come to be like him: "The greatest fruit of the mission consists in the conversion of the men; for if the men remain bad, the women will also be bad". In 1774, he was protesting strongly against the suggestion that his Congregation might accept the great church of the Gesù in Rome after the papal suppression of the Jesuits: "As soon as we are in the midst of prelates, nobles, ladies and courtiers, then goodbye to the missions, goodbye to the country places; we would quickly become courtiers ourselves".[3]

There was a backing for his common-sense view that those who flock together become birds of a feather in contemporary exegetes' understanding of 'likeness' in the *Genesis* creation narratives. While 'image' was taken to stand for our natural rational capacity to live with

119

God, 'likeness' was related to the gracious actualization of that capacity through our living with God. The description of Adam's walking familiarly with God in the garden, in the cool of the evening, was commonly understood to present a figure of the first human beings' realizing this likeness to God. Chaos comes upon the race when Adam and Eve wish to be like God out of God's company. They listen to the serpent's deceptive promise of likeness: "You shall be as Gods". But there is no 'being like' apart from 'living with'.

Our ordinary experience and our ordinary assessments of that experience and this reading of *Genesis* combine to give a clear sense of what is meant by the gospel announcement that "It is enough for the disciple to be like his teacher". We can appreciate how it is that the disciples, through their experience of the Galilee fellowship with Jesus, did not just pick up a few characteristic phrases and gestures from Jesus, but were themselves empowered to be effective announcers of good news. Alphonsus encourages ordinary folk to read the gospels as presentations of the possibilities of their own lives. They too may 'live with' the Lord and 'be like' him.

It is usual with Christians to speak of Jesus of Nazareth walking and talking with his disciples and of the Eucharist as the Body of Christ. Alphonsus will certainly use such expressions when he is directly quoting a passage of the New Testament or Patristic writing or a decree of the Council of Trent, but in his own person he speaks in both contexts of Jesus Christ, of the words of Jesus Christ and the true body of Jesus Christ. His language expresses the identity of the Jesus of the gospels and the Christ of the sacrament. It expresses a personal identity. It suggests a possibility of the members of the eucharistic community now enjoying the same personal relations with the one Lord as were enjoyed by his first disciples. This appreciation of being with Jesus Christ at the eucharistic celebration and at moments of meditation before the Blessed Sacrament and of a continuing possibility of being like Jesus Christ when walking and talking in the southern Italian countryside, is expressed in the language of contemporary spirituality as the practice of an "imitation of Christ", *imitatio Christi*.

There may be some difficulty with 'imitation' today. In the early eighteenth century the encouragement of virtue was quite generally believed to depend on a young person's being given a proper model from life, history, or myth. Children's governesses were equipped from a great treasury of exemplary stories by which they were to train their charges in decent behaviour. Alphonsus never forgot some of them. He kept them for use on days of recollection for nuns. "A certain rich nobleman who had married a peasant, to prevent her from being puffed up with pride at seeing herself attended by servants and dressed in rich apparel, caused the miserable garment which she wore before her marriage to be preserved and to be kept continually before her eyes. You should imitate his example."[4] Other stories were told to encourage other virtues. Perhaps a stableman regaled the boy with less prudent tales of the great Marco de Liguori who had been Governor of the whole city of Naples in the twelfth century. It was certainly a part of a tutor's job to direct attention towards a range of heroes as exemplars of gentlemanly living. The bravery of Hercules, the chivalry of Lancelot, the political skills of the Prince, were set before the boys as models to be copied. And the same sort of encouragement was given to adults as they were brought to take up responsible places in the culture. In the opera house, Metastasio presented the emperor Titus as an exemplar of princely clemency for the emperor Charles VI. Alphonsus' experience in the Amatrice law suit made it difficult for him to take this imperial propaganda as seriously as the tale of the raggedy dress. While the librettist showed Titus wanting only to be gracious and generous, Alphonsus remarked wryly that "in reality he must often have deceived or failed in his promises".[5] In the Law School, Vico had suggested that the Norman warriors who rescued Salerno from the Saracen were imitating heroes who stood with their friends against many foemen, Ajax on the Trojan plain, Horatius at the bridge. It is unlikely that Vico was offering this more aggressive example as encouragement to the student leaders and their street gangs, or even to Alphonsus and his card-playing chums. He might have been looking for more support from his fellow academicians in his professorship candidacy. Still, it would not have taken any great rhetorical skill to transfer the example to Alphonsus and his Redemptorists preaching against the forces of unbelief.

Alphonsus' own preaching was scattered through with such exemplars. His hearers were to take the example of St Philip Neri, make efforts to be like St Peter, and seize the opportunity of imitating the conduct of St Catherine of Siena. They could take example from those who took such examples themselves. Alphonsus recommended their imitating

121

Bishop Emingo who was "like a saint" in his death, for he died in the midst of saying his usual prayers.[6] There were bad examples too. When he wrote of martyrdom, Alphonsus was quick to warn the Naples lady of the danger of dressing in high fashion simply to be like her social equals, and as quick to warn the nun against dressing like a man with wig and sword for a convent play, or a choir monk from singing like the opera house tenor in hopes of getting congratulated in the sacristy.[7] These and all of his hearers should rather contemplate the martyrdom of Mary, who was "in all things like Jesus".

Today, it is possible for Christians to talk of Jesus in terms of 'the concrete categorical imperative', 'the decisive moral norm', and 'the measure of serving and self-giving'. These are the terms of moral theologians who mean to disclose the peculiar Christian origin of their discipline. They would be very unlikely to use the language of 'an imitation of Christ'. In our ear, 'imitation' has resonances of 'insincere' and 'fake' and 'second-rate'. Even if these resonances are kept out of mind, our modern awareness of how much historical circumstances alter cases may make it difficult for us to understand some of the more simple-minded exhortations to the Imitation of Christ in yesterday's hand-books. We have notions of the past as generally looking unlike the present. We have notions of how particular past times looked. We may not be able to distinguish the look of Joseph's Egypt from Cleopatra's but theatrical producers know that our fancy may be tickled by a few deliberate anachronisms, Lady Macbeth's lighting a cigarette, say, or Siegfried's sporting a dinner jacket. They can get us to raise a superior, historicist, smirk. So, confronted by talk of imitating Christ we are likely to ask questions based on our simple notions of how Galilee looked, of how Jesus looked, of how he walked. "Are we to wear sandals? — His size sandals?" No difficulty of this sort arises when we are reading Alphonsus' meditations upon *imitatio*. His understanding of the irrelevance of history for our present experience of the Lord prevented his offering any historically conditioned version of the imitation of Christ. He quite appreciated that an eighteenth century *imitatio* could only be realized in a way of living which fitted the character and circumstances of his present Christian community. He could use his imagination. He could get free of historicist conditioning. He could imagine Jesus talking and walking with him. He did not have to imagine the length of Jesus' stride or the goods in the window of the Jerusalem shops. Nor did he have to place Jesus in the Via dei Tribunali. "These things are better left somewhat obscure."[8] He had to be precise only in imagining Jesus' presence and the call that Jesus made on him. There might, certainly, be a difficulty in identifying that fit life style of *imitatio*, but it would not be an historicist's difficulty.

Early eighteenth century Naples was teeming with religious persons who had notions of what it would be to hear the call of Christ and to imitate Christ, and they were very ready to propose their notions to anyone who would listen. Something may be learned of the context of Alphonsus' usage of *imitatio* from the claim of the Congregation of the Apostolic Missions to be called to a life that was "like that of the Word Incarnate", from the generalised determination of the Congregation of Taranto, founded by Falcoia in 1720, to "turn themselves into a perfect imitation of Christ the Lord" and to live "in uniformity with the life of Jesus Christ", from Matteo Ripa's presentation of the missionary purpose of the Congregation of the Holy Family in terms of "the imitation of our Lord in an active and contemplative life" among the eastern peoples, in accord with the Redeemer's words, "I have given you an example". These were all communities in the Kingdom of Naples with whom Alphonsus had dealings. Most especially, he must have considered, after his meeting with Falcoia at the Chinese College, and that enthusiastic missioner's telling him of the Scala nuns, the significance of their dedication to a "perfect copying of the original life" of Jesus.

In 1719, Falcoia had been one of the Pious Workers invited by the bishop of Scala, a small town in the hills above Amalfi, to renew the spirit of nuns in a local community in decline. By 1720, the convent of Our Lady's Immaculate Conception was receiving postulants again. Decisively, in 1724, Falcoia brought in the three Crostarosa sisters. Julia, the most distinguished of them, took the name of Sr Maria Celeste. She had been Sr del Cielo in her previous convent. She certainly had had heavenly gifts, mystical graces, visions, since she was a six year old child. She had them at Scala. The Lord appeared to her and revealed that he wanted her to found a new religious institute. Celeste's Rule under which the nuns were to live was a record of her conversations with the Lord. After a declaration of the Eternal Father's Intent that the community of the Holy Saviour be "a living remembrance" of the divine love manifest in the life and work of his Son, the Idea of the Institute is announced by Christ himself. The community's work will be done in "a remembrance of the works that I accomplish", and, in the very structures of the community, Christians should recognize the Sisters' likeness to their Lord, for there are to be thirty-three choir nuns in each house, "in memory of the thirty-three years I have spent among men", twelve members of an advisory board in each convent, "in memory of my twelve apostles", and a superior who should "resemble me as much as possible". This community remembrance, *viva memoria*, was to be expressed in an *imitatio* through which the Sisters would revivify the meaning of elements in the usual conventual regime. Imitative virtue would witness to the Saviour's presence in community and individual. So the Lord then goes on to dictate rules of harmony and charity, of poverty, purity, obedience, humility, mortification, recollection, and love of the cross. These are the rules to be followed "if you desire to imitate me truly".[9]

Falcoia boasted to Alphonsus at the Chinese College about the mystic, wonderful, things that were happening at Scala. Alphonsus was sceptical. He had heard something of the acrimonious proceedings in the community. But he was also intrigued. He persuaded the unenthusiastic Pagano to give him leave to preach the convent retreat. Alphonsus' conferences explored the meaning of *imitatio* with the nuns. Gradually, he became convinced that Celeste had indeed been chosen by the Lord to found a new Institute in the Church. Pagano's warnings against getting mixed up with the mystic Sister and her imperious director were repeated by Torno, now Director of the Apostolic Missions. But Falcoia looked much more respectable and his spiritual judgement seemed to be properly approved when, in 1730, he was consecrated bishop of Castellamare de Stabia, just over the hill from Scala. And Celeste was proving to be not at all that "nun filled with illusions", as those whom he had always trusted were asserting in Naples. Rather, she was herself convincing evidence that "the work is indeed from God". But then, again, how was it that not every good nun in her community was sympathetic to "the work"?

These were, doubtless, unquiet times for Alphonsus. He was still young enough to think that only by some exaggeration could he communicate his real emotion. Classical references came back to mind from both days studying Homer with his tutor and evenings in the opera house with his friends. And with them, perhaps, some fearsome tale of his sea-faring father. He felt himself thrown this way and that, uncertain how to steer his way. He felt himself to be the sailor Odysseus, "in the middle of a tempest", tossed by such huge waves that "sometimes I can see neither heaven nor earth". Then, thrown ashore, "I find myself", he wrote to Mother Angiola at Scala, "in a dark cavern where there is no order, only a terrible horror".[10] He was, again, in a moment of intensest quandary about God's will for him, joining scripture with myth. After this *Odyssey IX* memory of the cavern of Poliphemus, echoing with his dreadful shrieks, and Odysseus cowering as the blinded cyclops groped to find his torturer, Alphonsus was coming immediately upon *Job 10* and the terrors of that land "where there is no order, only the shadow of death and everlasting horror". It is evidence of the general civilization of the Scala nuns that Alphonsus was sure that Mother Angiola would recognize the mixed sources of his language. He would not have been so discourteous as to write confusingly to her. Especially when he was so conscious of the terrors of his own confusion. He was simply assuming that they shared a culture in which myth and scripture went easily together.

They went together in Alphonsus' public expression of such perplexity. His verses on *"The sorrowing Soul"* begin in conventional neo-classical mode, *"In a grove remote and shadowed"*, but very soon shift, intensifyingly, into a language of pagan dread:

> Every way I look and reach
> Horrors I see and feel,

and then slip, through Homeric resonances of Penelope waiting on Ithaca for her husband, Odysseus, to return from Troy, into echoings of the Bride in the *Song of Songs*:

> Beloved, have a care for me,
> Come, do not abandon me here,
> See, I am sorrowing,
> Sighing, always, for thee.

Perhaps, indeed, he composed, or at least roughed out, these lines at this distressful time. The lonely soul, unable to find a way to go, abandoned to its own arid devices, is an image which very well fits Alphonsus' loss of his sense of direction in 1730.

Myth gives him, with Scripture, a language for his personal feeling. This was their general function at the San Bartolomeo. Ladies and gentlemen heard in the long-held high note an affirmation that the emotions of the mythic hero or the scriptural heroine at centre stage were of real significance. They were persuaded thereby that their own emotions were of real significance. This was an element in the popularity of opera. More, music and plot and characters offered a language in which opera-goers might speak their feelings, express themselves. Alphonsus heard the tensions of his own feelings in the theatrical music. With the other young gallants, struggling to articulate a new self-awareness, he had received the language gratefully. But he could not rest, in his letter to Mother Angiola or anywhere else, on a sense of his own significance. "But may the will of the supreme God always be done. If that is that I should be damned, then if it is for his greater glory, so be it." He waited for the sign of his proper *imitatio*. Events at Scala were about to settle his course.

After Falcoia had given an episcopal push to get the convent re-organized along the lines of the new Rule, Celeste had a further series of visions. This time she talked to Alphonsus. "Celeste saw my name written in the heart of Jesus; I am predestined", the young priest wrote in his note-book. He would, like Odysseus, come home. He would find the Beloved there. Celeste had seen Alphonsus in the company of the Lord. He was to found a male Institute in parallel with her community. In this he would discern his proper *imitatio*. Alphonsus' being with Christ was to issue in his being like Christ the preacher accompanied by his preaching disciples.

Alphonsus readily accepted that the Rule which the Lord had shown Celeste for her community should, with whatever adaptations to differences of circumstances proved necessary, be received as the pattern for the Rule of the preaching Institute. But a significant difference in their personal circumstances was that while Celeste had received the Rule from the Lord, Alphonsus had put himself under the rule of a spiritual director. Later he was troubled by remembrances of differences between Celeste and Falcoia, and of his own young priggish treatment of her at this time, but he remained steadfast in his preferring obedience under a director to enthusiasm for a vision. "Should Jesus Christ appear to a religious she would not be certain whether it was he that spoke or an evil spirit, who, under the appearance of the Redeemer, wished to deceive her; but when her Superiors speak, she knows for certain, from the words of Jesus Christ, that in obeying them, she obeys him. 'He', says the Lord, 'that heareth you, heareth me'."[11] But, on being told about this "Congregation of the Most Saviour", Falcoia himself urged Alphonsus to follow the example of Christ in accepting a dangerous and demanding vocation. The presbyteries of Naples buzzed with unsympathetic talk of yet another vision and yet another unnecessary Order, and, on the gleeful rumour that the whole enterprise had collapsed, Falcoia counselled Alphonsus to keep his intentions to himself. This too would be an imitation of Christ. He had "made as if to go further" along the road when he really meant to stop with the disciples at Emmaus. Alphonsus was to act as if the idea of the Congregation had, indeed, been surrendered. This instruction on how the imitation of Christ might be practised in the world of the Amatrice lawyers remained with Alphonsus until he could put it into its proper place in his Moral Theology.

In August, 1732, at Pagano's own suggestion, Alphonsus accepted Falcoia as his spiritual director. It was just about this time that Celeste was tiring of the bishop's re-writing of the Rule given to her by the Lord himself, and which was, she knew, already perfectly expressive of "the gospel pattern" of Christian living. On 3 November, 1732, Alphonsus arrived at Scala for the first ceremony of the new Institute for preaching men. During the three days of prayer before the Blessed Sacrament in Celeste's convent, a great many persons, including Bishops Antonia Santoro (1681-1741), of Scala and Falcoia of Castellamare, saw an image of the instruments of Christ's Passion on the host exposed in the monstrance. This was a vision which Alphonsus could interpret for himself. It figured the connection of the Cross with the Eucharist, and of both with the commissioning of those who, being now with Christ, were taking up their vocation to be like Christ. But he was anxious that the Congregation should not provide more curious material for the chattering classes of Naples. The two bishops said nothing at all about any inauguration of the Congregation of the Most Holy Saviour when they gave their evidence about the marvellous image to a pontifical commission of enquiry. This silence, too, might be an imitation of Christ. He, after a miracle, had instructed the cured man, "See that you say nothing to any one". It was left for the commissioners to assume that the bishops just happened to be at the chapel door together. Alphonsus kept this example in mind, too.

The visionary nun and the spiritually expert bishop had now been joined in their enterprise with a hard-working missioner who was determined that this Congregation should be structured according to "my own judgement", as he wrote in his note-book. He was certainly ready and able to prevent the adoption of any formulation of the imitation of Christ for the Congregation which went against his understanding of "being like". In a "summary of observances" in July, 1733, the "Idea and End" of the community is presented in terms which all three of them could accept. According to the pattern and the example of Christ, the members of the Congregation are to live lives like the life of Jesus Christ, making themselves "living copies of that divine model". But then the "Idea" quite specifyingly identifies the novices as imitators of Jesus in the womb, the newly-professed religious as imitators of the infant Jesus, and the philosophy students, who, like the twelve years old Jesus, have gone looking for wisdom among the doctors, can be expected to "imitate the childhood of the Lord".[12] This scheme, as artificially structured as the patterns of thirty-three and twelve in Celeste's *Rule*, is continued up to the Retreat that the senior fathers are to make before preaching missions and hearing the confessions of women, for this is "in imitation of that which His Divine Majesty did in the desert". Alphonsus must have seen the danger of some disjunction, one imitation being quite distinct from another, the imitation of Jesus as infant, child, and grown preacher, becoming discrete stages in the Redemptorist's spiritual life. There might have been a hint of "beginning, process, and end" in all this. When Alphonsus talked of imitating Jesus in his infancy, he made a careful paraphrase of a Circumcision sermon of St Bernard, "Let us go to Bethlelem and there we shall find what we are to imitate". We shall find, says Alphonsus, that Jesus is there "teaching us by example" what he was afterwards to teach by word of mouth.[13] Together, Christ's lying in a manger and his declaring that "the Son of Man has nowhere to lay his head" offer a single paradigm of the life of poverty that a Redemptorist is to imitate.

Something of the disjunctive language remains, however, in the *Great Rule*, the *Regola Grande*, which the bishop spent the next decade drafting and revising for what he considered "his Institute". Something remains, too, of Falcoia's pious assumption of the freedom to invent dominical speeches which enforce his own view of '*imitatio*'. At the very start of the *Great Rule*, Jesus himself announces that eternal truth has been made known "by my preaching", "by the examples of my life", and "by my sorrowful death on Calvary". He directs "my followers" to make it their aim "to imitate what I have done". It is as if there has indeed been another vision. "You, therefore, most beloved souls, chosen by me to be to the world the living images of my life, must copy in yourselves, most of all, my charity and love towards your neighbour." The missioners are to live "after my pattern", having been "refashioned into my likeness".[14] In thus casting the directives of the *Great Rule* as express commands of Christ to the members of the Institute, Falcoia was going quite against the sensitivities of Alphonsus. He had thought, he told Alphonsus early in 1732, that some proposal of the rules of the Redemptoristines "as if they came from the mouth of Christ" ought to be tolerated because "that way they would make more impression". But those expressions in Falcoia's successive drafts which suggested that the proposed rules for Redemptorists were to be observed "as if actually said and commanded by the Lord himself" should, Alphonsus insisted, either be removed entirely or recast according to the text of the gospels until they were indeed quotations from the Lord to his disciples.[15] The bishop seemed oddly unable, as he sat to compose the *Great Rule*, just as he had been unable when he was reconstructing the *Rule* for Celeste's community, to distinguish individual, private, conversation with the Lord, whether in the body or out of the body, from ecclesial, public, revelation to the Church. Alphonsus had repeatedly to persuade Falcoia that references to "the intent and idea of his Divine Majesty" which kept occurring in Falcoia's drafts, should be changed to "the law and counsel of the holy gospels". It never occurred to Alphonsus that such changing would imply any lessening of the immediacy of the Lord's command to the Redemptorist. We should listen at the reading of the Gospel in the liturgy, he wrote to his priests when he was bishop of Sant'Agata, "as if we heard the words of our divine Saviour instructing us himself".[16] At this reading of Scripture, most plainly, "Jesus Christ speaks". Alphonsus had no need to devise new speeches for the Lord in order to express the eternal elements of *imitatio*.

During the years that the drafting and re-drafting of the *Great Rule* was continuing, there were occasions when some short interim explanation of the Institute, its purpose and way of working, was required. At the founding of a house in a further diocese, for example. Such explanations were also put together in the language of *imitatio* and of conforming to "the gospel pattern" of Jesus' life. Alphonsus gave his authority for Falcoia's 1736 letter to the Marchese Montealegre, King Charles' Minister, which declares that it will be the chief aim of the proposed community "to imitate closely the life and holy virtues of our Lord". The *Compendium* of the proposed rule presented to the Bishop of Bovino in 1745 begins by stating the aspiration of the members of the Institute to "imitate as much as possible by divine grace this divine Master and Model". The 1747 text presented to the Archbishop of Conza, which seems to have been almost wholly the work of Alphonsus himself, similarly defines the purpose of the Institute in terms of "the closest imitation of the most holy life of our Saviour".[17]

To use the same language is not, necessarily, to have the same meaning in mind. Reports of national and international politicking show us this every day. It would even be a matter of some delicacy to determine just what Alphonsus himself is saying when he remarks that a wise man will distrust the claims of "a democratic regime".[18] And *"imitatio"* is no less patient of meanings than "democracy". But if there be a suspicion that such a language may, like so much of contemporary Neapolitan talk of "the spiritual life", have something too self-regarding about it, that it is too concerned with a Christian's making her or his soul, too little concerned with the enlivening of the community of Christians, such a suspicion should not attach to Alphonsus' use of *imitatio*. In the Lord's presence, Alphonsus felt himself to be a friend among friends. He is our companion, and those who "keep company" together with him, may make it their prayer that they shall always stay together.

Whatever eagerness for community was felt by Alphonsus, it was certainly an effect of grace. The largeness, extravagance even, of the language of Alphonsus' eucharistic devotion, contrasts with the reserve of his ordinary conversation. He was rarely able to express a human affection. He would never risk, in his relations with women, even the restrained courtesies of polite society for fear of slipping into a sin. He could not often acknowledge an affection for the men about him. He had had colleagues in the law school, and fellow gamesters at the card table, but during his priestly life, Don Giovanni Olivieri was, Frederick Jones says, perhaps Alphonsus' only friend "at this human level".[19] There must be some comfort for those of us who are not generally jovial or festive, in Alphonsus' finding his way to employ his talents for others despite this imperfect appreciation of their human attractiveness. He had even a scruple, after his retirement from Sant' Agatha, about playing with the community's dog. These are matters of temperament,

130

for sure. And, as Thomas à Kempis says, "Those things that a man cannot emend in himself or in others, he ought to suffer patiently 'til God order them otherwise". It is, at any rate, evident that Alphonsus' temperament was re-ordered by the eucharistic celebration. His living with others in the community round Christ, "our friend", prevents any slippage into a self-centred spirituality.[20]

If the general conversation of zealous persons in the Kingdom, and the particular notions of Falcoia and his friends at the Chinese College, constituted the context for Alphonsus' use of the language of *imitatio*, his particular understanding of its significance in his Congregation was shaped by his reverence for the *Imitation of Christ*. John Wesley had been, at least at first reading, "very angry at Kempis for being too strict". But for Alphonsus, Thomas à Kempis is the perfect expressor of *imitatio*. He is "that great servant of God", he is "the devout Thomas"; the *Imitation of Christ* is "that golden book", which the Christian should read, quote, paraphrase, and read again.[21] It is for Alphonsus a sure sign of the holy good sense of Teresa Maria de Liguori (c.1700-1724), when he was writing in 1761 a sketch of her life, that she read a chapter of the *Imitation of Christ* every morning in her Carmelite convent. He was himself another such constant reader. He wanted to be such a writer. Alphonsus told Remondini in 1773 that he had just finished a little work, the *Devout Reflections*, which was designed to be "rather like the chapters and reflections of Thomas à Kempis". The recollection of the *Imitation of Christ* occurs at small and large moments throughout Alphonsus' writing. At his wry comment on the lessening of religious fervour in the history of religious institutes, for example, at his grim reckoning of the shortness of human memory, at his meditation on the mental sufferings of Christ in the womb of Mary, or at his contrasting pilgrimages to historical sites with visits to the Blessed Sacrament, "Thou present with me here". The *Imitation of Christ* expresses the Christian life in ways that fit happily with the configurations of Alphonsus' enterprise. His use of "Jesus Christ speaks" represents a characteristic enlargement of Thomas à Kempis' exclamation, after a clutch of New Testament quotations, "These are Thy words, O Christ, eternal Truth; though not uttered at one time, nor written in one place". It must have been Falcoia's best argument for his employing invented conversations with the Lord in his drafts for the new Rule that Thomas à Kempis had shown that having his Divine Majesty speak with his beloved souls was a perfectly religious thing to arrange.[22]

" 'Whoso followeth me, walketh not in darkness', saith the Lord. These are the words of Christ by which we are admonished to imitate his life and manners." The very first sentences of the *Imitation of Christ* determine the sense of *imitatio* for Alphonsus. There is a perfect symmetry with the *Imitation of Christ* in the formulation of Alphonsus' 1733 *Idea*. The "whoso followeth me" and "to imitate his life and manners" of Thomas à Kempis are positioned again in the *Idea* as Alphonsus puts "following more closely in his footsteps" with the Redemptorists' vocation to be "living copies" of Christ. This symmetry recurs in Alphonsus' succinct formulation for the *Ristretto*, the outline of the Institute's character and purpose prepared for the negotiations with royal and ecclesiastical authorities in 1747. There, he nicely positions following and imitating in a single phrase, simply declaring the Redemptorist's vocation to "follow the example" of the Saviour.[23] Alphonsus never again put these things so conflatedly, but he went on expressing his sense of his vocation in just this way. In his 1750 *Considerations for those who are called to the Religious State*, the petition "Give me courage by Thy example" is put between the thankful declaration "I am one of those happy ones whom Thou hast called to follow thee" and the affirmation "I will follow".

Alphonsus did not, of course, deny himself the full scope of that language of *imitatio* employed in the rules of those various Neapolitan communities he was encountering. While in *The Treasury* he more usually writes of the priest as "the one who wishes to follow", who is "invited to follow" and must deny himself in order to become "the true follower" of Christ, he is still content to quote what others have written of a priest's imitating as much as possible the purity and sanctity of Jesus Christ and of the priest's "conforming to his true likeness". These languages can often muddle along together. So, towards the close of those 1750 *Considerations*, the prayer of the follower for the effective grace of an *imitatio* is expressed as "make me like you". Nevertheless, however it may be for others, "imitating Christ" remains best defined for Alphonsus in the *Imitation of Christ* terms of "following".

Thomas à Kempis wrote for his companions in religious life. Alphonsus is announcing the calls of the Lord upon "the priest as priest, the married man as married man, the trader as trader, the soldier as soldier"[24] and of the shepherd's wife as shepherd's wife, "with an infant crying for five or six hours without stopping, and she never able to get a night's

132

rest". Each Christian, trading and marching, tossing and turning, is called to a true *Imitatio Christi,* and must at the gracious *finale* be found "living according to the life of Jesus Christ". So *imitatio* is, in the early documents of the Congregation, often expressed in a language suited to the condition of every Christian. In the *Compendium* of Bovino, whose vocabulary and style reflect the influence of Falcoia, the opening declaration that the members of the community purpose to "imitate as much as possible by divine grace, this divine Master and model" leads into sections devoted to the practice of faith and hope and the love of God and one's neighbour which have an universal reference. The Redemptorists all recognized this large application of their sense of *imitatio.* Some more drastically than others. Hearing that his sister was seriously ill, Paolo Cafaro let himself say "I wish that her pains may become still greater that she may thus be more conformed to the suffering life of Jesus Christ".[25] Still, even Falcoia, even Cafaro, needed to distinguish the vocation of Redemptorist as Redemptorist, of follower as follower, in the Congregation.

In an attempt to specify a peculiarly Redemptorist *imitatio,* Falcoia first proceeded in the *Compendium* to formulate the poverty, purity of body and mind, and obedience which must characterize the religious who would imitate the virtues "practised by his Divine Majesty". The Redemptorists must, as Jesus taught the first ministers of the Gospel, "learn from me" to mortify themselves, they must live in conformity with the life of our Lord, and must honour by their recollected bearing "the hidden life of his Divine Majesty".[26] Alphonsus could hardly object to such generally well-meaning encouragements to the good life. But, even as he was sanctioning Falcoia's rather muddled and muddling pieties in these early documents, Alphonsus was considering how he might himself better frame the particular reference of "following" to the vocation of the Redemptorist.

"By this Jesus Christ wished to give his servants to understand what ought to be the life of those who wish to follow him: 'If any man will come after Me, let him deny himself, take up his cross, and follow me'."[27] What is true for each follower is true in a particular way for the Redemptorist follower. Alphonsus talks of each one, as he says in his admiring account of Paolo Cafaro, "crucifying his inclinations". There may be an application, as he remarks in his 1773 reflections *On the Passion,* "to the death of every just man" of the words "that the Jews said when Jesus was on the Cross: If he is the true Son of God, he will accept him and deliver him", but there is a particular martyrdom in the Redemptorist life towards that death.[28] And this especial witness of the Redemptorist is set out in the draft constitution *On Preaching* prepared for the General Congregation in 1747. This asserts that it is precisely in their following as preachers that the members of his Congregation are "especially dedicated to the imitation of Jesus Christ". The gospel declaration of the disciples' congruence with Christ, "As the Father sent me, I also send you", is to be interpreted by Redemptorists in the precise terms of the life upon which Jesus was sent by his Father. The Redemptorist, like Christ, is to live according to the terms of Isaiah's prophecy: "The Spirit of the Lord is upon me. He has anointed me to preach the good news to the poor". This is a defining injunction. Alphonsus remarks approvingly, in his *Notes on the life of Sarnelli*, that his hard-working colleague had often told him that he felt a special call to apply the words of Isaiah to himself, that he would, indeed, be damned, "if he did not devote all his energies to this purpose".[29] This is an imitation of Christ, preaching in Galilee and Judaea, which perfectly corresponds to Alphonsus' habitual celebration of what is "always the same".

The "always" of "I am always with you" impelled Alphonsus into the recognition of the "always" of "the poor you have always with you". The poor of Galilee are to be met in the poor of the Naples countryside. The Redemptorist is to live with these poor. And to live like them. It is "by enduring poverty, despisals, and sorrows" that "the saints have come into the eternal glory".[30] So the Redemptorists must "follow, like poor people, Jesus Christ, who himself was poor". They must "like poor men be content with frugal fare". And content with the simplest clothing. "Their habit, cloak, and stockings shall be of ordinary wool; however, the use of under-stockings of linen or cotton is allowed", "shoes shall be simple", and, as Alphonsus wrote to all members of the Congregation in August, 1758, about these dress rules, "let Superiors be careful to have them mended as long as they are worth mending — the Congregation is to be most pitied if the members are ashamed to appear in patched garments". He noted happily that, in accord with this vocation Paolo Cafaro's clothes were so shabby that "once when his brother met him looking as ragged as any beggar, he treated him as a madman, and loaded him with reproaches in the public street". Alphonsus wore such a patched cassock himself as he moved between villages on the mission.

It had taken Alphonsus a little while to discern this particular vocation to preach in the countryside. In the first rush of his enthusiasm, on that 29 August, 1723, he had insisted that Pagano receive him into the Girolamini community at once. St Philip Neri remained always one of his favourites, but while he had made the large city parishes the sphere of an Oratorian's vocation, Alphonsus' further experiences brought him to appreciate that there was an especial meaning for his life in Jesus' ministry in the villages. This is "the absolute difference" of the Redemptorist from members of all other Congregations as the *Ristretto* says. Conclusively, Alphonsus laid it down in the 1750 *Considerations* that "he who is called to the Congregation of the Most Holy Redeemer will never be a true follower of Jesus Christ" unless, in the spirit of the Institute, he work for the salvation of "the poor people in the countryside".[31]

Thus it is that this apostolate of preaching to the rural poor is emphasized repeatedly in the documents prepared for the Institute's application for papal approbation. Andrea Villani (1706-1792), the indefatigable representative of the community in the Roman negotiations, opened his "petitionary statement" of their cause with an historical account of Alphonsus' observation of the great neglect in which the poor people found themselves, "especially in the countryside", and to his forming the Institute with Bishop Falcoia in order "to assist the souls of the rural poor by missions" so that they should not die "ignorant of the necessary mysteries of the faith". Reiteratingly to a point at which he must surely be in danger of tiring the poor Pope, but knowing that this is the main matter for Alphonsus, Villani declares that the members of the community have from their early days together "gone on helping these poor people, moving about the countryside, from the little towns, into the most abandoned places", pursuing the shepherds of Puglia. They have now come together to live in houses "outside the populated areas" of the Kingdom. The Pope is asked, therefore, to approve what is being done for "so many country people", and to enact that the Congregation shall continue in "a work not only useful but also so necessary for the assistance of so many souls living in the country places of this extensive Kingdom". When the Pope referred the matter to the Congregation of the Council, and the Congregation referred it to Cardinal Spinelli, Alphonsus wrote to him in April 1748, to insist on this "countryside" character of the Redemptorists' peculiar mission. After some remarks putting aside any wearisome doubts the cardinal might have about yet another new piece of religious enthusiasm and yet another group of religious, Alphonsus moves quickly to indicate the lack in the Naples archdiocese of those who will work "in the country places", "the townships of the countryside", and "those little villages", or will establish religious centres "outside the populated places". Cardinal Spinelli took up this idea of a wholly rural mission. He wrote to the Roman Congregation in October, declaring that he was "of a mind to think this kind of Institute is most useful for country people" and suggesting that whoever formulated the rules for the Congregation should state plainly that the houses should always be "outside the cities".

The curial supervisor of the business, Cardinal Joachim Besozzi (c.1689-1755), after some canonist's further revision of the text of the Institute's petition for recognition, for the original "referred only to a life patterned on the norms of the Gospel", passed the papers upstairs. By an Apostolic Brief of 25 February, 1749, Pope Benedict XIV established the Congregation in an *imitatio* which would be fulfilled by "preaching the Word of God to the poor" who are "scattered in the countryside".

Of all the cardinals and secretaries, canonists and bureaucrats, who looked over Alphonsus' petition for papal recognition and the accompanying correspondence, it was Cardinal Spinelli who had found the fit phrase for the Congregation's work. He had made the necessary imaginative, scriptural, connection between Alphonsus' *imitatio* of preaching to the country folk, the demands that such a life would make on the missioner, and the apostolic testimony of *Hebrews*. It is "outside the city" that Jesus suffers, and it is to an *imitatio* beyond the walls that the author of *Hebrews* urges the christian missionary: "Let us go forth, outside the city". The author of *Hebrews* has an image of crucifixion in view. But there is more than one sort of martyrdom. For men, as for women. The first generation of Redemptorists suffered from the particular psychological anxiety which afflicted most Neapolitans when compelled to live at any distance from the city: "No one wants to leave Mama". Young Giuseppe Melchionna (1733-1803), thought the house at d'Iliceto, seventy miles or so from Naples, as a place of exile. Alphonsus found it difficult to get anyone to contemplate living across the water in Sicily. The foundation over the border in the Papal States had been most piteously opposed by his Consultors. Alphonsus understood this anxiety. "They are far from Naples", he admitted, suggesting to Francesco de Paola (1737-1814), the Superior of the Scifelli house, that he be "very kind and understanding with them". It was certainly prudent of Alphonsus to have taken the counsel of Cardinal Spinelli that he drop from the proposed Rule the obligation that these men should be ready to go off obediently on the foreign missions. Whatever romantic requests the novices made for oriental assignments, they would all, when it came to it, naturally, want to stay within the walls. Alphonsus persisted in the translation of this grand geographical imperative into a demand for a local martyrdom.

"It will be useful", he writes in the 1773 *Pious Reflections*, after quoting the saying at *Luke 9.23 : If anyone will come after me, let him deny himself and take up his cross daily, and follow me,* "to make a few observations on these words of Jesus Christ." Alphonsus becomes the textual critic for this important moment. "He says, *If anyone will come after me,* he does not say *to me* but *after me*". Alphonsus continues to divide and examine each word of this significant pericope. Comments on *take up, his cross, daily,* and *deny* lead, at *let him follow,* to the climactic declaration that "we must follow in the footsteps of Jesus Christ right up to death".[32] That witnessing death is sometimes to be caught of overwork, like the death of the forty-two years old Gennaro Sarnelli at Naples in 1744, sometimes of being forced to sleep out of doors on a cold night, like the death of the thirty-nine years old Vito Curzio at d'Iliceto in 1745, or, again, of a sudden fever, like the death of the forty-seven years old Paolo Cafaro at Caposele in 1753. But that following which required of the missioner is always to be completed in such witnessing.

Each Redemptorist would discover the demands of *"following"* in his own experience of the Congregation's preaching among the poor. And of living with the poor. Dying with them: "Christ lived poor and died poor". Alphonsus makes this plainest, perhaps, in his 1776 treatise on *The Sacrifice of Jesus Christ,* where, starting from the pre-figurings of Christ's sacrifice in the Hebrew scriptures, and leading then from the gospel accounts of the Passion into a characteristic elucidation of the significance of the Eucharist for the community's present share in the death of the Lord, he re-states the final demand contained in that "following" proposed in *Hebrews*: "He was led forth from Jerusalem, whence the Apostle invites us to follow him by sharing in his shame: Let us go forth, therefore...."[33]

137

(I)   Jesus began to preach, saying "Repent"

What had been figured in the helio-centric orrery was plainly declared in the *Imitation of Christ*, as Maggie Tulliver discovered as she read "the old-fashioned book for which you need only pay sixpence at a bookstall": "All the miseries of her young life had come from fixing her heart on her own pleasure, as if that were the central necessity of the universe". There were many others besides that unhappy girl, as George Eliot observed, writing in *The Mill on the Floss* of nineteenth century England in terms that surely applied to eighteenth century Naples, who felt the want of meaning, "life in this unpleasurable shape demanding some solution even to unspeculative minds". Alphonsus knew many of these. He was eager to speak with them of a meaningful solution. His *Moral Theology* represents his effort to relate freedom and obedience and meaning through considerations of Conscience and Law and the Sacraments so that confessors shall be able to make that solution open to their penitents.

While a practising lawyer, he had spent time each week with the sick of the *Incurabili* hospital, and had, as a member of the *Misericordiella* fraternity, worked with the prisoners in the Archbishop's gaol. While a young priest, he had joined the *Bianchi della Giustizia* who attended condemned criminals in the cells and on the way to execution in the Piazza del Mercato, and made representations for their widows.[34] Being put as a curate in the parish of Sant'Angelo a Segno, he had a care for the urchins running wild in the Via dei Tribunali and began to collect them for street classes. Meeting the hawker, Bartolomeo, who took his tray of books up and down the same street, Alphonsus had brought him to the *Capelle Serotine* where, for six years from 1727 on, he and Cesare Sportelli and Gennaro Sarnelli trained labouring men to be catechists for their fellow workers. He had, during these years, become very well acquainted with the urban poor. And, from that day when he put ashore at Amalfi in May 1730 and was confronted by the herdsmen and their families at Santa Maria dei Monte, be began to understand, too, the needs of the rural poor. The needs, as George Eliot says again, of those whose lives are "spread over sheepwalks, and scattered in lonely houses and huts". There was in the Kingdom of Naples too, an urgent need for whatever would "give patience and feed human love when the limbs ached with weariness and human looks are hard upon us". Alphonsus heard them cursing and understood how their circumstances had brought them to curse. And he recognized that their greatest need was for some forgiveness of their own hardness. There was a need for a patient and kindly and knowledgeable priest who would hear their confessions.

It was Alphonsus' experience that there were far too many simple priests in the Kingdom. A simple priest was, in Alphonsus' vocabulary, a priest who has not impressed the bishop enough to be trusted with faculties to hear confessions, or who has not bothered himself to seek faculties. Simply to be a priest is to be a manifestly incomplete imitation of Christ. It is to neglect the offer of being a forgiver like him. Exactly like him. For, were the Redeemer to sit in the next confessional, he would say *Ego te absolvo* over his penitents, and the priest in the next box would likewise say *Ego te absolvo*, and the penitents of each would be equally absolved.

But if the priest is to be like Christ and do his work of forgiveness, he must do it knowledgeably. It is "very difficult and dangerous work", for at his rendering his own account, the confessor will have to answer for the guidance he has given to penitents, and it must, therefore, be a dread matter to undertake to hear confessions "without the necessary learning". Such dread cannot, however, be turned into an excuse. "You may say that you are not qualified for the office of the confessor, because you have not studied theology; but do you not know that a priest is bound to study?"[35] If he is to fulfil his vocation, to be and do like Christ, the priest must study the moral law declared in the Church.

Alphonsus himself had been careful, as he came to this "most important and most difficult" of all studies, to find out a distinguished theologian and take him as his tutor.

"The illustrious and learned Torno"

Successively a member of the Naples cathedral chapter, Superior of the Apostolic Missions, and Bishop of Arcadiopolis, Giulio Torno was a scholarly man.[36] Even if he seem now an antiquarian rather than an historian, Torno knew enough about the tradition of the local church to put together a very respectable booklet in response to the anti-papalist gibes with which Pietro Giannone (1676-1748), had diversified the surly passages of his *Civil History of the Kingdom of Naples*, 1723. Vico let it be known how much he approved Torno's pamphlet, and it was perhaps this publication which suggested to Alphonsus that he would find Torno a congenial tutor on his abandoning his law practice that same year.

Though he found the forward-looking Vico a congenial supper-table companion, Torno himself liked rather to snuffle amongst the older theology. In 1720, he had put out his expensive edition of the posthumous commentary composed by Willem Hessel van Est (1542-1613), ("Estius" to his learned colleagues), on *The Four Books of the Sentences* of the mediaeval compendiarist, Peter Lombard (1100-1160). Most teachers are surprised by some oddment of their instruction that remains in a former pupil's mind long after everything of any importance has been forgotten or wantonly abandoned. It may well have been as they anticipated Matins together after class on a Friday afternoon, that Torno told Alphonsus of Estius' suggestion about the Chaldean storks at *Psalm* 103:19. This cheerful scrap of information remained with him until it could find a place in Alphonsus' own commentary on *The Divine Office*, fifty years on. Torno was certainly encouraging in Alphonsus, as they took their tutorials together, that taste for unconsidered trifles which he shared with Estius and Peter Lombard. So Torno remained in Alphonsus' recollection as a man of "vast erudition" as well as "untarnished reputation", he was "most distinguished and most learned" at his every appearance among the authorities Alphonsus cited in the *Moral Theology*.[37]

Torno's teaching method, putting moral questions alongside scriptural exegesis and patristic commentary, and keeping all together by his consistent reference to the anecdotal tradition of the community, had, clearly, its influence upon Alphonsus' own teaching method later. As did Torno's enthusiasm for the *Summa Theologiae* of Aquinas. Reminiscing about his own student days, when he was the favourite pupil of the noted Dominican scholar, Gregorio Selleri (1664-1729), Torno thought it safe to boast that he had been a Thomist from earliest childhood.[38] Alphonsus learnt the lifetime lesson that it would be enough to clinch an argument if he could finish upon "as St Thomas says", or even more determinedly, "such is the teaching of St Thomas". He would always aim to keep himself in concert with that "healthy teaching of the Angelic Doctor".[39] Each time a censor paused at some

140

opinion put forward in Alphonsus' later dogmatic or moral writings, he was ready with a substantiating reference to the *Summa*, as Salvatore Ruggieri (1724-1787)(?), and Giuseppe Simeoli (1713-1779), both learned rather too fast for their comfort. And nothing, it seemed to Alphonsus, self-condemned his scholarly adversary, the Dominican, Giovanni Patuzzi (1700-1769), more decidedly than his remarking that "the view of St Thomas is no longer to be accepted". But, whether they were claiming to be Thomists or not, Alphonsus was not much attracted by contemporary dogmatists. There was much amiss with those manualist theologies which proceeded according to their dull lines of argument, clarifying point after successive point, towards a conclusion *quod erat demonstrandum*. He recognized a likeness in these procedures to the inappropriatenesses of history, to "beginning, middle and end" according to the order of time. His sense of the irrelevance of such linear structures to the study of the eternal wonder of God was expressed at a characteristic stopping-place: "Why should we trouble ourselves about the opinions of scholastics as to whether predestination to glory precedes or follows the prevision of merits?"[40]

Still, Torno had not thought it practicable to teach directly from Aquinas' text. Not in moral theology classes, at any rate. He needed something a little more likely to deal with some modern problems. Alphonsus remembered in 1782 that Torno had recommended the *Medulla theologica*, 1650, of Louis Abelly (1603-1691), as treating complex questions "with great distinction and briefly". He recommended it himself.[41] But Abelly had already proved too easy-going in his moral judgements for the taste of the French bishops, and his *Medulla* had been replaced in the Aix diocesan seminary in 1676 as soon as the first volumes of professor François Genet's *Théologie morale* came from the printer.[42] Torno took up this Gallic text-book and employed the 1705 second, latin, edition of the *Théologie morale* in his classes. "The first volume of moral theology which was put into my hands was that of Genet."[43]

François Genet, the "more probable" and the "safer"

The seminary professor had in due time been rewarded for producing so useful a text-book by being made Bishop of Vaison, a diocese straddling the border between the Pope's Avignon territory and the

141

King's France. He had been, in his *Théologie morale*, quite explicit in affirming that "we sin when we act against either ecclesiastical or civil laws", but he allowed that the laws of princes could not oblige in conscience if they were founded, as they might be, on a false presumption. Spies accused the bishop of encouraging political discontent. And there were further complaints. Genet was suspected of circulating books banned by Louis XIV's censors. He certainly had received into his diocese the poor *Filles de l'Enfance* who were being pursued by the state troopers. And he had been active in a diocesan mission with a pair of priests who had been arrested, in his presence, on charges of anti-royalist pro-papalist propagandizing. In 1688, the King's soldiers occupied Avignon. Genet was arrested and thrown, untried, into prison. He did not get out until 1690. He at once resumed both his conscientious pastoral visitation of his diocese and his revision, for a new edition, of his text book. All this was well-known throughout Europe. The telling of the author's story cannot but have helped to promote his book.

The recently-graduated Alphonsus may have been charmed, as he perused the "brief explanation", over three hundred pages, of the *Institutiones* of Justinian in volume VIII of Genet's work, for there Genet, like Alphonsus, like Torno, a Doctor of Canon and Civil Law, was observing that "ignorance of civil law makes those who are in charge of the conduct of souls fall into many errors".[44] Alphonsus would have recognized in article after article of Genet's course that they both belonged to a lawyerly tradition reaching back in its argumentative modes, and, often enough, in its examples, to Cicero and, on special occasions, to Aristotle. But while in the civil courts the lawyer was employed to win the case, manipulating precedents, arguing for exceptions, pleading extenuating circumstances, to secure his client's success, in the tribunal of the confessional Genet was demanding that his student defend the law itself.

Theologically, Genet was associated in Torno's mind with those who took Selleri's limiting view of human openness to divine grace. This was a way of talking that Torno liked. It was re-inforcing what he had read in Estius' work, in the writings of Estius' Louvain relative, Johann Hessel (1522-1566), and of Estius' own teacher, the proto-Jansenist, Michael Baius (1513-1589). Genet had in his sights an array of opponents who, by their low expectations of humanity, their excusing appeal to what was practicable, and to what was reasonable, and their reliance on God's being ever-forgiving in the face of human insult, would bring Christian society near to collapse. The hard-working bishop looked about him at a reckless aristocracy, a rationalist intelligentia, a money-grabbing bourgeoisie, an abandoned and cursing peasantry, and determined to train priests who should preach a more demanding doctrine.

It should be a doctrine that dealt with a range of disobedient sinners. In a format of question and answer, supplemented by illustrative case histories, Genet set out his view of life and law, sinners and circumstances. His choice of cases was wide-ranging. Don Giuseppe, on the bridge of his galley-ship, might have been surprised to learn that, "since it is against the order of nature, the keeping of slaves is no longer practised among Christians". Don Ercole, turning over Alphonsus' reproachful letters, might have been reassured to learn that there was a real moral difficulty in deciding whether a man be obliged to pay out a bequest to a member of his family who has become a religious.[45] Every reader might have learned something from a sequence of cases exampling what could be done for Peter the Florentine in a scrapeful life. Arriving in Naples with letters of credit, Genet's youngster was hurried into a most unfortunate history, providing plenty of opportunities for the moralist to pose and answer various hard questions. Had Peter, in changing his money, taken part in a sinful usurous transaction? What could be done for Peter once he had bought a ring which turned out not to be of gold? What, again, once Peter had made a marriage contract with Catharine, upon her turning out not to be an heiress? And what, when, at the wedding reception, on lifting the bride's veil, Peter discovered he had married not Catharine but her sister Joanna? There would not, perhaps, have been the same wide-spreading interest in the case of the clergyman playing games of chance. But this, like the rest, could be neatly settled, Genet showed, by an appeal to law.[46]

Sometimes, he admitted, it was not immediately obvious what the law-giver meant to impose. There might be a doubt about whether the law had been promulgated. The most technical terms might yet admit differences of lawyerly interpretation. Questions might be raised about the general scope of the law's provisions. The facts of a particular case might be obscure. So informed opinions might differ about what the confessor should say to the penitent. Acknowledging these uncertainties, Genet confronted those priests who supposed it was enough if they could assure their penitents that some approved authors had approved an opinion that the law did not apply in their cases. Since the opinion was approved by an expert, *probata*, it was therefore probable, *"probabilis"*. Such confessors were encouraging penitents to act on "probable" opinion without fear of any offence against the law, or at least without fear of any culpable, sinful, offence against God. Genet set up a *probabilist* questioner to be knocked down. "Are we not always secure in conscience when we act according to a probable opinion?" This is a question, Genet answers, of the greatest moment. "It involves the largest of all the difficulties of moral theology."[47]

It was, Genet thought, the great deceit of the probabiliorists that they were suggesting to Christians that they were often confronted with a true choice between one properly approved way of acting and another, one probable opinion and another, one way of pleasing the Law-Giver and another. It is, rather, he was sure, almost always possible to identify the opinion which is more approved, more probable, *"probabilior"*, than all others, because it is almost always possible, for those who attend to the law with adequate seriousness, to draw the true consequences by consulting a great Tradition of Christian moral teaching. Genet's one reference to Estius was to dispute his account of the workings of that Tradition. By taking some care in selecting quotations and neatly altering some of them, Genet was able to demonstrate that Aquinas was just his sort of *probabiliorist*. He made a similarly accommodating exegesis of what the great moralist St Antoninus had to say about honest conjectures of what is likely. The Tradition was manifestly a probabiliorist tradition.[48]

As he read further, Alphonsus would have discerned that Genet himself was a deliberately inconsistent probabiliorist. Genet allows that when the more probable opinion is that an action would be within the law, Christians are certainly free to act on this opinion. But, he adds, if the less probable opinion be in favour of the law's imposing an obligation in this case, it would be better, more Christian, to refrain from an action which just might be outside the law. Still keen to show that the Tradition is with him, Genet cites, quite out of context, St Augustine's judgement during the Donatist campaign that "in cases of doubt the safer path is to be chosen". Alphonsus, as he read, would not have been encouraged to look for signs of the freedom of the children of God. Torno was unable to help him find his way. It was, unhappily, precisely in the midst of contemporary disputes about the divine offer of grace that Torno failed to respond to anything liberating in the teaching of Aquinas. He fell in line, here, with Genet, agreeing that when it came to the Judgement, it would be better to have been safer. There was, anyway, much to attract a scrupulous young man in the notion of a "God-fearing", safer, way of conducting one's life. And the conduct of the Medici lawyers in the Amatrice affair and their success in thwarting equity had shown him how careful the good man has to be to defend the law from the attacks of special pleading. "As a consequence, I was for some time myself a defender of the rigorist view."[49]

Cursing the Dead

From 1727 onwards, Alphonsus was taking an active part in the work of the Apostolic Missions in both the city and the scattered parts of the Kingdom, and in 1731, at Poligno a Mare, he was given charge of the arrangements for confessions on a parish mission. He got a few shocks. Genet and "that sort of author" had not warned the young man how wearying mentally, as well as physically, it would be for the confessor to keep himself in sympathy with sinners. Nor, even, had they, as they claimed, provided answers to all questions likely to be raised as he sat listening to the recital of their sins. Alphonsus' first published effort at tackling a moral problem, the 1746 *Letter concerning "cursing the dead"*, *bestemmia de' morti*,[50] witnesses to his being driven by pastoral experience to think out for himself and his penitents the particular reference of the law of the Kingdom of God to the actual state of women and men in the Kingdom of Naples.

It was a habit of Neapolitans of every class to slip into blasphemies upon the slightest disgruntlement with their condition. "In the piazza there is blaspheming against God, in the market-place there is blaspheming against God, in the card-rooms..." wrote the severe Sarnelli in his *Against Cursing*, 1740, " ...in the inn, the town house, the country road." Alphonsus knew exactly what Sarnelli was talking about, especially when he came to condemn the blaspheming on board ship "if the sea is not calm, if the wind does not blow". Alphonsus knew also about the common expletive "a curse upon your ancestors!" Text-book authors were suggesting, and the reservation to themselves of absolution for this blaspheming the dead by local bishops seemed to prove the text-book men to be right, that this cursing was a mortal sin against one's neighbour in Purgatory. Putting his notes together for his 1746 *Letter* explaining the true significance of that cursing along alleyways, across field boundaries, and up and down the rigging of his father's ship, Alphonsus had not found much to assist him in the manuals. The universally respected authorites had not bothered themselves with this little Neapolitan difficulty, not even the near-neighbouring St Thomas Aquinas. And the local foot-noters were nervous of any meddling with existing curial estimates of the matter. Alphonsus had to set out the evidence of how ordinary Neapolitans viewed their cursing, how experienced confessors felt about the certitudes of the diocesan canonists, and apply general principles of moral theology to the resolution of the difficulty. He had to acquire the skills of a moralist and to acquire them fast. "Cursing the dead" should not, he concluded, be considered serious sin. The Neapolitan cursers were not venting anything like the malice of serious sin.

There was a ready reception for this conclusion. Everyone of pastoral and academic respectability whom he consulted before having his *Letter* printed, the members of the Apostolic Missions, the Pious Workers, and the Pavone missioners, agreed that Alphonsus had made his case. The pamphlet did its work. The reservation of "blaspheming the dead" to his extraordinary tribunal was quietly rescinded by one bishop after another in the next few years.

The like acute awareness of the particular circumstances of others informs all that Alphonsus says later about a game of cards bearing along with it the possibility of the loser's losing his temper, and a night out on the town bearing with it the similar possibility of obscene jokes among the boys, about the ambiguous language of lawyers and the equivocations of accuser and accused, about what the confessor should ordinarily say to the concubine of the parish priest and how he might respond to her extraordinary signs of sorrow, about the temptations to sexual unruliness that may come upon an adolescent boy working with women on the fishwharf and upon a bishop having his hand kissed, about the temptations to despair of the slave at the oar, the condemned man on his way to the gallows, and the holy woman on her convent death-bed. He takes into account what the villagers would say and do if a man, whose concealed impotence rendered his attempt at marrying null, were, wishing to avoid sinful embraces, to shut out of his house the woman they all supposed to be his lawful wife. What they would say and do if their priest, on finding them too stimulating to his sexual imaginings, simply stopped hearing women's confessions. It was at the prompting of such real questions that Alphonsus picked his way delicately among definitions of "occasions of sin" which might be remote or proximate, *per se* or *per accidens*, necessary or voluntary, as he improved the successive editions of his *Moral Theology*, the three volume Italian manual, *Instructions for a Confessor*, 1757, which he had derived from the *Moral Theology*, and, for the more educated but even busier pastor, the short latin manual, *The Apostolic Man*, 1759. Less expectedly, to those who keep the moral theologian's concern with one's dealings with one's neighbour in a separate compartment from the ascetical theologian's concern for one's dealings with God, these cases and the distinctions necessary for their solution are reviewed again in *The Treasury* of helpful hints for priests.[51]

Alphonsus' 1746 *Letter* thus signals his undertaking a vocation in which his lawyerly experience, his bookman's learning, and his missioner's eagerness for Christian reconciliation, would be placed at the service of confessors and penitents. He did not think the vocation of the learned pastor to be in any way peculiar to himself. It is a consistent theme in his letters that to hold any office in the Church is to be summoned to such a service of study. He wrote to the 1774 conclavist cardinals, with a startlingly modern sense of his episcopal responsibility, that the Church required them to elect a pontiff who, among other virtues, had kept up his reading in dogmatic and moral theology, and who would thereby be best equipped to deal with the complexities of the age. He wrote, rather more ingratiatingly, to the expectant Canon Simeoli that "learned cardinals are necessary for the Church", most especially in their time.[52] And all his experience of life among the lower reaches of the Neapolitan clergy led him to discern the great need for priests who would appreciate the relation of reading and thinking and preaching and hearing confessions. He was the more insistent when he could hope for the greater effect. He urged each Redemptorist Rector to ensure that his house should have a working theologian's library. "If you have any money to spend", he wrote to Gasparo Caione at Caposele, "I would rather have you buy the works of Bellarmine, Spondano, Rinaldo (the Compendium of Baronius), the Mansi collection." They were certainly to buy several copies of his *Moral Theology*. And to sell them. "The *Moral Theology* is sold at twenty carlini. An appendix has been added, and it cannot be sold for less. The *Pratica* costs one carlino."[53]

Reconstructing Busenbaum's *Medulla*

What became the *Moral Theology* began with Alphonsus' publishing, in 1748, a set of notes to the 1650 *Medulla theologiae moralis* of the Westphalian Jesuit, Hermann Busenbaum (1609-1668). Busenbaum's *"Medulla"* and Genet's eight volumes which Alphonsus was now discarding, had for some time been set against one another. They were competing in the same market. And, by 1748, were generally recognized to be offering different wares. But Alphonsus professed a non-combative reason for taking up Busenbaum's handy account of the essentials of moral theology: "I selected Busenbaum from the rest because of his clear exposition, his discernment of what was important in a discussion, and his restraint in the matter of scholarly apparatus".[54] Still, Busenbaum's text did require some ever-lengthening annotations. For the second Naples edition, published in two volumes in 1753 and 1755, as well as revising and expanding his original notes, Alphonsus added others, some of them of short-essay length, on topics which he judged needful even in a handy text-book. Even for the third edition, three folio volumes, Venice, 1757, however, Busenbaum retains his place as the author, and Alphonsus as annotator is now followed by Francesco Antonio Zaccaria (1714-1795), as forwarder of their enterprise.

This most learned Jesuit, whom Alphonsus thought "well-balanced in his opinions, neither lax nor rigorous", and whom he had been pleased to accept as the Venetian censor, was an assiduous promoter of the interests of the Society. In 1749, he had edited the *Theologia moralis* of the Belgian Jesuit, Claude Lacroix (1652-1714), adding his own *Liber Prodromos de Locis Theologiis* in which he took several swipes at the inconstant scholarship of the Dominican moralist, Daniele Concina (1687-1756).[55] Zaccaria revised this little history of casuistry into a preface for the third edition of Alphonsus' *Moral Theology*, and placed the Jesuit device on the title-page. He proved a fine public relations man for the work, penning a ferocious review of the more severe Concina's *Instructions for Confessors*, 1753, in which he contrasted Alphonsus' methodical arrangement of topics and his pastoral care for confessor and sinner with Concina's "confused rag-bag of unbalanced opinions"

148

which must make confession a terrible experience for both of them. In 1755, he felt that it might be useful if he brought out his own moral text-book so that readers could see how good were the ideas of the three Jesuits, Busenbaum, Lacroix, and himself. He mis-timed his publication. His book was burnt along with Busenbaum's "*Medulla*" in the Toulouse bonfire of 1757. Zaccaria, resilient as ever, got his revenges in his *History of the Banning of Books*, 1774.

It was not until the publication of the sixth edition of the *Moral Theology*, 1767, that Busenbaum's name disappeared from the title page. Alphonsus realized that there were disadvantages to his being so closely associated with the Jesuits. They had, that very year, been expelled from the Kingdom. Still, he retained Zaccaria's opening essay "On the origins of casuistry" until the eighth edition, 1779. Alphonsus' own text had kept getting longer. He had gone on altering, deleting, adding, re-arranging, expanding, while he still had command of his energies, his faculties, and his secretaries, right up to the ninth edition which appeared in 1785, two years before his death. Some things remained at the last exactly as he had first read them in Busenbaum's "*Medulla*", the descriptions of the three ways a person may lawfully obtain an ecclesiastical benefice, for example, the estimate of dispensations granted by the Sacred Penitentiary, and the opening paragraphs of an article on Indulgences.[56] But, generally, Alphonsus' text was getting longer because he was becoming more and more discontented with the evidences, the arguments, the arrangement of topics in the "*Medulla*". "God knows how many times I have repented of not having from the beginning made the *Moral Theology* my own, without using Busenbaum at all", but since "I have followed the text and cases given by him" there was nothing to be done now about the order of topics. He could however, as he told Andrea Villani in 1773, alter the tone of the book. Most particularly, Alphonsus wanted to establish a larger range of authorities. He liked to work towards the point at which he might indicate the Catholic witness to his theses: "as all the Fathers, theologians, and masters of spirituality teach". The patristic authors who have directed the course of dogmatic theology, the authoritative moralists who occupy the footnotes of the manualists, and the ascetical writers, his dear patroness St Teresa among the masters, are to have each their say as the discussion continues. No jurisdictional disputes here. And no worries about chronology. As he starts on his consideration of "the scrupulous conscience" for example, Alphonsus takes evidences as he needs them with no regard at all for temporal order; in one short paragraph Alexander Natalis (1639-1724), St Antoninus (1389-1459), St Bernard (1090-1153), St Philip Neri (1515-1595), St Francis of Sales (1567-1622), the Blessed John of Avila (1500-1567), St Bernard again, St Ignatius Loyola (1491-1556), Cardinal Humbert, who died in 1061, come leaping happily together towards the *Sentences* of Denys van Leeuwen (1402-1471), and the *Speculum* of St Bonaventure (1221-1274).[57] Alphonsus is always able to find moral authorities, as he could always find authorities for all that he wanted to say, on the circling rim of Christians round Christ, each one still active in the present. By that affirmation "all teach", Alphonsus gives himself and his students the freedom of the Church. The truth which they share has been articulated by all honest and orthodox women and men at all times, "always the same".

Becoming an Authority

"Read my *Moral Theology* for half an hour each day", Alphonsus wrote to one of his priest students in 1756, "so that you may be able to hear confessions." His experience of that "cursing the dead" had shown him the need for his manual to be fitted to the conditions within which the Redemptorist missioners were working: "I have done it only for you, my brethren". Like Aquinas' *Summa*, Alphonsus' *Moral Theology* was designed to be a schoolroom text-book; "for our beginners".[58]

Certainly, Alphonsus did not write the *Moral Theology* for pleasure. He talks ruefully of God's only knowing how tedious and troublesome the whole enterprise has been for him. Not for pleasure. And not for money. "In regard to my royalty", he wrote to Remondini when arranging the Venetian publication of the *Moral Theology* in 1755, "that will be entirely according to your good pleasure." He might, though, allow himself a little pride in authorship. "I should like to have one copy." Remondini sent him a good number, and when Alphonsus offered to buy others from him at cost price, he sent him another twenty and then thirty more, all free. They both come off well from this exchange. Alphonsus felt "my dear Giovanni Battista" to be a real friend. One of very few. The feeling was, no doubt, partly in response to their having endured so much together. They had suffered from pirates by sea and by land. Cargoes had disappeared between Venice and Naples. Unauthorized editions of the small ascetical works, from which Remondini might well have expected to get a quick return on his investment, appeared on the Naples bookstalls.

150

They were reproductions of the small printings that Alphonsus liked to use as proofsheets before he sent off his final version to the Venetian publisher. "The booksellers are the cause. Seeing my works have a good sale, they print them again and again. I cannot help it." Only substantial volumes were protected by copyright in the Kingdom. Not for money, then. And not for fame. Though he acknowledged that *Visits to the Blessed Sacrament* would sell the better because "the publication of my *Moral Theology* had made my miserable name more known". And putting together the *Moral Theology* had clearly established him as a notable member of the academic community. But "I did not undertake this labour... to acquire a reputation", and Alphonsus knew that "if I had only wished to be applauded" he could have managed that far less tiringly. Still, his reconsiderations of different topics in moral theology had been very quickly deemed respectable enough for him to be accepted as a worthy antagonist by some distinguished controversialists.

Alphonsus' enlargement of the range of authorities in his moral theology had the effect, as he intended, of lessening the importance of such controversialists. Alphonsus was as sure as any of them that he had found out the right method of doing moral theology. He was as willing as any of them to impress confessors with his confident saying so: "I regard that system as certainly the true one". So he could not permit uninformed discussion to be carried on by the Redemptorist students. "I do not wish", he told one lecturer, "that there be taught opinions which are contrary to those we hold in the *Moral Theology*", and "I wish that the common opinions and those that I myself teach in my *Moral Theology* should be followed and maintained as much as is possible", and "if the Lector hold a contrary opinion, let him keep it to himself". On the other hand, the confessors in the Congregation who had some experience of the practical workings of his moral theology should go on observing, thinking, and discussing. When these Fathers were deliberating, "I do not pretend that my opinions must be followed", but he did intend that they should be given appropriate respect as this discussion went forward. "Before you reject them, at the very least, you should read my book." Reading that book with care, they would surely realize that they were being invited to something very like a common-room discussion. At the very first *caput* of the *Moral Theology*, there is a deliberately conversational disruption of the academic structure as Alphonsus comes to the end of distinguishing six conditions of Christian conscience. "We ought to talk more of this."[59] Alphonsus puts aside the thesis in order to chat with a friend. It is entirely in accord with Alphonsus' understanding of this continuing conversation that Newman should trust that he would not lose the intercession of the saint "who was a lover of truth" if, at the end of an enquiry into a moral question, "I follow other guidance in preference to his".[60]

As Newman again recognized, "St Alphonsus made many changes of opinion himself in the course of his writings".[61] This process of correction began almost as soon as Alphonsus began writing. The revised first volume of the *Moral Theology*, 1753, was prefaced by a catalogue of the fifty and more topics on which Alphonsus had changed his mind between the writing and the printing of the book. The second volume in 1755 took the number of these emendations, reconsiderations, retractions, up to a hundred. Each successive edition of the work was taken as an opportunity for further revisions. "My originals are entirely covered with marginal notes and erasures, as I am never content."[62] Such changes were certainly not made with an eye to forcing purchasers of early editions to buy the later one as well. Like the great Jowett in a similar situation, Alphonsus made sure that those who had spent their money on the *Moral Theology* received the alterations free. "I send you a package containing copies of the *Elenchus* for the second volume", he wrote to Caione in June, 1755, "I have them distributed among those that have the first edition of the work." He was so aware of himself as a man who moved from opinion to opinion that he collected precedents for such changings. He had ready a nice remark of Aquinas: "I have written differently about this somewhere else". And he meant his brethren to notice that he was changing. In a long letter to the whole Congregation, August 1754, he particularly directed the confessors to notice "those opinions which, as may be seen in the second edition of my work, I no longer allow to be probable".

With this allusion to *probable* opinions, Alphonsus might seem to be alerting them again to that rowdiest of the disputes among contemporary moralists. Some of the more ingenious of them might be happy to take part in that contention of *probabilists* and *probabiliorists* which had so occupied Genet. The dispute made so much noise not simply because a confessor's choosing sides would affect every piece of advice he gave penitents in the midst of personal anxieties, but also because it was, after all, a dispute among moralists about the value of their opinions, about their academic dignity, and their status in the Church. But Alphonsus whatever the professionals' worries, was simply recognizing a duty, as further considerations had to be made of further evidences, to point out for his students a principled way forward towards that *Ego te absolvo*.

The first principle is recovered from the New Testament contrast of "the spirit of slavery" and "the spirit of life who made me free". God, the giver of Law, has a mind for us to be free. So "that is lawful which is not prohibited". Freedom is in possession. Here, Alphonsus quite cheerfully directs his reader to the *Elements of Natural Law* of the German jurist, Johannes Gottlieb Heinecke (1681-1741), which had been put on the *Index of Forbidden Books* in 1743; there is evidently no harm in recalling Heinecke's remark that from God's direction against the eating of the fruit of the tree in the Garden a reader should infer that the fruits of all other trees were freely available.[63] The second principle is that if an opinion in favour of a law's applying to this Christian in these circumstances is "certainly more probable" than the opinion that the law does not oblige, it must be followed.[64] And there is a third principle that while the masters of theology are discussing, a matter is evidently discussible, and "one may freely embrace that opinion in favour of which we can cite the testimony of wise and prudent persons".[65]

It might appear simply that "the pressures of pastoral experience" combined with "the native kindliness of the saint" would bring Alphonsus to be on the outlook for probable reasons to question the certainty of any opinion that the law did apply. And, indeed, Alphonsus was able in 1756 to tell Remondini that "I have ever maintained in the past and still maintain the system of Probabilism and not that of Probabiliorism or Rigorism". But Alphonsus was never a Probabilist in the simplest sense. He knew this, and tried in 1749, 1755, 1758, 1762, 1764 and 1768, to find the precise way of distinguishing his position from that of the general run of probabilists. "I felt considerable unease that some of the arguments they put forward simply would not stand examination." It is in the sixth edition, 1767, in which his tract 'On the Conscience' was given its present shape and in which he inserted the revised, latin, version of his pamphlet *On the Moderate Use of the Probable Opinion*, that Alphonsus begins to phrase a truly helpful solution to his contemporaries' problem. He finds his way by means of a negative. It would not be right to follow the probable opinion in favour of freedom when that in favour of law is "notably and certainly more probable". In the seventh edition, 1772, refiningly, Alphonsus omitted "notably", since it was impossible to define with the necessary precision, and made his most significant contribution to the discussion in his notice of what is "certainly probable". He pointed out that where no opinion is "certainly more probable" there will also be an opinion or even opinions "not certainly less probable".

An honest Christian will recognize that the probabilist is wrong to suggest simply that "he who acts on a probability acts prudently". Probability alone, "Note, I say *alone*", is not enough.[66] Nevertheless, the very existence of two probable opinions establishes, if they really are equally probable, an "equi-probability" on which a Christian who wants to act honestly and within the law has to make a prudent judgement. It cannot be simply a matter of embracing the opinion in favour of liberty because this is still only a probable opinion. But the existence of equi-probable opinions among serious moralists about what has to be received as law itself demonstrates that there is a real doubt about the law's promulgation. Vico had demonstrated that it was by first establishing precisely what had been promulgated that the civil lawyer proved himself the guardian of common civility. Ordinary folk must be assured that a law that is not promulgated does not bind. Complementarily, in treating canon law, "St Thomas teaches this doctrine not in one passage only, but repeatedly" and "it is the common teaching of all the theologians".[67] Even that unfriendly Patuzzi, Alphonsus notes in an explanatory paper for a Royal Commission in 1777, declares in his tract against Alphonsus' *Moral Theology* that all agree that promulgation is absolutely necessary for a law to have binding force. The confessor can, in this uncertainty about the promulgation of law, advise according to the certainty of freedom.

Alphonsus was well pleased by the simplicity of his solution: "Before my book appeared this point was obscure; now, however, everyone confesses that it is as clear as daylight".[68]

Swearing in either scale

If the confessor were to be a judge like the judges in the civil tribunal, then the moralist could have contented himself with the recommendation of something along the lines of Justinian's equity or Vico's "kindly reasoning", something, perhaps, along the lines suggested by Mrs Do-as-you-would-be-done-by. But to be a judge in the tribunal of the confessional is not to administer that sort of law. The golden rule does have its place in Alphonsus considerations of confessor and penitent, but it is given a necessary theological turn. It is precisely because God treats us well that we ought to treat others well: "Be kind to one another, tender-hearted, forgiving one another, as God in Christ forgave you". Alphonsus is, assuredly, always aware that the judge in the tribunal of the confessional is also to be the accused at the divine tribunal, having to answer for his conduct towards penitents. It's a great comfort that "we are not going to be judged at a probabiliorist tribunal".[69]

It was an effect of Alphonsus' effort to think a way through the thickest of contemporary moral debate and his becoming an authority himself, that he attracted a set of partisans identifying themselves as equi-probabilists against probabilists and probabiliorists. And it was an effect of his encouraging the confessor to kindliness that equi-probabilism, as professed by those who were less delicately aware than Alphonsus of the claim of justice, seemed sometimes to be collapsing into a scandalous laxism. At any rate in 1864, Canon Charles Kingsley (1819-75), the creator of Mrs Do-as-you-would-be-done-by, had come across a couple of those seminary casuists who followed, or claimed to follow, "the blessed St Alphonsus de Liguori": Scavini, whose manual was used at Oscott, and Neyraguet, whose manual was used at Maynooth.[70] Referring to these text-books, Kingsley felt entitled to point to "those permissions to deception which may be seen to be formalised and detailed in the works of the Roman casuists, and especially those of the great Liguori, whose books have received the public and solemn sanction of the Romish see".[71] What they said of *aequivocatio* seemed to provide ammunition in that battle against Catholic priests and their notions of Christian morality which climaxed in the publication of *Apologia pro vita sua* by John Henry Newman (1801-1890).

As one gentleman with another, Newman shared Kingsley's notions of decent behaviour. "Much as I admire the high points of the Italian character, I like the English rule of conduct better."[72] But Newman noted, rightly, that the manualists' use of *aequivocatio* was not the Englishman's use of *equivocation*.[73] *Aequivocatio* is, first, a neutral technical term in rhetoric, most especially in the rhetoric of lawyers. It has to do with an ambiguity, a play on words, an evasion by which the advocate diverts his hearers' attention from matters that he wishes to keep from them.

There is an equivocal ambiguity in the Baptist's reply "I am not Elias". There is an equivocal evasion in "I am not going up to the feast" when Jesus is not going up openly. There was, it seemed to both St John Chrysostom and St Thomas, and so to Alphonsus, another dominical equivocation in the Lord's saying "No one knows" when the Day of Judgement will come, not even the Son of Man. The saints took it that Jesus is the Son of Man, that he does know when the Day will come, but that he does not know it "as man", so no man knows it, no one knows. Later moralists, Honoré Tournely (1653-1729), in his *On the Incarnation*, and Vincenzo Gotti (1664-1742), in his *Theologia scolastica-dogmatica*, revived a suggestion of St Augustine that Jesus reserved his knowledge of the Day on the ground that "no one knows for telling to others who have no right to know". This was a line of argument which would be deployed in quite extravagant ways as moralists referred it to human beings who just did not want to reply to a questioner. There is the equivocal gesture, too. Jesus "made as if" to go on from Emmaus.[74] Falcoia acted as if the plan for a new Institute of priests had collapsed. And there is equivocal silence. Bishop Santoro of Scala did not mention why he was at the chapel Benediction when the miraculous image appeared on the host. The great Salamancan, Dominico Soto (1494-1560), had begun the reference of dominical examples to the ordinary conduct of human affairs in his 1552 lectures on *Reasoning about and Concealing Secrets*. His thesis had been developed in the complex set of *Moral Solutions*, 1629-1659, of the witty Palermo casuist, Antonio Diana (1585-1663). Alphonsus had read these books and he had taken note of those contemporary episcopal examples.

Genet had, of course, laid it down that "equivocations are never lawful".[75] Kingsley might have been tempted to approve this strictness. But he, like Alphonsus, had been taught the domestic use of "Her ladyship is not at home", understanding, "not at home to you now". And Alphonsus had learnt, too, the street use of "I have no money to buy bread for the children", understanding that "if I had any children" and "after spending money on drink" then "I would have no money".[76] It is thus that butlers and beggarwomen bring *aequivocatio* near to the more notorious *equivocation*.

Equivocation is chiefly employed in reference to the untruthfulness of foreign folk, particularly Romish priests, most particularly foreign-trained, clever, Jesuits on trial in English courts. These priests are brought to mind each time a play-goer hears Macbeth's porter let through his hell-gate, "an equivocator that could swear in both the scales", or each time a novel-reader comes in *Pamela* to Richardson's accusation that "for equivocation, no Jesuit ever went beyond you". But "although an Italian" as Baron Angot des Rotours observed in his 1916 study, "Liguori had personally an intense horror of untruth".[77] Alphonsus had to deal with others, whether Italian or not, who had not had such a horror and had come to be forgiven their sin.

It is plain to Alphonsus that for anyone anywhere to take an oath there must be grave reason, one can swear only in a matter of importance, there must be just cause, one can swear only in an honest business, and there must be truth, one can swear only to how things seem to oneself to be. But can one ever back an equivocal statement with an oath? Whatever Englishmen thought, this was not a simple question for Alphonsus. The answer must depend, as Gotti had suggested, on who was asking the question and the circumstances within which the question was being asked. It is remarkable that Alphonsus' example of the questioner is the violent husband, ready to inflict injury on his suspected wife.[78] The man may have no evidence of unfaithfulness, simply a suspicion, unless she admit the offence. Alphonsus judges that she should not be condemned for resorting to some *aequivocatio* in answer to the bully's demands. She may declare, "I swear by God that I am innocent of this sin", meaning not "I have not committed this adultery" but "I have been freed from the guilt of this sin by going to confession and being absolved". This might be her only means of keeping the family together. And what would happen to the children if she did not have this equivocal means of defending them all? It is noticeable today that Alphonsus is controlling the genders of Latin grammar as he puts this *caput* together. When writing of the accused in court cases about inheritance or debt or cheating in commercial ventures, he is always using the masculine. The accused is always a man. When he is considering a charge of adultery, he is always using the feminine. The accused is always a woman. Alphonsus does not suppose that a husband is going to be accused in his society, or, if accused, that a man would have any need to hide his adultery with an evasive answer. *Aequivocatio* becomes on this occasion an instrument for the defence of a vulnerable woman against the male conventions of society. We, in our society, are likely to be more disturbed by his considerations of the prisoner in the dock.

157

There is something very attractive in Alphonsus' persistent effort for truth-telling in courts that he had himself quitted on account of a judge's disregard for the truth of a case. Courts in which a private offer to commute the death penalty, even acquit altogether, might be made in exchange for the guilty man's giving up his daughter to the judge. Courts in which the judge had had a suspect tortured in order to start the hearing from a convincing confession. These things were common enough in Naples for Alphonsus to think it right to spend several paragraphs of his *Moral Theology* on them.[79] And all the while, as he guides his reader through such evidences of human corruption, he is sustaining the reader's sense of moral theology as truly Christian theology. In a 1776 *Meditation*, he enables his fellows to put what happens in the Kingdom's courtrooms with the suffering of Christ; "when an innocent man is sentenced, left in the hands of his enemies, so that they may make him suffer and die according to their pleasure" they are to recognize a likeness with the Passion of the Lord. There is always some unjust accuser. Always some unjust conviction. "Such, truly, is the way of the world."[80] Meditating upon the Passion may disclose a meaning in events. Studying moral theology makes the demand that Christians do something. In February, 1769, he was writing to the Royal Administrator of Nitre about a poor man of his diocese, "prevent an innocent man from dying in prison... he was arrested solely on account of a calumny... he has nothing... you could not perform a greater act of charity".[81]

There are, however, some just judges in these courts. There are, therefore, questions whether a man who had given equivocal evidence, had even sworn an equivocal oath, before such a judge were guilty of grave sin. It is always in the context of a court case that being "economical with the truth" will have its greatest impact on the public sense of morality. Naples was not different from anywhere else. And, since he has come to confession, it is apparent that the ambiguous oath-taker has already his own real sense of having gone wrong. The confessor has to make the best of a bad job. The moralist must help the confessor to find the appropriately charitable way of expressing the justice of God towards the equivocator. This is evident to every manualist. Hence all the talk of "capable of conveying the truth" and "ambiguity", of "allowing him to deceive himself" and of "just cause" and "venial sin", in the manual accounts of *aequivocatio*. Hence some further shocks to the public's sense of morality.

It seems to Alphonsus that "anyone who is asked a question by a legitimately appointed judge, must speak the truth".[82] Therefore, anyone who, in a legitimately constituted court, takes a trial oath to an equivocation sins against justice. But how gravely? Is there no cause which could lessen the guilt of the equivocal answer under oath? In the shorter *Apostolic Man*, Alphonsus says plainly that everyone, witnesses and accused, is bound to answer with "the whole truth" when asked about the matter in such a court. But things are never quite simple enough for short form treatments. In his *Moral Theology*, Alphonsus considers the instance of a witness being asked if he knows of any crime's having been committed by the prisoner in the dock. No judge should proceed like that. Charges should be preferred before arraignments. It would be to compound the illegitimacy of the judge's 'fishing trip' for the witness to reveal some hidden crime of his neighbour. And the judge who asks such a question is unlikely to be the sort of person who is contented by the witness who claims a right to silence. It cannot be gravely sinful for the witness to put him off with an equivocal reply. The witness knows nothing that he should tell. Alphonsus considers, too, the instance of the accused man who, if convicted, will be sentenced to execution, or permanent exile, or a lengthy prison sentence, or a life in the galleys.[83] Alphonsus has taken his turn among the *Bianchi della Giustizia* to stand with a condemned man on the scaffold. To speak of the Tabernacle as "the prison" of the Lord in his 1750 *Considerations on the Religious State* had been no empty resort to metaphor; he shuddered in recollection of the degradation in the Archbishop's cells. He had had to deal with the panic that afflicted Neapolitan Redemptorists when assigned to houses at any distance from their city. Terrible memories of those poor slaves, tied to the oars, under the deck of his father's ship, rise again. Having declared himself "Not guilty", meaning "Not yet convicted", can the culprit, under such fear, be expected to incriminate himself when questioned? Can he be expected to tell "the whole truth"? It seems to Alphonsus that in such a case, if the accused man, coming now to confession, had not lied, but had found some evasive form of words to conceal his guilt, even taken an equivocal oath of his innocence, he should not be deemed by the court to have committed the grave criminal offence of perjury. The oath had not been taken to the truth of a falsehood.[84]

Alphonsus, limiting consideration of the uses of *aequivocatio*, even though they were so much more carefully put together than the tracts of both earlier and later moralists, had been attacked long before Kingsley made his thrust. In Alphonsus' life-time, the Fiscal Advocate of Naples was accusing him of encouraging craftiness and lying and perjury, and generally upturning the honest order of His Majesty's courts.[85] But Alphonsus is not suggesting that confessor and penitent cease to recognize various equivocations as sinnings. He is simply anxious not to label a sin as grave sin unless it actually proves on examination to be so. And, equally, not to miss recognizing what is grave sin. And, most importantly, not to forget that he is dealing with those who are sorry for their offendings. "God does not wish me", he told the people of Foggia in opening the mission of 1745, "to speak to you of justice and punishments but of peace and pardon when you stop offending him."[86] The man "that could swear in both the scales against either scale" would not enter, unrepentant, into the ecclesial company of the eternal Lord. Alphonsus will have nothing to do with those "falsehoods which are not lies" countenanced by Milton and Dr Johnson, and even by Archdeacon Paley.[87] Alphonsus knew that falsehoods are always lies. But the poor sinner, retreating from the rough power of her husband or the rack of the police chief to seek forgiveness will find a kindly confessor. "How can you", he asked in *The True Bride*, "imagine that a confessor, who is bound by his office to show charity to those that come to the tribunal of penance, should treat you with harshness and severity?"[88]

The Law and the Custom

Kingsley's instinct for demonstrating the linkage of Alphonsus' account of equivocation with everything else in his appreciation of human experience was unerring. His pamphlet *"What, then, does Dr Newman mean?"* was scattered through with clever references to "the feeble old woman who first genuflects before the Blessed Sacrament, and then steals her neighbour's handkerchief", "the Carmelites of the Reform of St Theresa", "some tale of a vision of the invisible world", "a holy Jesuit preacher who died in the odour of sanctity", "the liquefaction of the blood of St Januarius at Naples", "the Glories of Mary", and a funny story of a holy person and a donkey. These things are, as Kingsley said, connected with "the economic views of Alphonsus de Liguori".[89] They witness to a coherence of Alphonsus' enterprise. He had discerned the good example of Torno's teaching method. He practised and taught moral theology with dogmatic and ascetical theology as a member of a community which expressed itself in such connected ways. What he knew of those who handed down laws and those who sat on the magistrate's bench, along with what he knew of the feeble old woman and her neighbour, and of the glories of Mary, informed not only what he said of the particular problem of the accused man and his oath, but also what he said of law-givers and the law itself.

There was a risk in any talk of the law-giver, especially in any talk of the law-giver as a member of society. It was the common belief of eighteenth century princes that not only the judge's appointment but the law he was set to administer depended on the good pleasure of the ruler. Whether they were right to hold such a belief had been a matter of delicate modern debate since the Belgian Jesuit, Leonard Lessius (1544-1623), had given the question a new airing in his work *On Justice and Law,* 1605. The scholar's discussions had become more lively upon the publication by Idelfonso of the Angels *(fl.c.*1720), of the final volume of the great Salamancan *Cursus* in 1721. It seemed to some shocked academics that "the Carmelites of the Reform of St Theresa" were coming near to identifying civil "Law and Order" with the exercise of force by the army and the police. Idelfonso took it that a moderate use of such force was permissible because it depended ultimately on the people's having somehow agreed to exchange freedom for protection. The ruler rules by the ancient and consenting silence of the people. At any rate, he allowed that if a tyrant maintained his order unopposed, his laws should be obeyed. Alphonsus thought this a sensible recognition of things as they were. But there remained some questions for the lawyers to answer. Alphonsus was particularly interested in establishing the necessity of a law's being properly promulgated. He would have been as indignant as Alice upon the King of Hearts suddenly applying Rule 42. Others were asking questions about popular opposition to the ruler. How could it be expressed? This whole discussion had been moved forward by Muratori's reforming critique of the *Defects of Jurisprudence.* His book had been ill-received by the princes. With an eye to the fount of promotion, several Neapolitan law professors, Piero Cirillo, in *"Observations on a Treatise by L.A. Muratori",* and Francesco Rapolla, in his *Defence of Jurisprudence,* lauded the present state of the King's courts. The sturdier analysis of autocracy was more often conducted by members of religious orders who had surrendered all ambition. Busenbaum had even given space to a speculative consideration of tyrannicide. The European kings had not cared for this anti-tyrant talk. While the sheets of the third edition were being set by Remondini's printers in 1757, Busenbaum's *"Medulla"* was burnt by the public hangman in Toulouse, and Zaccaria's 1755 M*oral Theology* along with it. Alphonsus hastily removed whatever in his own text echoed Busenbaum's offending section. Still, *The Apostolic Man* was banned in Portugal. "They thought me a Jesuit." They had made, though Alphonsus protested that "I do not follow the Jesuits either in Dogmatic or in Moral Theology", an understandable mistake. Those who favoured the divine right of kings could not have been happy at the way in which Alphonsus' 1776 pamphlet on *The Fidelity of Vassals*, whose title promised so well, was neatly turned into a review of the divinely-imposed duties of kings to choose God-fearing ministers, to dismiss flatterers, and to be slow to believe sneaks, along with delicately warning phrases about "the freedom of the heart" of the kings subjects.[90]

That freedom, which is encouraged by the good laws of the good king, is further protected not only by the occasional countermanding of civil law by a canonical law, but Alphonsus suggests in the *Moral Theology*, by the continuing influence of custom in an enlightened society. Perhaps he had been first startled into thinking about these things when Vico quoted, as he liked to do, the disturbing remark of Chrysostom that "custom is like a king and law a tyrant". Perhaps this was the start of Alphonsus' life-long interest in the writings of this stimulating saint. For certain, he is anxious that his reader should notice the peculiarity of his emphasis on the uses of custom, "There's nothing like it in Busenbaum".[91]

In developing and enlarging a notion of custom that Idelfonso had taken from Aquinas, Alphonsus was careful to define more precisely than they the bases of a subject's proper appeal to custom against princely law. His sense of the actual community prevents his muddling true custom with what the curate, the alderman, and the widow declare to be, or not to be, "our sort of thing". Alphonsus' first requirement for any custom having legitimate force in the running of the community life is that it shall promote the common good, not benefitting men more than women, or clerics more than lay people, or shop-keepers more than their customers, or notables more than the generality of people. Then, he says, the custom must be seen to promote what is reasonable, and this means that it must conform to the demands of natural and divine law even as it is being invoked against a human law. Then, to be authoritative, the custom will have to have been established and observed for some considerable and continuous time. Say, a ten-year period. The custom has also, if it is to be alleged with any seriousness in a dispute with the law-giver, to be itself concerned with a serious matter. Not just the preservation of a piece of harmless fun. Alphonsus is not about to preserve the hobby-horse. Finally, the people's custom has, as Aquinas noted, to have been, for that ten years or so, at least tolerated by their prince. With that last safeguard, there cannot seem now to be anything at all revolutionary in all this. And, indeed, the elements of this scheme are not presented by Alphonsus as original. They have figured in the discussions of the great Francisco Suarez (1548-1617), the Sicilian, Antonio Diana (1585-1663), and the Belgian Jesuit, Claude Lacroix (1652-1714), and the others who engaged in the difficult study of moral theology with more seriousness than the run of manualists. Alphonsus' originality here, as everywhere in the *Moral Theology*, is in his recognizing the complexity of the question as it occurs in the lives of those who come to confessors for advice. Neither a quick conservative nod in favour of obeying the government, nor an equally quick encouragement to resistance, would serve. There would be times when a local appeal to custom would have to be disallowed. There would be times when the priest should assist the people to obtain their customary rights when the prince was re-animating a law that had long ago fallen into disuse or when he was imposing a new law quite against the forms of community life. In doubtful times, whoever is attempting to frame a decent public policy will need to step very precisely. But there is nothing timorous in what Alphonsus is saying. It should be possible for free women and men to make a successful appeal, certainly an honest appeal, against any law which contradicts a custom which stands the five tests that Alphonsus proposes.

Most likely, Busenbaum kept quiet about the force of custom in civil society for fear that such a discussion must raise the questions about the force of custom in the Church. Seminary rectors might not approve a manual for use by their students if it hinted at limitations of their powers. And then there were rumblings of that old "Gallican custom" in the French universities. More brusquely, Genet, in the last quick article of his opening *Tract* dealing with the principles and rules of moral theology, had observed that custom was of interest only to those who were looking for an excuse not to obey the canons and statutes of the Church. Lacroix, Zaccaria's favourite among his fellow Jesuits, had taken custom to be another form of law, simply imposing added obligations. The custom of fasting on the vigil of Pentecost should, for example, be observed "as if it were imposed by law". These manualists went on providing work for other manualists. There had been a controversy recently about the binding force of the custom of abstaining from milk-products on vigils outside Lent. Alphonsus had read these authors, and the commentary upon their antics in Juan de Cardenas' *Crisis Theology* in the Venetian edition, 1700. He knew all about the degenerative process of such disputes. He felt disinclined to talk about these text-book examples. He would rather refer to the comfortable custom of the clergy's still reciting the psalms of the Breviary in a version which everyone admitted to be less accurate than St Jerome's second translation. He himself liked the swing of the old latin rhythms. He would rather refer to the custom "recently introduced throughout the diocese of daily public adoration of the Blessed Sacrament", or "the custom of giving a sermon about the Blessed Virgin during each mission", which was, when he wrote in 1781, well past its ten-year probationary period. Customs of that sort encourage Christians to some larger recognition of the graceful community within which they are living. And he felt able to rely on the good sense and local knowledge of a bishop to effect the abrogation of any custom which was proving unhelpful for the Christian life of his diocese.

That reference to the powers of the diocesan bishop, like his cheerful acknowledgement that he had recently established a custom in his diocese, hints at an essential difference in his conception of the relation of custom to law in the Church from that which he thought obtained in a civil society. It is evident in the whole conduct of Alphonsus' priestly and episcopal life, as in his rule of the Congregation, that that "freedom of the heart" which is sometimes defended by custom against the presumptions of a prince, is, in the Church, most perfectly realizable in the Christian's observance of law. There can be no question of setting any popular custom against law in the Church. For, while it may be a matter of debate amongst those who are interested in kings, "whether the force of a law depend on its being accepted by the people", Alphonsus knows that "it is certain that the Pope does not receive legislative authority from the people, but from Christ".[92] It is in this Christ-given authority of the papacy that Christians may put their certain trust. It is through the enactments of this authority, as it is ordinarily exercised in the Church, that Christians may discern the definition of their moral life. It is, most wonderfully, from this authority and its ordinary delegation that Christians receive forgiveness of their sins.

There have, Alphonsus knows, been objectors, even Christian objectors, to such a bald statement of papal authority, its origin and its scope, and he knows how they must be answered. In one of those pamphlet-length essays which occur occasionally in his *Moral Theology*, he puts the answer into a structure provided by *Proposition 29* condemned, along with thirty other Jansenist errors, by Pope Alexander VIII in 1690.[93]

Pope Alexander and the Jansenists had both been interested in questions about papal infallibility and papal sovereignty over a general council, and Alphonsus does review the usual arguments about these great matters in his dissertation. He is here and everywhere strong in attacking those who refuse to believe in the infallibility of the Pope, "the French are known to do such a thing", he wrote to one obstinate Redemptorist, "but it is too much to hear that an Italian priest holds the definitions of the Pope to be fallible". But it is not to be expected that he would be much interested in Pope Liberius' private slip into Arianism or Pope Honorius' unfortunate letter to the monothelite Sergius. He can rattle through evidences for the Pope's superiority to a council from the "confirm your brethren" of *Luke 32*, the eighteenth canon of Nicaea, and a curious deduction, "from reason", that monarchy is the best form of government. But he proved so tired of arguments about councils that, having announced that he would deal with three objections to his orthodox account of Lateran V, he tackled only two of them before giving up the discussion.[94] Whatever fascination such historical debates had for others, Alphonsus is really concerned only to clarify again the significance of the scriptual commission to Peter: "Feed my sheep". He is happiest when repeating Aquinas' exegesis of "one sheepfold and one shepherd". That is where what is "always the same" is to be discerned. "Feed my sheep" opens upon the exercise of what Vico had called divine wisdom, proving in its practicality that, as Vico again had said, not only are divine providence and human prudence derived from one work, they are forwarding to one goal. Alphonsus is chiefly aiming to demonstrate the bases of the ordinary workings of ecclesiastical authority which affect the lives of those around him. This essay on *Proposition 29* prepares the way for that exposition of law which shall occupy the body of his *Moral Theology*, confident that Christians may thereby come to appreciate that they are fulfilling Christ's will even as they practise obedience in the Church.

"That beautiful order of obedience"

Like Kent on meeting Lear, Alphonsus was himself eager to serve authority. He was always sensitive to occasions for obedience. Adolf von Harnack (1851-1930), most famously, declared that Alphonsus' moral system, while defending the freedom of the individual against the pretensions of law, depended from an assumption of a confessor or spiritual director exercising an absolutist regimen over his penitents.[95] Harnack was a thorough reader. "He who acts in obedience to a learned and pious confessor, acts not only with no doubt, but with the greatest security that can be had upon earth."[96] It is the more noticeable that Alphonsus should have been so steadfast in his championing of a director's authority when he had seen how unhappily such authority had been exerted at Scala. Falcoia being long dead, the venerable Celeste allowed herself to write without bitterness of his direction: "The Lord placed me under the guidance of this priest in order that I should experience the precious fruits of the cross which I had not yet suffered; still, he was a great servant of God".[97] She had had no success in persuading Alphonsus to take Falcoia's place as her director. And her next lighting on the charming Silvestro Tosques led inevitably to the collapse of all that she had hoped to achieve in the Scala convent. At that awful crisis Alphonsus seems, perhaps, something of a prig. He felt, a little too easily, entitled, on account of his "following at the beck of obedience", to rebuke Celeste for her disregarding "that beautiful order of obedience which Jesus Christ has left us in his Church to make known to us his holy will".[98] But that language of obedience remained real for him as he matured into the energetic Rector Major and on into his final frustrating years when he knew that "if obedience is lost, the Congregation will be ruined". He was, in one confrontation with the Ciorani community in 1779, driven to the most plain speaking about what he took to be their wilful neglect of this necessary virtue: "As for you, who are not Rectors Major, you have only to obey". More gently, the little "lives" he had written of his earlier companions reach to the ultimate praise of Vito Curzio whose "favourite virtue" was obedience and whose death declared him to be "a martyr to this virtue". But whom should he himself obey? "I have in the Institute", he complained, "no Superior on whom I can depend in what concerns my vows, hence I am a prey to terrible disquietudes."[99] He, therefore, instructed Bartolomeo Corrado (1733-1797), who was being sent to Rome to negotiate a reunion of the Redemptorist houses in the Papal States with those in the Kingdom, in 1781, to "ask the Pope for a special audience and make known the trouble that agitates me". Corrado took the problem to the Sacred Penitentiary who told Alphonsus that he should obey his confessor on this as on other matters.

It may seem to us, as to Corrado, a little importunist to trouble a Pope about such things. But the papacy was for Alphonsus not simply the source of remote ecclesiastical authority but the source, too, of that prudential wisdom which showed him how to put his will to be obedient into gracious practice. Confronted by the demands of the King's men in 1752, Alphonsus had had to surrender much that had been granted in the papal Brief approving the Congregation in 1749. But he assured the Nuncio of Pope Benedict XIV that he had got "sufficient to maintain our way of life" in which the Redemptorists were practising their mission. The Nuncio silently accepted the new arrangements, as Alphonsus had been sure he would. Even at the *Regolamento* crisis of 1779, in which his obedience to the civil power brought him into disfavour with Pope Pius VI, Alphonsus stayed confident in the workings of that prudential wisdom: "We must address ourselves, not to the King (for the King will never abandon his line of conduct), but to the Pope; by virtue of his supreme authority, he could find a way out".[100] This time, the papacy was not served by silent advisers. Pope Pius VI listened to the implausible but very loud accusations of "king-serving" against Alphonsus and shut him and his Neapolitan brethren out of the Congregation, fixing the Presidency of the Redemptorist Houses in the Papal States upon the equivocating Isidore Leggio (1737-1800). So, having returned, in his letter to the Pope in December, 1780, to "Feed my sheep", asking that "the universal Pastor of the flocks of Jesus Christ" should be zealous to "feed the sheep entrusted to your care", Alphonsus brought his courtly petition to the quite simple statement: "We hope to receive help from you".

Only by some practical exercise of papal authority would he and his companions again be able to work in imitation of Christ. Unless the

Pope renewed their old privileges, granting them faculties to forgive those who had committed the gravest offences, they would be kept in something like the condition of simple priests and the people would remain in their sins. Nothing else could be so important to Alphonsus. Not even papal favour. "The Pope lets me hope that he will restore to me the office of Rector Major. It is not this that affects me. The blow that has hurt me is the withdrawal of the faculties proper to the missions, faculties without which we can render to souls but feeble services."[101]

A Petrine Question

With a complementarity of divinely-given freedom and divinely-established authority which is realized in obedience, there is, evidently, a complementarity of that authority with the divinely-given grace of repentance which is realized in forgiveness. There is an imperative for the activation of papal authority towards forgiveness in the Lord's answer to Peter's question: "How often shall my brother sin against me, and I forgive him?" And there is a coincidence in the celebration of that forgiveness in the Sacrament of Penance, just as there is a coincidence of eucharistic adoration: "whatever you bind on earth shall be bound in heaven and whatever you loose on earth shall be loosed in heaven". This is the liberating solution offered to that hard question which occurs even to unspeculative minds.

The petrine question, its staggering answer, and the realization of that answer in the confessional, remain with Alphonsus as he tackles every topic in his *Moral Theology*. Whatever delight in legal intricacies spoil the work of some other authority as needless distinctions were encouraged to increase and multiply, whatever prurience concerning matters which that Enlightenment gentlemen, Edward Gibbon, thought best left "in the decent obscurity of a learned language", Alphonsus, in the hefty volumes of his Latin *Moral Theology* and in the Italian handbook he derived from them, is only concerned to disclose to the confessor a way of bringing the penitent into forgiveness. This is most clearly what he is doing as he considers the recidivists who come back to confession again and again with a sorry repetition of deliberate lapses into the same sin, "seventy times seven".

The recidivist is likely to protest to the confessor a determination to overcome temptation, but there is, Alphonsus observes "a strong reason to suspect that the sorrow and purpose of amendment of the penitent are not sincere". He tells the confessor to require "the words which proceed not from the mouth but from the heart" of the recidivist as of anyone else.[102] But just when it may appear that Alphonsus is slipping back into the company of the rigid moralists, he brings the student to recognize the possibility of absolving in just the way that he had brought him to the possibility of following the equiprobable opinion in favour of freedom. As an uncertainly promulgated law cannot bind as if it were certain law, so an uncertain recidivist cannot be bound as if he were certainly a recidivist. The recidivist's coming to confession itself makes it impossible for the confessor to be certain that the penitent has not put the necessary distance between himself and the habit. The confessor cannot, therefore, simply settle for a sharp rebuff before he sends each recidivist away unabsolved. He must, rather, be alert to the difference between the complacent, word-perfect, recidivist and the one who comes to confession only after withstanding great internal or external pressure not to come, doing great violence to his feelings of repugnance, or trudging a great distance to the church. And the confessor must be ready to differentiate between the sinner who chooses to remain in the situation which prompts him to sin and one who is trapped in his own temperament. If the confessor cannot persuade the one to leave the sinful situation, it would be better to defer absolution for a while. But if the other, caught in the toils of a personal weakness, collapsing, for example, into "self-pollution" or "morose delectation", come to confession, expressing sorrow with the words of the heart, it is seldom right to defer absolution. After all, there must be great hope that more good will come from the grace of the sacrament than from deferring that grace. Whatever rigid modern authors say, St Thomas had long ago remarked that grace would always prove a greater remedy for sin than any of our strenuous efforts. If there must be deferment, then, against the men of "intolerable rigour", Genet, for example, who suggest that absolution be deferred for months, even years, Alphonsus can quote his old tutor, now "the most learned and illustrious bishop", Giulio Torno, who deems that no deferment be longer than ten days. "And though the confessor should be obliged to defer absolution, he ought to dismiss the penitent with kindness, fixing the day for him to return, and indicating the remedies that he must practise meanwhile, in order to prepare himself for absolution: sinners are saved this way, not by harshness and reproaches which drive them to despair." Alphonsus himself, Tannoia records, could not, in his old age, remember having ever sent anyone away without absolution.[103]

Writing again of the priest and the recidivist in *The Treasury*, Alphonsus tells some stories which together constitute a delicate and deliberate pattern of forgiving which nicely compliments the recidivist's pattern of sinning.[104] Matter and form are, in these narratives, perfectly balanced. Alphonsus starts with a story of "a sinner addicted to the grossest impurities" who knelt one day in the confessional of a Jesuit. The Father did not rant against the penitent but prescribed, as Alphonsus would have him, "the remedy for his wicked habits", telling him to recommend himself morning and evening to the pure Lady, saying three *Hail Marys* each time. As one may in story-telling, Alphonsus jumps to "several years later" when the sinner returned to the Jesuit. He was now free of those vices in which he had so repeatedly indulged before. "Through that little devotional practice of saying the *Hail Marys*, he had obtained the grace to change his life." Alphonsus next tells the story of telling the story again. There is a recidivism of story as of sin. He returns to the Jesuit. This Father, with his penitent's permission, had told the pleasing story of the *Hail Marys* in a sermon. There is, this time, a soldier in the congregation who is himself addicted to just such impurities. He, on hearing the story, begins morning and evening to recite the *Hail Marys*. "In a short time", he is enabled to renounce his sin. Alphonsus is not yet renouncing his story. He returns to the soldier. Like every skilful story-teller, like, for example, the teller of "Goldilocks and the three bears", he gives the third element of his story a twist away from the pattern established by the first two. The story is still concerned with recidivism. But it has rather a different impact. One day, the converted soldier, confident in his new-found freedom, presented himself at the house of the lady with whom he had so repeatedly sinned, thinking to convert her. This time there's no re-telling the story of the *Hail Marys*. "He was suddenly driven back and found himself transported a considerable distance." Just as he had been about to knock at her door, the recidivist had been rescued from himself. "Had he been placed again in the occasion of sin", the narrator tells the reader, "he would probably have relapsed". Alphonsus was fond of those stories. He had told them for more than ten years by the time they found their places in *The Treasury*. They represent a realization in popular, receivable, terms of all that he had been working out for himself in the technical language of the *Moral Theology*. He was always telling such stories.

170

(II) "He said nothing to them without a parable"

Putting any particular sermon together was no easier for Alphonsus than for any other effective preacher. But he came early to the working method that sustained him for over fifty years. He first wrote down in the disorder that they occurred to him, "promiscuously" as he was happy to admit, "the opinions, arguments, similes, examples" which he hoped to fit into a sermon. He read these through. Then he took another sheet of paper and wrote out, this time with hopes of an order coming into view, the headings "to which the sermon may be reduced". These he numbered. Then, "again promiscuously", he would try to fit the material on the first sheet to the numbered headings on the second. Then, on further sheets, each heading's material was juggled, rejected, brought back, differently placed, until the desirable direction of the idea was established in outline. Alphonsus could then begin to work out the actual text of the sermon.[105]

Perhaps, through this informal structuring and re-structuring, Alphonsus' sermon came close sometimes to exemplifying the very nine-part sequence that seminary professors proposed in rhetoric classes. But, when attempting to share his own practice with students in his *"Instructions to Preachers"*, Alphonsus is content to reduce these parts to the three that Vico had expounded in his lectures on Quintilian's *Institutio Oratoria*: the *exordium* as the priest settles himself and his congregation into the subject of the day's discourse, the *proof*, by which the congregation is assured that they may credit the priest's message, and the *peroration*, sending them home with a thought that should last them at least for the week. However confused by the precise analytics of the professors, the student should be able to apprehend this simpler structure and come less tiredly to the critical selection of words for his sermon.

The Amatrice law-suit had turned upon the single word "new" in the grant of the fiefdom. Alphonsus had learnt then, if he had not learnt before, to be watchful of the ways in which others were using words. Coming, among the elegancies of *The Eternity Counsellor*, 1653, of Daniello Bartoli (1608-1685), upon an unreferenced citation of Chrysostom, "O happy unhappiness by which a poor man was led into eternal happiness", *"pauperem ad aeternam felicitatem"*, Alphonsus knew at once that his especial Father would have put his emphasis upon "eternity". We poor women and men are brought by Christ into "the happiness of eternity". It is this present wonder which the missioner must announce as he sets out *"evangelizare pauperibus"*. Chrysostom would have secured the complementarity of grammar and theological truth. He would have had a noun where Bartoli was putting a mere adjective. He would have written *"ad aeternitatis felicitatem"*. Alphonsus restores the text accordingly.[106] Reading in a treatise *"On the Trinity"* ascribed to St Justin that "the Word employs the Virgin as sequestratrix", Alphonsus first explains that *sequestratrix* signifies an arbitress whose decision "the disputants bind themselves to observe", and then points out that in this context St Justin "means to say that Jesus lays before Mary all his reasons for punishing a sinner who, on the other side, places himself in her hands".[107] *Sequestratrix* opens upon the large prospect of the present economy of salvation and the doctrine of a mediatrix of all graces. Other words prompt the recollection of an apt story as he gets his sermon ready. Consulting Aquinas at "Give not what is holy to dogs" in his study of *Matthew* , the one word "dogs" is enough to remind him of a story for those who too often resort to angry words. He tells his congregation of a woman, just one of themselves, who, in order to receive Communion at a mission, merely pretended to forgive her neighbour, and, on her later refusing to stop her cursing, fell down dead, and was carried out of the village and thrown on the dung-hill, "just like a dog".[108]

He was as watchful of his own usage. Each word mattered. In 1746, he began to put the *Brief Comments on the Tuscan Language* together as a set of guidelines by which he could keep himself linguistically consistent in his lecturing to students at d'Iliceto. In the 1750 published version of these short notes on usage, Alphonsus provides a list of useful nouns, with their proper pronunciation and spelling, which at its first member, *abbate*, and his ruling against *abate*, expressly contradicts the authoritative 1612 *Vocabolario* of the Florentine Academy. But not all matters of dispute about a word and its use were settled so dictatorially. In 1770, Alphonsus and the equally bi-lingual Tannoia had a fine match about whether *aedes* signified "house" or "room". And usually, Alphonsus understood, there was more at stake in choosing a word than addressing a priest correctly or even determining the scope of a curial document. There was an *imitatio* in selecting a word as in all else. "The preacher occupies in the pulpit the place of Christ, and speaks to sinners on the part of Jesus Christ".[109] He must, therefore, be careful

172

to use words as Jesus used them. "Jesus has imposed this same obligation on his apostles, and through them on all priests who are called to be preachers." Their sermons will be put together "in a manner entirely apostolic", as he says in his prescription for the *Exercises of the Missions*, "in a simple and popular style".[110] "Simple and popular", as he says again in his *Letter to a Religious*.[111] He had been reading the contrary opinion of the fashionable preacher, Alessandro Bandiera (1699-1770), in the preface to his *Gerotricamerone*, but there were both scholarly and operatic encouragers of such a simple and popular communication of truth.

The posthumously published essay *"On Popular Eloquence"*, 1750 of Ludovico Muratori (1672-1750), is one of only three works besides the *Imitation of Christ* that Alphonsus describes as a "golden book".[112] He was keen that young priests should read it so that they should come nearer to preaching as Jesus preached. In the face of the "extravagant hyperboles, fantastic notions, and silly conceits" that highly praised preachers were adopting from the mannerist prosody of Marini, "piling up gems and flowers together", Muratori, whom Alphonsus judged to be "one of the finest literary men of the day", recommended that however many learned and sophisticated persons might be seated among the congregation, a Christian should preach a plain doctrine in plain words. Other learned persons could be found to agree. The anti-clerical historian, Pietro Giannone (1676-1748), who so annoyed both Torno and Vico, says in his *Autobiography* that he ever counted it his good fortune to have listened to the saintly Pious Worker, Antonio Torres (1636-1713), as he expounded "the true and reliable Christian morality" and by precept and practice persuaded the congregation to put no faith in the displays of preachers whose oratory was more pagan than evangelical. And Alphonsus' mother had told him of Nicholas Capasso, "a man so distinguished for learning", going day after day to hear her uncle, the unpretentious Francesco Gizzio, preach a series of sermons "in an apostolic manner". Capasso came later to hear the young Alphonsus preach, and for the same reason.

The convoluted oratory of "Mannerism" had had its beginning and middle and was approaching its end in the theatre even if this were not yet recognized by those who climbed into the pulpit with a sheaf of rhetorical paragraphs in their hands, ready and willing to suit the extravagant action to the words. They were offering an old-fashioned

173

entertainment. Such stuff might still be acceptable in the court chapel as in the court theatre but city audiences now expected something more popular, more immediately intelligible. Alphonsus could rather discern examples in the librettos of contemporary operas for the preachers' making efforts to speak popularly. Leonardo Vinci, who had preceded Alphonsus in Greco's classes at the Conservatorio dei Poveri, was making operas whose action took place on the streets of Naples, with characters like the neighbourhood barber, the laundress, and the irascible sea-captain, all chattering away in the local slang. The words came across. Dr Burney noticed that Vinci's score was the friend of the libretto, calling attention chiefly to the voice part and aiming above all at a dramatic clarity. Feo's operas were not being performed during Burney's stay in Naples, but as he read the scores he was again struck by the Neapolitan handling of the words, "full of fire, invention, and force".[113] And getting ever more popular. Rospigliosi had gone down to the palace kitchens for the three comic servants whose colloquialisms mock the formalities of the noblemen's language in the Landi *S Alessio*. But Burney registered the especial importance in this democratizing of operatic language of the later works of the great Giovanni Battista Pergolesi. Having tried setting "exquisite poetry" in the Roman theatre "instead of the Neapolitan jargon", Pergolesi had returned home where "clearness, simplicity, truth and sweetness of expression" were welcomed on the stage. The librettos of his *Monk in Love* and *The Clever Peasant Girl*, 1734, had a colloquial force, and Pergolesi enjoyed such a success with them that he ceased to write any other sort of opera, ending his career with the hilarious *Flaminio* in the autumn of 1735. Leo saw what was happening and made such play in his 1739 *Girl from Frascati* with the possibilities of the local language that his public very soon put aside the original title and simply referred to the piece by the comic catchphrase *"That is to say...."* The careful academic training that these composers had received in the Conservatories had given them so expert and easy a command of the formal elements of composition that they could put what they wanted to say in a language which would be at once understood by the most unsophisticated listeners.

None of this was forgotten by the missioner. The best of his little songs were written in Neapolitan dialect. He so far abandoned the rules of prosody taught by Don Bonaccia and the university rhetoricians as to throw, conversationally, the odd Spanish word among the Italian. And he would preach in as familiar a manner. "The merit of such sermons consists in employing the language and figures which usually make an impression in common conversation." It would of course, be the common conversation of the master going his rounds of the stable and the barn rather than his supper table discourse to the family. In his 1761 episcopal letter *"On the Manner of Preaching"*, which he sent to his fellow bishops with the advice that they should send it on to their priests, Alphonsus summed up his notions of the appropriate language "in the wise words of the celebrated Muratori": "The preacher must speak to the people in the language in which a man of learning would endeavour to persuade a peasant". From his very first sermon, which it must be supposed his mother if not his father attended, Alphonsus employed the street pronunciation of the name of Jesus, *Giésu* rather than *Gesù*, which he would have used at home.[114]

There was, he realized, a danger in this popular language. When Rospigliosi made his contrast between the comic servant and the sententious squire he was not, perhaps, quite aware of how the familiar language of the nurse was undermining the moral sentiments of St Alessio's aristocratic relations. Alphonsus had noted where the laughs came in the opera house and the Oratorian entertainments. He was not going to allow the preacher to be his own underminer. "A facetious remark, naturally suggested by the occasion, may perhaps be allowed", but "to reduce the exhortation to a comic scene, as some do, by introducing silly trifles or funny stories, with attitudes and gestures designed to make the hearers laugh", that is not only impious at the time, it leads to the congregation's losing more time later at the chuckling recollection of the story. But then there was at least as great a danger in the mannerisms of the fashionable preacher. Alphonsus had been told a frightening story of the Jesuit rector of the Majorcan College. While he was preaching a dainty sermon, Jesus whispered in the ear of the Venerable Alphonsus Rodriguez as he sat in the congregation, "Your rector will have to pay for this sermon in Purgatory".[115] So it was with no hint of regret that Alphonsus recollected how, "on hearing a young man of our Congregation preaching in a grand and learned style", he had made him quit the pulpit in the middle of his sermon, more, "I forbade him to say Mass for three days". Only those who share the common language may share the common celebration.

Alphonsus' objection was not to the literary forms themselves but to poor Alessandro de Meo's inexperienced misuse of them. Anticipating, in his *Letter to a Religious,* 1761, some older priest's raising an objection based on St Basil's remarks about "the sacred school's not observing the rules of the rhetoricians", Alphonsus confidently declares that the saint, whatever he may have said, cannot have meant that the preacher is not to use whatever art he has, he must have meant that he should not imitate the emptiness of the professional speech writers. Alphonsus was, indeed, insistent that the preacher in his Congregation make the effort to acquire the elements of rhetoric. In his precepts for the young Redemptorist's conduct during the *Exercises of the Missions,* Alphonsus' recommendations for the construction of an effective sermon include a happy reference to the way in which Quintilian's theoretical account of amplification and attenuation is illustrated in the practice of St Paul. In Alphonsus' view of these things, the preacher should have so studied the argumentative art of the barrister and the persuasive skill of the opera house librettist that he might turn them, quite unobtrusively, to use in his simply-worded sermon. He therefore casually advises the young man to get a firm purchase on the six tropes, Metaphor to Metonymy, and the thirty-seven figures, Anaphora to Zeugma. There are popular metaphors and simple metonyms after all. "A sower went forth.." and "a hope that enters into the inner shrine..." And apostolic instances of anaphora and zeugma. "By faith the people crossed the Red sea... by faith the walls of Jericho fell down... by faith Rahab the harlot did not perish" and "let all bitterness and anger and indignation and clamour and blasphemy be put away".

Alphonsus' care for the scriptural language as he studied, for the parables of the Lord in the Gospels, for the exemplary homilies of the apostles in *Acts,* for the rhetorical elegancies of *Hebrews,* together with the family instance of Gizzio and his lively remembrances of such popular pieces as *"That is to say...",* fixed his understanding of a good sermon. Alphonsus worked to bring his own preaching into a form which would be both "like that of an apostle and like that of ordinary conversation", *all 'apostolica ed alla populare.* And, most like that of the composers and their librettists in this, he would persuade by telling stories.

True Narrative

Vico had taught his students to recognize a fitness in Quintilian's delaying the discussion of how to tell a story until he came to speak of lawyers and their trial pleadings. In Book IV of the *Institutio Oratoria*, Quintilian writes of the lawyer as a story-teller who makes a statement of fact sound plausible. He distinguishes this story-telling from the fable of the fantasizing poet and the reportage of the historian. Alphonsus must have been pleased with Quintilian's suggestion that the lawyer's plausible narrative is unlikely to present events in the order in which they occurred. Credibility could never depend for him on temporal sequence, but his being taught to ignore the categories of the great rhetorician was of importance for his understanding of story-telling in the ecclesial community. Vico had demonstrated that Quintilian's lawyer, if he is to present the true state of a case, must employ at least some of the arts of the fabulist. He had, indeed, defined the fable of the poet as "true narrative". His own *Autobiography*, 1728 and 1731, is such a fable, a reconstruction of memories in a way that enables his readers to recognize and approve the principles and practices of his life. However disillusioned with lawyers and courts, Alphonsus is still acknowledging the validity of this version of "true narrative" and giving it a community sense in his mature theological work.

Alphonsus is ever aware of his sharing the living memory of the Lord's death with the apostle, with the evangelist who re-told the story as he had heard it, and with all those Christians who are still hearing and re-telling the story. The true narrative recited at the Canon is a reconstruction of the gospel histories of Maundy Thursday which enables those at the liturgy to better appreciate the life which the Lord is sharing with the community. Christian handing-on of true narrative is not confined to this original liturgical situation. Alphonsus is sharing in the tradition of the first stories told and re-told by Jesus of the mugged man and the stranger, the father and the wastrel, the king and his wily steward. These have been retold again by the first disciples, and retold again and again after the evangelists have set them down. In his carefully distinguishing chapter on the sermon in *Exercises of the Missions*, Alphonsus preferred, as a matter of terminology, to reserve fable for "a fiction in which one displays impossibilities, such as animals or plants talking", and to use parable for "a fiction in which one displays

177

possible facts". He told the young Redemptorists, eager to practise an *imitatio Christi*, that "sermons more easily admit parables than fables", but he was taking a generous view of parable.[116] He was happy to be continuing the handing-on of parables from his nanny, his tutor, the wisest aunt telling the saddest tale, and his spiritual director.[117] If he were to fulfil an *imitatio* of the story-telling Christ, and preach as Jesus preached, then the missioner would be re-telling these parables as well. It is at such tellings that women and men recognize each other as members of the atemporal community. Those who hear a story as *"our story"* are realizing a relation not only with those hearing it with them but also with all those ancestral folk who have kept the story going for them, and those for whom they must keep the story going into the future.[118]

Perhaps Alphonsus made up his tale of "the gay young warrior", but he received the nurse's bed-time story of "a certain poor shepherdess", and the retreat-giver's parable of "the bad-mannered abbess", and the galley-master's anecdote of "the ungrateful son".[119] And though there were no Naples productions of Shakespeare's plays in Alphonsus' time, some Spanish visitor to Grimani's court could have told him about a Madrid performance of a tragedy of "a blind man, placed at the top of a cliff, rejecting guidance" who looks so very like Gloster in *King Lear*. Perhaps it was this same literary gossip who quoted a line from *Hamlet* about "he that plays the king" and another from *As you like it* about "our exits and our entrances" that Alphonsus brought back to mind years later.[120]

He certainly did not invent the one about an excessively criminal nun, for he is careful to say that he had that story from Fr Cagnolio, who had it from Fr Patrigiani.[121] Alphonsus had a great many of his stories from such priestly gossips. Returning missioners knew that he would relish a parish anecdote and find some improving use for it. The tale of the sacrilegious tourist was "told me by a priest, a companion of mine, as happening to himself". Another companion reported the long story told by "a very old man who in one of our missions, after the sermon on the Blessed Virgin Mary", came to tell one of the Fathers his autobiography with its delightfully mariological ending. Alphonsus, repeating this story in the *Glories of Mary*, was careful to remark that it was community property, "He gave the Father leave to publish it".[122]

"Rhetoric indicates to us the places whence we may draw", Alphonsus notes in his directions for the mission sermon, "the proofs needed for a sermon." The old man's story is an example of the "Common Places" which are "serviceable for every kind of discourse". It might be re-told at almost any time, anywhere. But the missioner should be prepared, on arriving at a township, to take, as the 1747 *Constitution on Missions* puts it, "the circumstances of the place, the people, and other things" into account.[123] It was more likely that the missioner, would, on discerning the character of the town, have recourse in his sermons to some of the "Particular Places" to establish "the fitness or unfitness, the necessity or special utility of that which one wishes to persuade them". Alphonsus' own sense of the differences that circumstances make is, perhaps, most happily declared in his dealing with situations that he did not know at all. His acknowledging that in the Low Countries it was quite the custom for a woman to be an altar-server. Or his recommending that the Redemptorists not attempt to conduct themselves in Austria as if they were still on the Italian side of the Alps. "These missions", he told the doubtful Tannoia in 1784, "will be different from ours."[124] His careful consideration of equi-probable opinions demonstrates not only how readied he was in temperament to accept such a possibility of good folks re-acting to life differently. Of there being more than one Christian way of receiving the divine proffer of grace. It witnesses also to an interplay of temperament and experience. His moral theory has its beginnings in his mission-giving. He had learnt, for example, that city folk might not respond well to ceremonies which could excite devotion in country folk. They might yet be equally active members of the community. Then, again, things would be different for the Spring mission to a village, when the preacher might start his evening sermon in daylight, from the Winter, when, on account of the farm-workers having to come from distant fields, "it will be necessary to begin half-an-hour after sunset, sometimes even later". Anyone planning to preach earlier would find that the sermon would be attended "only by priests, a few people of leisure, and a small number of devout women who can leave their occupation, while most of the women and, decidedly, the men, who need the mission most, will not be able to attend". And it would be no use their attempting anything in the Summer. "To give missions during the hot weather", he warned Francesco de Paola in June, 1774, "would be to risk the health of more than one subject." However, in Spring or Winter, in city or village, they should make a start on the very day of their arrival, "unless the fatigue of the journey prevent it".

What was practical sense in the arrangement of a mission, and uncommon politeness in the conduct of an academic argument, was an inward necessity at the re-telling of the community's stories. Alphonsus finds it difficult to put stories into shape for other preachers' congregations and their circumstances. Story-telling occurs only within the familiar company. Those "true narratives" which happen when he is himself preaching to a congregation, when he is judging the temper, appreciating the character, of those present with him in their church, finding the proper tone, are not patient of any simple exchange from pulpit to pulpit. He cannot rely on present stories surviving from his sermons into those of another in another place at another time. So he does not often risk their transportation. It is most noticeable that the model *Sermons for Every Sunday*, each of which, he told Remondini wearily, cost him fifteen days labour, and which are packed with dullish pieties and conventional accommodations of the scriptural readings, are almost entirely story-less or have stories that collapse after a single sentence. And a depressing sentence at that. "The divine mother revealed to the great Servant of God, Benedicta of Florence, that a boy of twelve years was damned by his first sin."[125] Alphonsus had prefaced this collection with some remarks about the preacher's extending the matter of the sermon points "according to his pleasure", but it is not a case here of the preacher's being expected to make much from Alphonsus' narrative hint. Alphonsus is not looking for him to fill his sermon with devotional descriptions of the Blessed Benedicta or prurient details of the twelve-year-old's vice. There is nothing to be done with the story. Nothing more to be said. Except, of course, the mean application of this instance and the drawn-out denunciation of every sinner "above the age of reason" huddled in the congregation. It cannot have done much to increase the paschal joy of any parishioner of any age to be told, in the Easter Sunday sermon, the story of the young Englishman who confessed his sins and died what seemed a holy death, but who came back ghoulishly to admit to his confessor, as the poor priest vested for the requiem, that, being tempted to indulge a bad thought at the moment of death, he had yielded, "and thus was lost".

In part, this shift from *Ego te absolvo* reflects, like his efforts to deal with *aequivocatio*, a difference between the pulpit situation, where the priest is condemning sin, and the confessional, where he is recovering the sinner.[126] In part, it reflects his having to write sermons for diocesan curates. Alphonsus prefaced his guide to sermon-giving in the *Exercises of the Missions* with a warning that he was offering examples "written in a familiar style proper for the missions"which must be "very different from the style of preaching Sunday sermons".[127] He had made it plain that Redemptorists, priests and brothers, and their lay helpers, were all to be story-tellers. Alphonsus' "practical introduction" to the outline of popular instruction he made for catechists retells a *Genesis* story, an anecdote of St Catherine of Genoa, an episode from St Augustine's *Confessions*, a moral fable from Pallius' *Lausaniac History*, and a Neapolitan folk-tale of the Hungarian Franciscan who flew through the air.[128] In this domestic work, Alphonsus is writing for people he knew well, and when he would instruct them how to tell a story he leads them through the parable of the father and the prodigal son, bringing them to a final gracious sentence. They shall say to the catechism class, "You see in this example, my dear children, how good God is towards those that return to him with a repentant heart, etc. Let us, then, have confidence, etc. Jesus Christ will embrace you and if you make today a good confession, etc."[129] That conjunction of repentant and confidence and, mirroringly, of embrace and confession at the close of a story-telling in an *imitatio Christi* is peculiarly Alphonsian. It was not characteristic of the diocesan preaching which his mission sermons interrupted for the ten days or so every four years. The young Redemptorist priests were, therefore, showing their discernment in not following the pattern provided in those *Sermons for Every Sunday*. "My brethren do not read them."[130] They knew that they had followed a gracious story-teller into the Congregation and that they were, according to the differences of talent, to share Alphonsus' vocation. It is a sad irony that so uncharacteristic a body of sermons, written for someone else, anyone else, to preach, should have so often been received as the most personal expression of Alphonsus' faith, and it is more than sad that he should have, thereby, been loaded with a reputation for damning enthusiasm.

"So do you"

Riding from village to next village, stopping to greet a goatherd, sitting down to persuade some minor Count to lighten a peasant's taxes, exhorting the members of his episcopal household to sterner virtue, encouraging a city fraternity, preaching before the Cardinal, Alphonsus tempered his story-tellings to his company. Now and again he plunges *in medias res* with the literate confidence of the man who enjoys the *Aeneid*. He gives the story of the ulcerous hermit such a start.[131] He can slip down, equally, into the slower tone of the old men on the piazza bench, leaning across to the reader with all the gracious informality of his father among the magistrates of the *sedile* of Portanova. "I may add", he says after one depressing tale, "that this very morning, a layman remarked to one of my brethren that such priests make one lose one's faith."[132] He slips down even further in telling the unedifying anecdote of the priest hit in the genitals by a thunderbolt, but he had been nudged into this piece of naughtiness by St Bridget of Sweden.[133] Mostly Alphonsus resists whatever pressures there were for a preacher to employ either the more sophisticated or the more vulgar forms of story-telling.

Alphonsus begins telling a story as every nanny and pub-pest knows one must begin. "There was this priest discovered in a lady's house...", "This monk from Brabant...", and "This holy virgin was educated with great care...."[134] And these characters are caught into traditional plots. The daring journeyer of Homer and Luke is recovered by Alphonsus as the old sailor who passes through so many dangers, being many times at the point of death, in strange lands among stranger peoples, until he come at last, like Odysseus to Ithaca and Paul to Rome, to the Redemptorist mission house. The journeyer is discovered again, this time crossing lands with Gilgamesh and Marco Polo, as the Blessed Virgin herself, harried by an unfriendly king, who sets out with her baby to find a safe home in Egypt. This, as Alphonsus has checked in several authors, was three hundred miles away, so, as his congregation in the Amalfi hills might calculate for themselves, it was a journey of upwards of thirty days, and Alphonsus has a picaresque incident a day to relate of snowdrifts, of pot-holed roads, of robbers behind every rock, and of wild beasts within every bush.[135] Mary and Joseph and the bambino travel through a landscape which the congregation would recognize both as their own and as that of folk-tale. We, as we read now, may recognize for ourselves the landscape of Frankenstein and the Ice Queen, of Dick Turpin and the Wife of Bath, of Robinson Crusoe and Robin Hood, of Hercules and Mowgli. It begins to seem, a delighted reader may smile to admit, that Alphonsus has his share of the beginnings and middles, if not of the ends always, of every story-teller.

182

The entire irrelevance of future as well of past when story-tellers are telling stories is apparent as Alphonsus employs just the devices which will recur in the frighteners of Edgar Allan Poe and the Hammer movie-makers. Alphonsus' narratives of one poor priest made to drink down poison by an angry husband, and of another's feeling a ghost's tug at his chasuble as he walked out of the sacristy, witness to his mastery of the macabre.[136] There is a truly late-night television quality to the tale of the student woken by a violent knocking at his door, and, on opening it, discovering his friend, broken-bodied and grimacing hideously, who has been strangled by a demon in the street below.[137] One of Alphonsus' stories, which he told a fellow missioner on his return to their lodging after a day's work, was so frightful that, the scared Redemptorist avowed, "it deprived me of sleep for nights after". "Tantalizingly", as Frederick Jones remarks, this nervous companion "would not dare to commit it to writing."[138] But Alphonsus did not often resort to such terrorizing things. The horror story and the horror movie are designed to prompt the momentary shock of fear. That delicious thrill achieved, what next? There's nothing more to be said. They inspire fear and even terror, and of course, they cause a great stir, as Alphonsus noted, "but conversions from this terror do not last".[139] Alphonsus is not telling his stories for such passing effect. He has too lively a sense of his own struggles to free himself from the image of a vengeful God for him to put others into such terror. He is eager for his hearers to feel the tug of divine love and to take their places in the remembering, story-telling, life-enhancing, community.

If he were usually cautious in his recourse to the story-telling techniques of the horror movie, Alphonsus was entirely free in his use of that narrator's device whereby the hearer is given at the start the one necessary fact to which all the characters in the story are struggling. Perhaps Alphonsus and the script-writers of the *Columbo* television series both discovered this device at the first verse of *Mark*. Certainly he employs it to great effect. Especially when he is telling stories of the Lord and his importunate mother. Thus, in the *Glories of Mary*, we are told first that "thou hast saved all who have had recourse to thee", and then we wait for the Neapolitan Jesuits to recognize Mary's hand in the Scotsman's happy death, we wait for the Franciscans to realize that Mary is at the top of the ladder set against the wall of heaven, helping her clients over the parapet, we wait, rather more impatiently, for the Redemptorist missioner to be quick enough to absolve the man with Mary's picture in his hand.[140]

Everyone likes a story which, as it is being told, makes a listener feel rather superior to the poor foolish characters muddling their way through the plot. But, as he tells one good story after another, letting his hearers into the lives of Charles V's courtier, Thomas à Kempis' brother, or the Venerable Serafina's mule, Alphonsus is guarding against their giving themselves over to complacence. It was not a matter of happy chance that at *Meditations for all Times of the Year*, LXXXVIII, Alphonsus set out his simple re-telling of the Prodigal Son parable from one of his missioner sermons. He set it out again in Sermon XVIII for the fourth Sunday of Lent. That parable was, for Alphonsus, the paradigm parable. And the prodigal himself is the paradigm of ourselves, listening as he re-tells the parable. On the son's rising from the filth and returning to his father, we hear what little is required of us in order that we shall be forgiven. "So do you." This is the immediate call of all his story-telling. The story of the nun and the mule, for example, is most elegantly directed towards the hearer's taking the narrative to himself. It is possible that Celeste Crostarosa told Alphonsus this story in a moment of unusual lightness. She had made her original religious vows at the Marigliano convent which was conducted according to the adaptation of the Teresian rule made by the neapolitan Serafina Pisa (1621-1699). More likely, he had the charming anecdote from Pagano who in 1723 was completing the authorized biography of the Venerable Serafina begun by Squillante. Just when Alphonsus was coming regularly to talk to him in the Naples Oratory about the direction his life should take, Pagano would have been full of stories of the discalced foundress of the convent of the Holy Saviour on Capri. Any of these might have suggested a direction for him to take, but none of them would have been so likely to remain in the memory as the one about her and the convent mule. "She began, full of compassion, to talk to it: 'Poor beast', she said, 'you have no knowledge of God and cannot love him'. Then the mule began to weep." At Alphonsus' putting the coda to this story years later, it may be that there is a pleasing echo of Pagano's repeated assurance that the young man need only respond to God's love and the future would settle itself. But there is also an Alphonsian twist to the story. "So do you, whenever you see such a beast, stir yourself, you who can love God, to some act of love." Neither the Venerable Celeste nor Pagano would have been telling the story so that we should concentrate on anyone but the nun. As Alphonsus tells it, the mule is the model for Christian living. The beast shows human beings that they are to weep. "So do you."[141]

Alphonsus was as ready to point the plain moral of a narrative in his dealings with difficult individuals. The young Giuseppe Melchionna, who imagined he had been sent to the d'Iliceto house of the Redemptorists as a punishment, wrote to Alphonsus demanding to be moved. He would leave the Congregation else. "Did you ever hear the story", Alphonsus began his reply, "of St Paul the hermit and St Antony?" Antony begged the reluctant Paul to open the door to him or he would die on the threshhold. Paul was not much impressed by this. "That's a nice way to ask for something, threatening dire consequences." "And I say", Alphonsus added at once, "the same to you."[142] There is in such story-telling the immediacy of the "Thou art the man" of Nathan's parable for the delinquent David and the "Go and do likewise" of Jesus' coda to the Samaritan parable. What will the hearer do now?

Such immediacy is characteristic of story. It is not usual for teller or hearer to be interested in putting a story back into chronological harmony with the facts of history. Even when the story itself assumes some historical backdrop. Hardly anyone worries enough to ask when it was that Dick Whittington or Roland or Vlad the Impaler flourished. Alphonsus is perfectly at his ease in this timeless story-telling *milieu*. He rarely mentions a date, perhaps only a couple of times in his own narratives: in his anecdote of the priest, the vipers, and the Naples earthquake of 1688, and in the even more disturbing story of the Virgin's setting fire to a dance hall in 1611.[143] We may, I suppose, place with these his rather awkward *apologia* for the miracle story of the stolen hosts at S Pietro a Peterno on 28 January, 1772, but that, in many ways, is an uncharacteristic piece of story-telling.[144] Alphonsus is generally assured that dates and acknowledgements of sources and other such footnoting apparatus are not likely to be missed. No decent Christian reading his story of the Archduke Albert and the raggedy nun is going to complain that there is not an accompanying genealogical table for this Spanish Hapsburg.[145] He and the nun are simply our sort of people. They inhabit our culture. We tell their story in our own time.

The atemporal order of the story-telling community is manifest in the characteristic structures of Alphonsus' ascetical writing. Not on every occasion, but generally, having first stated his main theme plainly, Alphonsus provides an introductory group of academic authorities, with short, simple, well-aimed, citations of their works. These authorities are not brought forward as successively contributing to the developing solution to a question. They are clearly manifesting the Church together, all at once. Thus, in a paragraph of *The Treasury*, he has a play-ground game of hop-scotch with the authoritative saints, landing free on quotations which a conventional commentator would have drilled into chronological line for the classroom exposition. It may be that we notice later, for we are such stuff as historians are made, that St Eucharius dies about 449, that St Thomas is probably born in 1225 and certainly dies in 1274, St Gregory the Great can be precisely dated at 1021-1085, St Bernard at 1090-1153, St Philip Neri at 1515-1595, St Francis Xavier at 1506-1552, and then, less surely, we time St Patrick at about 389 to about 461. But as each of them, contributing no more than a quick sentence, comes in and out of play in Alphonsus' paragraph, his readers are being brought to realize the present vitality of the communion of saints. Again, in one short passage of the *True Bride*, Alphonsus cheerfully connects the reader with the Psalmist and then at once moves on to St Maria Maddalena de Pazzi, to St Augustine next, and then, by a reversing hop, back to Scripture and the *Song of Songs*. In another, he jumps from the Venerable John of Avila to St Francis of Sales, then to our Lady and St Frances of Rome, alights for a moment on the *Catechism of the Council of Trent*, and then comes down with both feet on the common view of the Doctors.[146]

In another's meditations such leapings about might offer the reader nothing more than the author's feeling for rhetorical congruences. They might even represent a lazy refusal to put things into proper order for the poor reader. Certainly, Alphonsus responds immediately to a psychological pattern, an aesthetic design, a verbal correspondence, a play on names, a pun, but he is responding to these excitements as happy indicators of the time-released ecclesial order which we all inhabit. Such *catenae*, emphasizing communion and what we hold in common are manifestations of a theological understanding. They contrast significantly with the dis-spiriting chronological lists of unorthodox writers that Alphonsus makes in his final set of dogmatic writings. Bayle, Tindal, Rousseau, and the rest are duly catalogued according to their individual, self-important, birth, publication, and death dates.

The contrast of those who have put themselves outside the community and those who still enjoy authority among us is made clearer as the ecclesial witnesses press forward to give their evidence as stories. The preliminary academic references open themselves out and become one-liner anecdotes. St Francis Xavier, "alone, in the east, converted, it is related, ten millions of pagans to the faith". St Frances of Rome "perceiving that the enemy wished to prevent her going to communion, spat in his face". Such little elaborations, hardly more than smiling asides, among the citations of patristic and scholastic authorities and of the hagiographic literature, are being put in place as preface to further story-telling.

Alphonsus, commonly, next brings on witnesses who are allowed to tell their longer but equally achronological stories. In the *True Bride*, short references to those who had already been living with the problems of "combatting self-love" and "the obedience due to the Rule of the religious house" and "mortifying the appetite", and many more like matters, are followed by beautifully developed narratives. Alphonsus has fine tales to tell of the abbot who spent seventy years in his community without having one single day free of temptation and the woman who performed eight acts of self-despisal every time she ate an egg, of the dispute about obedience in small matters between Fr Oviedo and Fr Bobadilla in the Jesuit college in Naples and the religious of Jumieges who got his hair cut before the assigned day and saw a gleeful demon sweeping up the barber's floor, and of Brother Acardo who followed the smell of roasted fowl right out of a Cistercian monastery and the nun who, having eaten a forbidden lettuce, felt very unwell, and, on her applying to an exorcist, the little devil inside her protesting, "What evil have I done? I was sitting on the lettuce and she came and ate it".[147] In these and many like instances of Alphonsus' story-telling throughout his ascetical works, the introductory *catena* provides his reader with a necessary context within which each forwarding story is to be understood both separately and in conjunction with the others.

The pattern for this structure of a *catena* of citations and short anecdotes followed by a couple of longer narratives proposing the same appreciation of experience may well have occurred to Alphonsus in a moment of recalling his schoolboy acquaintance with Homer's *Odyssey*. It would be quite in accord with his ordinary habit of converting past experience into present missioner's material if he were employing memories of Don Bonaccia's translation assignments in shaping his announcement of the good news to the poor. The incidents of the

Odyssey set for his study as, after the Jesuit reform of the curriculum, for the study of every well-educated European Catholic boy, would certainly have included Odysseus' journey to the Underworld in Book XI. Vico, making his explanation of the theory of early cultures' concern with the cult of the dead, could assume that his students would have been taken through this passage by their tutors and schoolmasters.[148] The Book begins with the establishment of Odysseus' present purpose, he means to enlarge his understanding of human possibilities and fates, especially his own, by communicating with the dead members of his culture. Odysseus pours sheep's blood upon the ground and the dead come to him. Homer first makes a quick list of the diversity of the multitude of moaning souls. "Newly-wedded women, adolescent boys, old men bearing a life-time's grief, love-sick girls, and a great host of warriors." Then, stepping out of the crowd, come several spirits to tell their short stories: Elpenor the helmsman, Anticleia the hero's mother jostling for a place with Teiresias the seer, and a crowd of princesses eager to take their places at the sacrificial trench. "So each stepped forward and declared her ancestry in answer to my questions." This is a timeless region. The spirits are only with difficulty prevented from telling their stories all at once. These quick autobiographers are followed at the trench by the longer-winded general, Agamemnon, and the ill-fortuned Achilles. These two make grander statements of those ideas of justice and fate which had been swiftly noticed by the others. Remembering this tutorial text of the tale-bearing spirits, of their appearing first in quaint disorder, of their then coming forward with their little anecdotes, and of the greater ones among them at last setting out on their longer narratives, and of all these spirits gathering at the ceremony of sacrifice, some at least among Alphonsus' readers must have grinned to observe how he had read a paradigm for the shaping of his ascetical writing out of Homer's epic. The design of the *"Book of Spirits"* seems to have been nicely converted for the presentation of that cloud of witnesses summoned in *Hebrews*.

As in the *"Book of Spirits"*, the significance of each story in Alphonsus' structure can only be appreciated if the reader keeps in mind the opening statement of his theme, the *catena* of citations, and each of the previous stories. This is not a simple matter for most of us. And it was not a simple matter for Alphonsus as he composed. There was always some risk that he would discover that he had lost direction between stories, that the cloud of witnesses would have shifted its shape unaccountably from being like a camel to being like a whale. Even Homer nods. His hero had gone to the dead to discover what the seer Teiresias could tell him of his destiny, but, as the Book goes forward, Homer becomes more and more interested in the stories that others can tell and after the seer's departure he extends the scene for a range of other encounters. Now and again, in the fun of it, Alphonsus' own story-telling does spill over the boundaries of his argument. But Alphonsus did not expect that doing theology in this way would be a risk-free enterprise. And he knew that the saints themselves were assisting him to communicate their meaningful stories. These were no books he held in his hand but women and men of the redeemed community. The method proved itself time and again as Alphonsus' hearers and readers were turned around and came repentingly to the moment of *Ego te absolvo*.

These things are not patient of short-form demonstration, but Alphonsus' general competence in positioning stories so that together they communicate a theological understanding of our world may perhaps be particularly instanced in his statement of theme and his management of a preliminary *catena* and its six elucidatory stories in a section of the *Glories of Mary*.

"Hail, holy Queen"

Coming, in his meditations upon the petitions of the *Salve Regina*, "Hail, holy Queen, Mother of Mercy, hail our life, our sweetness, and our hope...", to the entreaty, '"Turn, then, most gracious advocate, thine eyes of mercy towards us", Alphonsus attends first to justice and merit and, with these, justification. Christ is the suffering hero who has earned "in all justice" the reconciliation of his race with God the Father. The possibility of our entering upon eternal life is Christ's just reward. This is the clear relation in justice between his merit and our justification. Alphonsus moves then to declare the equally clear distinction between what is due to merit and what is granted by favour. Christ wills us to be sharers in his merit. It is her sharing in this merit which prompts us to hail Mary as highly favoured and, in due order, Mary may be a hander-on of favour. So he encourages the Christian reciting the *Salve Regina* to remember that the prayers of every mother have power to win over her son, even if he be a great king sitting on his judgement

189

seat. So it is with Mary and her Son. He has established her "not as mediatrix of justice" but "as mediatrix of grace". This seems, says Alphonsus, to be a very pious and a "very probable" opinion.

It was, at any rate, as Alphonsus is pleased to show in his *Glories of Mary*, the opinion of that splendid Pope Innocent III, who advised "whoever is in the night of sin, let him cast his eyes on the moon, let him turn to Mary".[149] Alphonsus is emboldened by this to slip from astronomy to astrology in praise of "this auspicious luminary". Alphonsus knew, too, that he had St Thomas with him in his talk of "the King of Justice and the Queen of Mercy". And St Albert was there to help him place this wonder in a scriptural context with his re-telling of the story of Esther, "who was herself a great type of our Queen". And when he presents her as "mediatrix of grace", he knows himself to be supported by the common consent of good people. He has it from Fr Pepe that Mary sent Fr Martin Guttierez to thank Fr Suarez for having so courageously defended this "very probable" opinion.[150] With Fr Pepe there were Neapolitans enough to back him, but perhaps the most imaginatively congenial member of the larger ecclesial community was Jean le Crasset who, in his manual of *True Devotion*, had talked so well of centre and radii and circumference, and the concentric circles of Christians who received their gifts from Christ after they had been brought through the inmost ring of Mary's movement round her central son.[151]

His theme of Mary's advocacy, of mediatrix and grace, having been properly established, Alphonsus can set about displaying the snippets he has assembled for his *catena*. Here, after references to Ss Thomas, Luke, and Ambrose, to Richard of St Laurence and Cosmas of Jerusalem, to Ss Peter Damian, Germanus, and Anselm, the discussion is burst open by a little story which makes the clearest affirmation of Mary's status as advocate and mediatrix. "St Bridget one day overheard Jesus talking to Mary, and he was saying 'Ask whatever you will of me, for none of your requests can go unanswered', and he went on, 'since you denied me nothing on earth. I will deny you nothing in heaven'." There is a domestic ease in this scene of the Lord, his mother, and the Swedish saint listening behind the door of Paradise.[152] It is, for Alphonsus, a cheerful sign of the familiar closeness of all our present lives with Christ. St Bridget is a neighbourly gossip telling us what is going on in our Church.

190

This quick story is followed by another, equally sparely told, suggesting that we are all able to overhear such a conversation. We may before this have been reading the gospel carelessly but now we should attend to what the best exegetes, Ss John Chrysostom and Thomas, say about the Lord's not being able to ignore a hint from his mother at the Cana marriage feast.[153] That story brings Mary and her advocacy into community focus. "The mother of Jesus was there; Jesus was also invited to the marriage, with his disciples." Tenses never matter to Alphonsus. We know at once that we are there, among those disciples at the feast. We hear Mary tell her Son of our needs. And we have her confidence that Jesus will do something for us. This Cana story, too, is directed towards our immediate condition and makes its immediate demand on us: "Whatever he tells you, so do you".

It is a recurring temptation for those already seated at the festive table to cry out with the March Hare and the Mad Hatter, "No room! no room!", at the approach of someone who is not one of us. The party is all too likely to become the gang. There must be a danger, then, of the Church's becoming a sect. Such a thing would not be at all congruent with what Alphonsus wants to say of the Church in which Mary is mediatrix. After the short stories of the Cana marriage and the over-hearing St Bridget, Alphonsus stops in his tracks to make unaccustomed reference to Cornelius Jansen (1581-1643), and Pasquier Quesnel (1634-1719). He pauses for a moment so that the reader may bring to mind these Jansenists' opposition to frequent Communion and their complementary disruption of what Catholics have in common by the schismatic nomination in 1723 of a bishop for themselves alone.[154] The language of "outer space" and "black hole" would have suited his purpose very well here. These references and short stories are followed by a group of longer narratives designed to put the present Christian in closer relation with a variety of human beings. No exclusions here. Alphonsus is about to emphasize the nearness of human beings in pagan culture, in the scriptural community, and in that mediaeval society which contemporary, enlightenment, persons thought so old-fashioned. The *Glories of Mary* is proving to be, as Alphonsus himself wrote to Remondini, "the most elaborate" as well as "the most popular" of his writings.[155]

Those enlighted persons would have thought it entirely proper that Alphonsus should begin with a story from Valerius Maximus'

Memorable Facts and Sayings, the popular exemplar collection of the Roman world. Alphonsus' positioning the story here might be received by his old friends as a sign of his belonging still to the civilized class of Naples society. But he intends it as a sign of our all belonging to the Church. It is a story of a general's being unable to withstand the force of his mother's prayers. On Coriolanus' returning as the commander of the enemy troops, after being exiled from Rome, the supplications of his school friends and the representatives of the terrified citizenry were insufficient to persuade him to call off the advance of the Volscian army. The people of Rome, therefore, asked Coriolanus' mother to intercede for them with her son. As soon as his mother knelt to implore him to be merciful, Coriolanus could not keep up his anger against those who had rejected and exiled him. He immediately relented. He forgave them. There is a clear comparison to be made. "The prayers of Mary with Jesus are as much more powerful than those of Veturia as the love and gratitude of this Son for his most dear Mother are the greater." Alphonsus might rely on a good number of his readers recognizing that Coriolanus paid for this pardoning of the people with his own life.

This old Roman story is paired with another from the recent experience of Christians, "There was this young man...." On the death of his father, his mother sent him to be a page at the court of a great prince, making him promise to recite an *Ave Maria* every day, with especial fervour at the petition that Mary pray for us "at the hour of our death". He made the promise easily enough and set off into the world. Arriving at the court, the reckless youngster quickly fell in with the vicious habits of the place, squandered his inheritance, and declined into a highwayman. But each day he recited the promised *Ave Maria*. After one desperate escapade, he was caught, tried, and condemned to death. In his prison cell, he was visited by a demon in the guise of a beautiful girl who offered to organize his escape if he would only give up this daily *Ave Maria*. He would not. Rather, on the demon's departure, remembering his mother, he made a tearful confession of all his sins to the prison chaplain. The way to the scaffold, on the morning set for his execution, took him past a statue of Mary, the mother of God, to whom he now repeated his prayer, "Protect me at the hour of my death", and the statue nodded to him. He at once, despite his shackles, ran from the guards, and threw himself down before the statue. The Lady took him by the hand and would not let go until the authorities had pardoned him. So he returned rejoicingly to his own land and lived thenceforward a life of affection for Mary whose prayer had delivered him from both temporal and eternal death. These stories have to be heard together. The Roman history and the news report share a single significance. Coming to the happy close of this second story, the reader is to put the reprieved young highwayman and the relenting Coriolanus into imaginative coherence. The mother is always interceding. The son is always forgiving. Jesus is the same, yesterday.

Alphonsus has another pair of stories ready as he makes his next move in his exposition of Mary as "most gracious advocate". If that story of Coriolanus shows that we must make a space for pagan signs, then, assuredly, we must see that there is something for ourselves in the scriptural narratives. Alphonsus takes up St Bonaventure's reference to Mary as "the wise Abigail" and enlarges it into a retelling of the Hebrew story in *I Samuel*. Abigail, the wife of the ungrateful Nabal, "knew very well how to appease King David by her prayers" when the king was righteously enraged against her boorish husband. Alphonsus' theological design had not required that he mention that Coriolanus had intended to establish himself as a fascist dictator, and does not now require him to extend his story-telling to the point at which Nabal suffers a fatal heart-attack. He is telling this old story only that the reader may appreciate its figuring the present condition of those who live in the Church. He stops, therefore, at the image of the woman pleading for her people. "This is just what Mary does." As at his presentation of the Coriolanus exemplar, Alphonsus has a pairing story of such a turning away of wrath, "There was this unhappy nun..." Sr Beatrice, the portress of her convent, fell for this handsome young man and ran away with him, leaving the door key on the pedestal of a statue of Mary. Her lover abandoned her. For fifteen years she wandered the country, until at last she came again to the town where she had been a nun. Worn out, miserable, she rang the convent bell. To her surprise, the door was opened by the most holy Virgin herself, looking just as she looked in the statue. Mary said to her: "Since you left the key with me, I have been portress, waiting for you here. Turn now, go to confession, do penance. My Son waits for you. Live a good life and keep up the reputation I have earned for you." So saying, she vanished. And Beatrice put on her habit again, took up her duties, and in gratitude, lived a holy life until she died a holy death. It is evident that Alphonsus means his reader to see some likeness of the wise Abigail, who takes her wicked man's place and pleads for David's forgiveness, and Mary who takes the sinning nun's place. These stories are to be read as a pair. We appreciate them, again, as figure and reality. Alphonsus does not need to show, in the second story, that Mary pleads for the Lord's forgiveness. He has already secured that understanding of the situation by the way he tells the first story. There is a continuity of forgiveness in the imaginative order. On Abigail's plea, David has suspended his sentence against Nabal. So we know that it is on account of Mary's advocacy that the Lord waits for Beatrice to repent so that he may receive her back into his company. Mary is hailed as "Our Lady". There is a continuity of her prayer for the nun of Fonte Eraldo and her prayer for us, Alphonsus' sinful readers. The imaginative power of the story-telling propels the paradigm of forgiveness into our own time. We know, as Alphonsus tells these stories, that Jesus is the same, today.

To contemporary readers of a certain education it was reassuring that Alphonsus should demonstrate his respect for classical culture in telling the Coriolanus story, and it was, in a different way, quite proper that even a sophisticated priest should make his bow towards the rougher writing of the Scriptures, but there was something distasteful, something throw-back, superstitious even, in Alphonsus' putting alongside these literatures the lore of those "middle" ages which yawned between persons of the Enlightenment and their Greek and Roman predecessors. But Alphonsus' theological perceptions prove to be perfectly expressible in the terms of mediaeval romance.

In the final paragraphs of his celebration of Mary as advocate, he brings forward a story from the *Moral Lessons of Job* of St Gregory the Great. Perhaps, this time, the genial Torno had told his class a story as they struggled to appreciate what was going on in that strange book, "There is this beast...." St Gregory had been ready, in his naturalist's expertise, to demythologize the story into an account of *rhinocerus iste*, but Alphonsus alters this, and encourages more pleasant talk of *il liocorno*, "this unicorn...." No hunter can catch this fleet-footed, nervous, creature. It is, however, "well-known" that, at the mere call of a virgin, the beast will come to her, and will let her put a cord about its neck, and be led by her. The virgin may bring the creature out of the dark wood. There is a present meaning for this mediaeval legend. There are sinners, now, "wilder than that wild beast", who run from God, but who, yet, at the voice of Mary, become tame and allow themselves to be led home. Alphonsus has, again, his pairing exemplar from present circumstances to substantiate this reference of the timeless legend. "There was in Fiorenza a young woman named Benedetta...." He cannot resist adding, because he enjoys such *aequivocatio*, that Benedetta should rather have been called "Maledetta", on account of her wicked ways.[156] One day St Dominic preached in her town and she, who had come in idleness to hear him, turned around and made a good confession of her sins. But it happened with her as Alphonsus knew it could happen with his own converts. When the preacher had gone on his way, she went back to her ways. However, being shown in a dream the book in which all her sins were recorded, she woke and ran to the nearest Lady Chapel to ask Mary to help her. The Virgin told her that if she would obtain that forgiveness which she sought, Benedetta must keep ever before her the Passion of Christ. This would prompt her repentance. She did as the Virgin bade her. And there came the day when, in another dream, she saw that the record against her had been wiped clean, and so she could die a happy death. Benedetta had run away from God. When the preacher supposed he had caught her, she ran off again. It is only when she comes to Mary that she may, consentingly, be led into the forgiven life. The unicorn yields to the virgin as unicorns always do. After Roman history and Hebrew scripture, mediaeval legend has been prised open so that Alphonsus' reader may appreciate that Mary is an advocate with the Lord who is "the same, for ever".

Stories from the New World

There may seem to us much in Alphonsus' response to the Roman history of Coriolanus and the legend of the Unicorn, as in his response to the Greek myth of Hercules, to encourage our looking to a range of human story-tellings for aids in the appreciation of the gospels, to the story-tellings of Islam, of the Siberian shaman, or of the Hopi, say, and even a little to encourage the most modern talk of a multiplicity of preparatory Testaments. His contemporaries had very little interest in comparisons and parallellings of that sort. If Vico is distinguished among Neapolitan academics by his taking seriously the tradition of myth, he is recognizable as a member of their cultural establishment in his assuming that the literature of the Greeks and the law of the Romans provide all that an educated man needed to master from other times and places. He talked in world-wide terms of how human beings "are led naturally to preserve the memory of those customs, orders and laws, which hold them within this or that society", but he was not really interested in anything but his own Western society. He nods towards the burial customs of the peoples of New Guinea and Virginia, and makes a reference to those other Americans who, still living in their mythic times, "give the name of god to anything which goes beyond their small understanding", and a further bow to the Japanese Emperor who "retains much of the heroic nature".[157] But when he wanted to say anything more of the native people, Vico found all that he required in the accounts of Tacitus. He assumed that whatever in the tales of returning travellers from Brazil or southern Africa is opposed to what is recorded in classical authors must be invention of these men to promote the sale of their books. If not their invention, then certainly their fault. Vico is convinced that these newly-known natives would not now be deviating from the normal course of human behaviour if they had not been discovered by interfering Europeans.[158]

Not all Europeans were deliberate liars or interferers. While he was telling the stories of the Algonquin, Huron, and Iroquois nations that he had collected in North America, the great Jesuit missionary, Joseph Lafitau (1670-1740), may have shared the classicist's pleasure at discerning in "this religion of the first Gentiles" some resonances with "things which are in the ancient Authors" and have shared the Christian's pleasure in finding, too, "a resemblance at several points with the beliefs of the faith", even to their mythology's disclosing "vestiges of the mystery of the most holy Trinity", but he was also capable of learning from those who had told him such splendid stories. In the preface to his 1724 *Customs of the American Savages*, Lafitau declared humbly that "a man should only study manners to form manners and he will find everywhere something from which to draw advantage". There was matter in all this for Alphonsus to consider. He was not satisfied by Vichian talk of there being enough to occupy a man in Europe. He did not share Lafitau's hope of discovering from the natives a way of reforming European manners. The strangers and their story-tellings prompted him to make a missionary response.

Alphonsus' earliest note-books show that before founding his Institute he was thinking to devote his energies to a preaching life among the heathen of the Orient. In 1734, he wrote to Pagano that Matteo Ripa had been telling him of the Cape of Good Hope and the idolatrous people to be met before a missionary got anywhere near China. No one was teaching them. So Alphonsus had to reconsider whether he ought not himself to go to southern Africa. He read carefully the opinions of the Salamancans, weighing the absence of any moral obligation to travel against the demand in charity to do something for the poor at the other end of the earth. His wondering about the Cape was checked on Falcoia's remarking cheerfully, "Why not those too, in the same necessity throughout the rest of Africa? Asia? America? And undiscovered countries?"[159] But Alphonsus went on reading about the Franciscan efforts in Japan, about St Francis Xavier in India, about St Louis Bertrand in the West Indies, about the Belgian missionaries in the Philippines, and the colonial lady in Lima who failed to secure the lasting conversion of even one of her singing Indians.[160] His *Truth of the Faith*, 1767, witnesses to his maintaining his earlier interest in stories of those Canadians in Lafitau's book who go hunting after human beings for their cooking pot.[161] And in the inhabitants of New Guinea whose women are burnt alive on the pyres of their husbands.[162] What he had read of the Aztecs sacrificing more than a thousand men at one time on the altar of their god had remained as a horror in his imagination for the rest of his life.[163] He was all this time positioning both delightful story and nightmare in the characteristic structures of his theology. The Kingdom might be realized to be everywhere the same as well as every time the same. Whatever he was going to say to the Neapolitans about the meaning of their classical myth-laden culture would have to be congruent with what he thought the missionaries should be saying to the Indians about their traditional lore. Their story-tellings would have to be considered together. He had read what Rochefort, du Tetre, and Sagard were publishing about Indians, Chinese, Africans and Americans, and was reassured by each of these people's having one chief among the gods.[164] This offered a starting-point for affirmations of likeness.

Others, with unfriendly intent, were pressing this same view on Christian apologists at home and abroad. Quite against Lafitau's intention, his book, together with others, Richard Blome's *Present State of his Majesties Isles and Territories in America*, 1687, and William Bosman's *New and Accurate Description of the Coast of Guinea*, 1704, for example, persuaded some readers that the likenesses between these native story-tellings and those of the Hebrews and Christians arose from a shared and primitive superstition which decent, rational, eighteenth century

Europeans could well abandon. This is a major element in the movement which begins with the British "Deists", John Toland (1670-1722), and Matt Tindal (1657-1733), and that is extended throughout our culture by the enlightened Voltaire.

Alphonsus produced his first *"Brief Dissertation"* against those who are "today called Deists" in 1756. He had not found it a cheering task to read through contemporary controversial literature of Deists and Catholics on God, the human soul, the scriptural narratives, and the claims of the Church. Coming to the end of this tiresome collection of chuffy pamphlets and cumbersome tomes of the Italian, French, Dutch and English debaters, he can only admit to Remondini that "the book cost me much labour". Still, there should be a great demand for his own work, he reassured the poor publisher, since it was "short", "full of matter", and its argument could be followed "very easily".[165] The group of apologetic treatises, to which this brief dissertation was the prologue, is not generally esteemed a climactic flourishment of Alphonsus' talents, but he thought the campaign against the mistakes, deceptions, and heresies of contemporary philosophers to be truly important. The enlightenment gentlemen's dismissal of the story of St Januarius' blood was a small but tell-tale sign of the terrible harm that this unchristian crew had been working in western culture.

Alphonsus' writing this group of treatises represents the last result of his being introduced by Vico to the unpleasing line which ran from *The Citizen*, 1642, of Thomas Hobbes (1588-1679), through the *Tractatus*, 1670 of Baruch Spinoza (1632-1677), and the *Essay concerning Human Understanding*, 1690, of John Locke (1632-1704), to Bayle's *Historical and Critical Dictionary*, 1697. In both the *Universal Right* and the *New Science*, Vico presents Hobbes as the example of those who would condemn us to live in a world governed by chance and the fear of chance. It seemed to Vico that Hobbes' social arrangement demanded that the weak simply obey the strong and keep up a hope that the stronger might chance along to deliver them. And to those who waited for such relief, the pantheist Spinoza seemed to deny the possibility of any human beings' making a difference and the possibility of any divine intervention. This stood to reason. It was the even more strict standing to such reason by Locke which made him the uncomfortablest philosopher, the least interesting, the most easy to dismiss. Society had not, Vico was sure, been brought to its present condition simply by philosophic human beings taking thought about plain evidence. And then came Bayle, recognizing the complexity of our history and our inability to put ourselves into rational order, and going on to declare the futility of postulating, for the comfort of irrational folk, the existence of a non-interventionist God. Bayle put all theism down to foolery and roguery. It was apparent to Vico that only by giving a silly credit to the lying stories told by returning travellers to excite an interest in their books could Bayle, and Arnauld with him, have entertained the notion that "peoples can live in justice without the light of God". There may seem to a modern reader something a trifle arbitrary in Vico's listing these '"skeptics" together, but he had identified a shared tone which was dismissive of our hard-won, socially necessary, ideas of natural justice and divine providence. These were both topics which, in the division sanctioned by the departmental arrangements of Naples university belonged in the Law School curriculum, and Vico's interest, as Professor of Latin Eloquence in the School, was certainly not only with the language in which these great matters were being discussed.

It is not clear from Alphonsus' writing what, if anything at all, he had read of Hobbes' work. Perhaps only the Latin treatise on *The Citizen* which, like Locke's *Letter on Tolerance*, was available in the Naples bookshops. He was content in *The Truth of Faith* to say that so far as he had acquainted himself with the man's work, Hobbes seemed to be proposing a merely ridiculous system in which phantasms take the place of reality. Hobbes' analysis in *Leviathan* of "memory" as a sensation in the process of decay, "fading, old, and past", must seem to propose such a phantasm just when Alphonsus would speak of real presence.[166] There's nothing in such theorizing to delay the page-skipping Alphonsus. Perhaps he was simply content to reconstruct what he remembered from Vico's Law School lectures. This may account, too, for the quick way Alphonsus takes with "the cursed system of Spinoza", and with the ways in which the errors of these men had been continued and elaborated in "the most pernicious system" of Bayle.[167] Whatever the differences of emphasis, everything that Alphonsus says about Bayle in that *"Brief Dissertation"* and in the *Reflections on the Truth of Divine Revelation*, 1773, and *The Truth of the Faith* is, likely, based on a recollection of what Vico was saying in class, or even a reading of relevant passages of the discussion in *Universal Right* and *New Science*. Alphonsus is giving Vico's sequence of Hobbes, Spinoza, and Bayle, his own sense of beginning, process, and collapse, and attending particularly to the horrid character of the collapse. But there are sad evidences both of his hurried reading of some articles and of his tiredness as he put together his critical assessment of what he found in Bayle's *Dictionary*. Alphonsus seems to let go his hold on so much that is individual in his thought and to fall into the commonplaces of contemporary pious scribblers. This is the period when he was writing those depressing *Sermons for Every Sunday*, 1771, and the *Theological Moral Dissertation*, 1776, describing a future hell and heaven. He is by now too weary to mount a defence on all fronts. Bayle had suggested himself as the new critic of all religions, pagan, Hebrew, and Christian alike. Alphonsus is perhaps a little too relieved at being able to distance himself and all Christians from the pagans and their gods in this debate. He allows himself not only to make fun of the Indians who reverence the cow and the Singhalese who worship a tooth of a monkey, but to abuse the deities of Greece. He writes brutally in the *"Brief Dissertation"* about "that parricide Jove" whom Vico had presented as the first law-giver, and of "the dishonest Apollo", and even, in *Truth of the Faith*, of "the incestuous Apollo", whom he had himself before taken to be an imaginative pre-figure of the Good Shepherd. Alphonsus gets this language straight from Bayle.[168] He is using it to clear a space to deal with the further nastiness of what Bayle boasted to be a new kind of commentary on the biblical stories.[169] Alphonsus' angry dismissal of Jove and Apollo as he sought to justify David and rebut the blasphemy against Christ could not denote him truly. He was being bounced out of the generosity of mind and civility of language usual with him. He would be uncomfortably aware of this. These things mattered to every educated Neapolitan. He could see that it would be improper to draw the dignified, church-going, Vico into an academic brawl. Even when Alphonsus came to write of the *Admirable Conduct of Divine Providence*, 1775, treating professedly a topic which had much occupied Vico, he kept Vico's name out of it. But he evidently thought he could adopt the controversialist manners of the foreigner when dealing with the foreigner.

Whatever restrained him from bringing Vico's name into the rough and tumble of theological controversy did not, evidently, seem relevant as he set about the British; Collins, Toland, Tindal, "il Tindall", Woolston, Shaftesbury, "il Schanfrerbury", and Sam Clarke. Alphonsus had clearly understood, as many who viewed these debates did not, that the original impulse for deism had been in the works of these English controversialists and not in the satires of the French *philosophes*. He had read, of course, what Rousseau was saying about "the noble savage" and "natural religion", and the more agreeable things he had said about Christianity's contribution to the stability of European society, and he had even quoted word for word, in *Reflections on the Truth of Divine Revelation*, 1773, Rousseau's contrast of Christian imperialism and the oppressive rules of Rome and China. He had noted, too, the story-telling effectiveness of *Emile*, 1762.[170] His *Reflections*, written to combat "the opposing principles of the deists", opens with several citations of the *"Profession of Faith"* of the Savoyard priest which was the most fetching section of the novel. There was evidently some danger of Rousseau's declaring himself the moral story-teller to rival La Fontaine, but Alphonsus recognized that Rousseau's priest was re-cycling the reduced language of Samuel Clarke (1675-1729), as he praises "the giver of all good things", and with sweet reasonableness, urges all women and men to maintain a civilized equity in their dealings with one another. Further, Clarke himself, Alphonsus discerned, was merely a decadent repeater of notions he had found in the writings of Toland. And everyone, as these things were repeated, was getting worse. It was another case of unorthodox beginning and progress. "The Calvinists of England and the Jansenists of France are no longer Jansenists and Calvinists but atheists and deists." But it was not yet a case of the unorthodox collapsing. A French translation of Toland's *Letters to Serena*, 1704, had been put out by Baron d'Holbach in 1768, making that troublesome deist's notions even more widely known. Appallingly, the deists were not content with an English and French readership. Their "pestiferous works" were continually arriving at the city gate. "In Naples these books are sought after and read even by women."[171] And their authors came too. Giannone delighted not only in the enlargement of the bookshop stocks but in the visits of the British contingent, Addison in 1701, Shaftesbury in 1711, Berkeley in 1717. Their enlightened conversation would, he surmised, help to lift the heavy yoke which "the philosophy of the cloisters" had put on the necks of the Neapolitans.

John Toland and the dismissal of 'Mystery'

Toland's *Christianity not Mysterious*, 1696, was a serious attempt, serious enough to draw Leibniz into the debate, at bringing the researches of the French Oratorian Richard Simon (1638-1712), and the Arminian biblical scholar, Jean le Clerc (1657-1736), to bear upon the general discussion of the varieties of religious practice in the new-known world. And to do so in some way which would preserve what Toland took to be the essentials of a story-free Christianity. "How little soever our Notions agree, and let our worldly Conveniences be what they will", Toland would have his reader understand that true religion "is always the same", being in this "like God its author". He would free Christian contemporaries from their subjection to both Hebrew narrative and Greek commentary. He would, according to the pattern of the Apostles, who penned the Gospel "with little or no Ornament", "no studied Expression", declare "the enjoyment of Christian Liberty to the slaves of the levitical and pagan priesthoods" and renew the offer of "Salvation to repenting sinners".[172] He took his apostolic and simplifying project further in his *Letters to Serena*. Toland had none of the educated gentleman's usual sympathy with all things Greek. He had turned its likeness to the tales of modern native religion back on Greek mythology. "The present Heathens, who inhabit the greatest part of Africa, vast Tracts of Asia, almost all America, and some few corners of Europe, agree very much with the Ancients" in their theology.[173] So modern men may take as quick a way with the gods of Greece as with those of other tribesmen. They were merely the figures, images, illustrative fancies of poets which primitive folk had accepted as realities. Toland, like Vico, had read Varro's thesis of a three-fold Theology and, unlike Vico, was prepared to apply the thesis to the history of Christian theology. He identified the mythical element in the gospels and proposed to eliminate it. He would then proceed to the next age of arbitrary ecclesiastical will, drawing snide parallels between ancient figments of imagination, modern heathen fetishes, and contemporary Catholic devotions. "The same may be as truly said of the modern Saints and Images" and "almost every Point of these superstitions and idolatrous Religions are in these or grosser Circumstances revived by many Christians in our Western Parts of the World." Modern Catholics, he judged, lived under a theology devised by clergy who were joined with princes to keep ordinary folk in subjection. There must come a third age of enlightened common sense.

Toland had, evidently, his own version of "always the same". Tackling his thesis, Alphonsus found it difficult to take command of the tone of the dispute. Just as he allowed Bayle to lead him into saying uncharacteristically disagreeable things about Greek myth, Toland's skilful mock of "figments of imagination" had its unnerving effect.

Reading *Christianity not Mysterious*, Alphonsus was led into placing an uncharacteristic emphasis upon "the facts of the Old and New Testaments" together. His 1773 *Reflections* plainly re-assert that "the New Testament clearly authenticates the truth of the Old and the Old authenticates that of the New".[174] He was coming near to making an appeal to prophecy and fulfilment as exhibiting historical rather than eternal truth. The 1775 treatise on *Divine Providence* was, again, designed to demonstrate a consistency of facts. Collating and juxtaposing "the facts" of the Hebrew and Christian narratives, he was "demonstrating the truthfulness of our faith" and the "matter of fact" against the British Deists "who have ruined France, Germany and Italy, and the whole of Europe".[175] Toland has led him away from the consideration of story as story, and the practice of mission as the handing-on of community story. For the moment, however, Alphonsus was confident that he had dealt an adequate blow against Toland, and, incidentally, against some others, the noisy Protestant Chillingworth "and his Oxford theologians". He was rather more agitated by "that Englishman Tindall" and "his pestiferous book", *Christianity as old as the Creation*, 1730.

Toland had shown to his own reductionist satisfaction that if true Christian faith had been always and everywhere the same, then it must always and everywhere have been as decently rational as the eighteenth century gentleman could desire. Tindal took up this line of reasoning. He gave it a moral application. It is luminously self-evident to Tindal that God has "from the beginning given mankind some rule or law for their conduct", that there is "a clear and distinct Light that enlightens all Men", by which they may acquaint themselves with "eternal Truths". The observing of this law, based on eternal truths, has always answered God's salvific purpose. Anything which has been held as revealed only at certain times and places of the race must, even if true, interesting, and beautiful, be regarded as inessential for salvation. Tindal thus, quite off-handedly, dissolves the difference, so essential to the structure of Alphonsus' theology, between the times "before Christ" and those "in the years of our Lord". It is, he thought, intolerable to suggest that "God had left all mankind for 4000 years together and even the greater part to this Day, destitute of sufficient Means to do their Duty". There was an immediate cause for Alphonsus' concern in this reduction of revelation to talk of "sufficient Means" and "Duty". And more troublesomeness in Toland's suggestion that since Christians themselves are saying that "those who lived before this appearance in the World" benefit from Christ's death, along with "those who have never heard of his Appearance, tho' they lived after it", Christianity must be simply a call to obey "the eternal and universal law of Righteousness" in decent human living. Tindal supposed, therefore, that the design of the Gospel was not to supplement this Law but to rid it of an accumulated load of superstition. Most dangerously, he appropriated the language in which Alphonsus was celebrating an eternal mystery of Christ and applied it to a pre-christian law: "True Christianity is not a religion of yesterday, but what God at the beginning dictated and still continues to dictate to Christians as well as to others".[176]

Since this law of reason "does not depend on the uncertain meaning of words and phrases in dead languages", much less on "types, metaphors, allegories, and parables", things "spoken after so figurative a manner" must be interpreted until they are brought into line with the plain sense of that law. The marvellous narratives in the Bible must be jettisoned by reasonable Christians. Then the consistent, reasonable and universal moral force of the divine message will become clear. "Tales make it a Mystery." Tindal is especially irritated by the story of "a Conference with a serpent (incapable of human voice) even before Consent had given any Meaning to Sounds". That odd story's being at the very start of the record of revelation was most provoking to a philosopher. His account of Adam and Eve, which exhibits an impudent relish of incest, reaches its climax in adducing the witness of "the poor Indians" of the Americas who demand of missionaries why a God who loves mankind permitted the Devil such scope. "With us, one who does not hinder a Mischief, when it is in his power, is thought not much better than he who does it." The whole race must revolt at such a sorry account of the Deity. With Hebrew story went Christian mystery. The heathen had at least not fallen into the absurdity of believing "that Jupiter and Mercury, the Sender and the Sent, were the same God".[177] The time had evidently passed when decent folk could nod contentedly as they perused Lafitau's remarks about "vestiges of the most holy Trinity" in the myths of the ancients and the tales of the Indians. The time had passed, indeed, when even scriptural story-telling could be proposed as offering a basis for credible doctrine or acceptable behaviour. Tindal would remove all story-telling from the reasonable Christian's account of the world.

Tindal supposes that it is only through the clergy's repetition of tales of Eve and the serpent, or Jacob and the wrestler, or Ezekiel and the dung, and the even more fantastic stories of the patristic and mediaeval churches, that "the poor Indians" abroad and "the common people" at home think themselves unable to comprehend God's will for their lives. Tindal presented himself as the defender of "the Bulk of Mankind", or at least of "the Generality of Christians, even those of lowest Capacities," as the articulator of "their common interest". He took this, he said, to be the duty of a free British man. "Whoever knows anything of France and Italy, not to mention other Countries, can't but know that the better sort are sensible of the prevailing Absurdities, but, overawed by the Priests and the Mob, are forced to submit." He sensed a connection of the exemplar collections and sacramental penance. "Can the Popish Priests any more believe their Legendary Traditions, than the Pagan Priests did their Oracles?"and were not these story-mongering priests claiming "a Power by divine Right to absolve People upon confession" as a means of keeping them in thrall to these legendary traditions? He sensed another connection between "this supposed Infallibility, which puts it in the power of that Church to make their Votaries believe Virtue to be Vice, and Vice, Virtue, or any other Absurdity whatever", and "the impudent Fogeries of Athanasius and such like Saints about Miracles done by Monks".[178] It is clear, long before the close of this biggish book, that in Tindal's estimate, as in Alphonsus', the telling of stories about "this monk of Brabant", the upholding of papal infallibility, the announcing of the presence of Christ in the Eucharist, the redeeming efficacy of his Passion, and the Triune life of God himself, belong together. Coming from a session with whoever excerpted and translated *Christianity as old as the Creation* for him, Alphonsus would have been the more convinced that to remove the story-telling would be to disrupt that ecclesial order which is always being declared in parables of the Kingdom.

(III) "...for the kingdom of heaven is at hand"

We can all see the Kingdom coming when, during the famine of 1764, Alphonsus sells his episcopal carriage and gets further into debt so that the people of Sant' Agata de Goti may have grain. When, in 1736, he tells an anxious nun that her vocation requires that she should be most careful of the comfort of the sick, "especially if they are servants", and "do not mind if on this account you omit your usual devotions". Or when he pleads with Marquis Granito in 1763 to release Grazia Castauro, "a very poor woman of Arienzo", who had been arrested on account of a package of "powder" she was carrying from one parish priest to another and who, after eleven days in prison, was starving to death, and asks the Duke of Maddaloni in 1769 to find a chaplain for his jail who would not simply treat the prisoners like ignorant children but would "break the bread of the word of God" with them.[179] These good works are clear signs of the Kingdom. But Jesus suggests that we should look about us for others.

In Jesus' parables, rock and sand and wind, field and seed, tree and bird, become signs of the kingdom of God. To some it might seem awkward now to preach as Jesus Christ preached, but Alphonsus had no difficulty in taking up such a way of talking about the elements of the natural world.[180] Recurringly, in his mature theology, he insists that we acknowledge "seas and rivers and fountains, mountains and plains, minerals, vegetables, and all kinds of animal", as signs of a divine order. In Jesus' preaching there is a place for women and men in this order. Sowers of seeds, hirelings and shepherds, housewives, vineyard dressers, have their parabolic parts. That desirable harmony of human beings in an environment is manifest again in Alphonsus' story of that "courtesy of love" when St Francis Xavier, having lost his crucifix overboard in a storm, was met on landing by a crab which held it out to him in its claws, and in his story of the wild beast which pawed out a grave for St Mary of Alexandria in the desert sand. For those who are impressed by newspaper reports, the most striking instance of this order will be that incident on 17 or 18 January, 1772, Alphonsus did not trouble to remember which, when the horse of Herr Hamm, refusing to step on ground where a host was buried, had suddenly bolted. Alphonsus is affirming, in an age of enlightenment, the order that had been figured by the mustard tree and the lost coin, and then, since the announcement of the Kingdom is always the same, by the lion sitting next to the cardinal's hat in St Jerome's cell, and by the herring scale that shone with the blood of Christ as Julian of Norwich prepared supper. He is affirming, in an age of restless questioning by philosophers who talk alarmingly of systematic doubt, that we should recognize ourselves as members of an intelligible order, of indeed, an intelligent order. He has another story of St Blaise in his Armenian cave. "Numerous crowds of persons used constantly to come to him for the cure of their bodily diseases as well as of their spiritual maladies. Even the most ferocious animals are said to have proceeded to his cave to be healed." These animals, too, understand the "courtesy of love", and "if they found the saint at prayer they would wait patiently until he had done", but they would not go away until he had given them their share of his blessing. The inarticulate beasts are aware of themselves as members of this Kingdom.[181]

Creation may be a dumb assister. Alphonsus has a story of St Stanislaus Kostka fleeing from his home to join the Jesuit novitiate and his brother pursuing him in their family coach and the horses, however he whipped them, refusing to let him catch the saint. Alphonsus has another story of Blessed Oringa of Valdrano running off to a convent where she might sing psalms in peace and of the river Arno's parting to aid her escape. There are resonances in these stories of the divine frustration of Pharoah's charioteering pursuit of God's People and of Miriam's singing her song of praise after their escape. These things, certainly, are always the same. Creation may be a dumb accuser. "St Teresa, when she beheld the plains, the sea, the rivers, or other beautiful creatures, felt as if they reproached her for her own ingratitude to God." This shaming sentence struck home. Alphonsus brought it forward time and again in his ascetical writing.[182] He keeps telling his reader to notice that "the very brutes are grateful to their benefactors". Look at the gratitude of the tiger and the lion to the zoo-keeper who feeds them. Seneca had noticed that. Look at the ox and the grateful ass at their master's stall. Isaiah had pointed to them. Look at the puppy at the monastery gate at Pagani. "When you see a little dog which, for a miserable morsel of bread, is so faithful to its master, reflect how much greater reason you have to be faithful to God."[183]

The Venerable Serafina had been wrong to suppose that the convent mule could not love God. It wept, in Alphonsus' telling of the story, at its incapacity to speak its love. Sometimes creation seems, indeed, to be struggling into speech. "While David was yet a king, but in a state of sin, he walked in his garden", and there it seemed to him that the plants asked him "Where is thy God? Wouldst thou seek thy happiness in us?" St Simon Salo got the same message. "When, in walking through the fields", Alphonsus told the *True Bride*, "he saw flowers or herbs, he would strike them with his staff, saying, Be quiet! be quiet! you reproach me with not loving that God who made you so beautiful for my sake, that I might be led to love him; I hear you; cease, reprove me no more. Be quiet!" Alphonsus has another story of creation actually finding Christian voice. There was this little bird that had been trained to talk which made good use of speech when it was suddenly seized by a hawk. On its crying out "Hail Mary", the startled predator let go its hold and the little bird flew away free.[184] But this was clearly exceptional. Parable has almost become fable. Alphonsus was more usually remarking the inability of the mule, and the natural world generally, to articulate the Kingdom. We, co-creatures with the mule and the mountains and the stars, we who can speak, have a vocation to speak for them. So, in *The Divine Office*, Alphonsus reminds his fellows how *Psalm* 19 is to be read according to *Romans* 10. The stars have had to be dumb all their existence, "there is no speech nor are there words, their voice is not heard", but now, the Christian community is to shout out for them, "their voice goes out through all the earth and their words to the ends of the world." As that psalm is recited within the liturgy, stars and mountains and mules are being brought with the psalmist and the Christian reciter to appreciate their inhabitation of one world and to appreciate that world as Kingdom.

It is most immediately at the thankful celebration of the eucharist that the integrating power of the liturgy may be experienced. Alphonsus tells a beautiful story of St Wenceslas of Bohemia which differs from the later version of Helmore and Neale precisely in its having a eucharistic emphasis. This is one of his favourite stories. He tells it more than once. Most effectively in *Visits to the Blessed Sacrament*.[185] In Alphonsus' telling, the duke gathers wheat and grapes and, having made the host and wine with his own hands for the morning mass, sets out on a winter night for the country church. "It is related" that the duke's manservant who accompanied him, having to trudge through the snow suffered much from the cold. Perceiving this, the duke commanded him to step only in his footprints. "He did so and never afterwards felt the cold." In this parable, night and cold and snow and wheat and grapes find themselves in one order with duke and servant. Alphonsus would have his Redemptorists see that what is happening in the story is happening in their lives. They are to think for a moment of the relation of duke and servant. Walking "according to Thy example" as Thomas à Kempis says, "in your footsteps", "striving to follow in my footsteps" as Falcoia has it in the *Great Rule*, they may receive the equerry as a figure for their *imitatio*. Anyone might make such a little leap of imagination as he hears the story of the follower who comes nearer the chapel and the liturgical celebration. Everything is coming into its eucharistic place. Thus, in *Conversing familiarly with God*, he is able in imagination to rearrange the sequence of the missioner's usual journey through the countryside to the next parish church so that natural sights are given a liturgical order. He begins, naturally enough, at "when you are in the cart drawn by beasts of burden and when you see a little dog running after the cart, and when you hear the birds sing". At these moments the members of dumb creation suggest that the missioner give their praise to God. But then, intensifyingly, Alphonsus imagines the missioner passing through a valley, tramping along the shore, his day's journey stretching into night. He imagines surreally. The missioner should see himself to be both on the road and already in the sanctuary, as we are, all of us, both on the way and already in Paradise. He constructs a paragraph of alternating phrases in which the pattern of an environmental liturgy is impressed upon his reader: "When you behold the valleys...when you see a beautifully decorated church...when you look out to sea...when you glimpse the candles lighted on the altar...when you look up at the sky, all studded with stars..." So, recognizing together the natural and liturgical signs of the Kingdom, passing the stable on the outskirts of the village, the carpenter's shop in the street, and the woodpile against the wall, and remembering Bethlehem and Nazareth and Calvary, the missioner arrives at the parish church, "when you see chalices and patens..." There, he is to "remember the greatness of the love which Jesus has shown us in giving us this most holy sacrament". And remembering, he will celebrate.[186]

The conversation of the servants of God

The paraliturgical "Hail Mary" allows the little bird to enjoy some further life. The liturgical praise of the priest and congregation not only gives the members of the natural order a voice, it opens upon further life for us. Alphonsus knows that various scholars, Xavier Mattei chief among them, have read that verse about the dumb stars and the rest of *Psalm* 19 as offering a merely astronomical description, asserting that the Hebrew text refers only to the positioning of bodies in the sky. They would have us read verse 5 as "He has set a pavilion for the sun among them". But Alphonsus prefers the Greek Septuagint and Latin Vulgate texts which declare the heavens to be divinely inhabited: "He has placed his pavilion in the sun". He proposes the scholar's justification for his preference. "It is", he remarks with a tug of his pince-nez, "reasonable to suppose that the Hebrew text was once less corrupt than it is today".[187] So, when we look up at the sun-lit sky, we ourselves are moved higher to sit with Christ and his mother and all his saints. We discover ourselves to be members of an intimate Kingdom. This is, of course, the eucharistic Kingdom. In that "presence chamber", where aristocratic Neapolitans, the *"nobilita de generosa"*, his father and brother on the fringes of the company, came into the presence of their king, poor commoners could at most hope to speak to him "through some third person". And then "only a few times in the year". But in this Kingdom, where "the throne of grace" "the cross on which Jesus sits", and where "he is present on our altars" as on "a throne of love and mercy", the present King "grants audience to all". "Always." Experiencing "what a Paradise it is" to be with him, moving among the martyrs, "those courtiers of Jesus Christ", we may talk familiarly with Christ, confiding our wants to him "as a friend to a friend".

Alphonsus' writing is scattered through with the familiarities of this conversation of Christ, the saints, and ourselves within that present Paradise. Maria Diaz lived in the tribune of a Spanish church chatting with "my neighbour" in the Tabernacle. The Venerable Francis of the Infant Jesus could not pass a church without going in to have a word with his friend.[188] Alphonsus especially delighted in a story of holy civility, told in Pietro Gisolfo's *Life of the Venerable Antonio de Collelis*, 1663, of a young man's joining in the conversation of Antonio Torres and Filippo Orilia when they were in the novitiate of the Pious Workers, and their suspicious novice master's discovering that this third young man was the Lord. "At the conversation of the servants of God", Alphonsus repeats with great pleasure from St Teresa, "Jesus Christ is always present".[189] There is a give and take within this cheerful conversation. Sometimes the talk gets very lively indeed. Alphonsus more than once recalls the spirited complaint of Maddalena Orsini that she had suffered for years while, as she told Christ, "Thou didst only hang on the cross for three hours", and he recalls Christ's indignant reply, "You don't know what you're talking about". But then, St Gertrude, one day meditating on the injuries done to Jesus in his Passion, began to praise and bless him, and the Lord was so pleased that he came to thank her. And then again when St Teresa pitied Jesus crowned with thorns, he changed the subject, "Pity me rather for the wounds inflicted by the sins of Christians". These are moments which display a personal diversity in the Kingdom. Saint differs from saint and conversation from conversation. When the Venerable Serafina thought she might have asked too much, Mary came smiling to reassure her, "Look, I have already obtained the favour". While on Blessed Alan of Rupe's nearly yielding to a temptation, Mary gave him a motherly box on the ears, saying, "If you had only asked me, you would not have got yourself into this mess". Alphonsus himself, in the *Glories of Mary*, wonders for a moment, like the Venerable Serafina, whether he might not be asking "for perhaps too much" but then tells himself that her Son "will deny thee nothing", and he is, in *Reflections on the Passion*, at least as bold as Maddalena Orsini, exclaiming as he stands in imagination beneath the cross on Calvary, "Ah, my beloved Jesus, Thou art in the wrong to make thy lamentation, saying *My God, why hast Thou forsaken me?*".[190] So it is not surprising that he is not at all backward in speaking his mind among the saints as questions of doctrine and the practice of the Christian life are raised: St Philip Neri's advice is "very profitable to some", but only, Alphonsus emphasizes, to some; when "my dear patroness", St Teresa, praises the faculty of imagination, "it is necessary to remark" that a couple of distinctions are required before letting her continue with a line of argument.[191] So St Teresa says..., St Thomas agrees..., St Maria Maddalena de Pazzi adds.... and then the eunuch of Queen Candace, Thomas à Kempis, Brother Vito, and all of us may join in. It is this saintly conversation which is being carried forward in Alphonsus' sermons. He would speak from the pulpit to the congregation "as if talking in a room, prompting them to some good work, or telling them a story".[192] And it is carried forward in his writings. Alphonsus is talking with the reader as a friend to a friend: "In my book on the *Glories of Mary*, I promised to write you another which would treat of the love of Jesus Christ", he acknowledges at the start of his 1751 *Reflections on the Passion*, "but on account of my bodily infirmities, my Director would not let me keep my promise." He is a little shame-faced here, making excuses as he stands before us. His sense of the reader's presence is at least as lively as he speaks out

211

strongly in his controversial works: "My dearest Christian brothers", he calls out at the close of his 1773 *Reflections on the Truth of Divine Revelation*, "let us thank God that we were born in a Catholic country" and "not in some heretical place where the intellectuals are slipping into atheism".

This is the familiar way with decent authors. "This is no book", Whitman declared to the reader of *Leaves of Grass*, "Who touches this, touches a man", and "It is I you hold and who hold you". Rather less violently, Shakespeare nodded to his audience at the end of *Love's Labour's Lost* with a self-mocking grin: "That's too long for a play". Reading Shakespeare at home, F. D. Maurice supposed that we all experience moments when "a light falls on the page of a book — someone seems as if he were showing you the true sense of it; why not he who wrote it?" So Maggie Tulliver, reading the *Imitation of Christ*, listened "while a low voice said..."

Above and beyond their acquaintance with him, Alphonsus hopes that his dearest readers, whom he imagines saying "This is certainly true", may as they read have parts in a conversation not only with him but with the saints. If, that is, they can get in a word. Telling the parable of the king with the handsome son, early in his *Reflections on the Passion*, he comes into a space where the saints seem, like Homer's spirits, all to be speaking at once: "But how is this?", asks St Augustine; "What could it signify?", enquires St Bernard; "Why, Lord, why?", exclaims St Bonaventure; "Who could ever explain it?" adds St Laurence Justinian. Then Alphonsus makes a place for us in this company. "Suppose, my brother, that Jesus had died for you alone..." And then, after our chat, "once a moment has been found to ask Jesus for some particular grace for yourself and for your neighbours", it would be a kindness if his readers would "pray also for me who composed this little book for your benefit".[193]

Reading his book, remembering the needs of others, talking with the Lord after communion, pausing then at the church door to say a friendly word to a neighbour, it may well seem that the Kingdom is come. Far too often, however, it proves impossible for us to sustain this conversation with others. Alphonsus had painful memories of childish games turning to rancour, of angry exchanges with his father, and, later, of Bishop Falcoia's rough treatment of the Venerable Celeste, of a nun

212

in the convent recreation room "ready to stop the sisters in mid sentence" and a thousand other uncomfortable occasions. He understood very well how such things happen. He understood that Francesco de Paola spoke sharply to others in the Redemptorist house at Scifelli only because "you suffer from hypochondria and this malady renders one disagreeable". He understood that the most hurtful things are often said in jest, "but you would not like it", he told a witty sister, "if you were made to look a fool in front of your community". And he understood that too few words might be as unpleasant as too many: "Brother Siniscalchi complains", he told Gasparo Cione, the Rector of Caposele, "that when he speaks to you, you scarcely answer him". He was not always able to achieve just the right conviviality in his own conversation. The stilted phrases of the final pages of *Evidence of the Faith* suggest his sense of performing a painful duty as he engages in parlour controversy with the man "under instruction". So he made allowances. "An uncharitable word that springs out of passion may", he granted the *True Bride*, "be excusable."[194]

Even if these domestic rudenesses are left aside, still human beings cannot be expected to sustain a conversation that should truly figure the eternal Kingdom. We are not "always the same" ourselves. We change our minds. We change the subject. We get ill. We lose our wits. Our talk becomes confused and confusing. We die. Maggie Tulliver heard that low voice say "All things pass away, and thou together with them". Alphonsus makes a louder assault upon the reader at the sudden start of one of his longer stories: "A young man dies". He continues, relentlessly, in characteristic present tense. "His parents are in a hurry to get him out of the house." This is the youngster who, a little while ago, was "courted for his conversation", who enjoyed a local fame for wit, graceful phrasing, urbanity and good humour. If today some still are saying "what a clever, funny, and delightful chap he was", in a very short time "no one will so much as mention him".[195] The cheerful chat of even the best of us is such a temporary, disappointing, substitute for the desirable conversation of the Kingdom.

We have a vocation to speak what the stars and mountains and mules would say of themselves within the Kingdom, to speak also of ourselves as inhabiting this same order, but our natural voice proves too weak. The psalmist, the bohemian duke, the missioner arriving at the parish church, together suggest that we should join them in the liturgy if we would make the appropriate acknowledgement of what is always the same.

Saying the same

In *Evidence of Faith*, Alphonsus offers three notes of the truth of Catholic faith: the healthiness of the doctrine, the conversion of the world, and the stability of dogma. The Catholic faith is encouraging human beings towards a good life under God, it is being received by the furthest-scattered peoples, and it is not subject to changing fashion. The truth we believe today was believed from the very first age of the Church. He offers examples of such truth: the freedom of the will, the effectiveness of the sacraments, the real presence of Christ in the Eucharist, the invocation of saints and the veneration of their relics and images. This is a neat selection of teachings. It points to the essential elements of the common life of Catholics: the definition of what it is to be a free human being and the affirmation of the time-released company of those who are fully freed are hinged upon the Eucharist.

His presentation of this note of Catholic faith suggests, unsurprisingly, that Alphonsus would have liked to make some simple re-assuring statement of the unchangingness of doctrine in the manner of Bishop Bossuet. Even in 1774, a dozen years after working on *Evidence of the Faith*, he was still interested in Bossuet's arguments, asking the librarian at the Nocera house to send him the Italian translation of the *Discourses on Universal History*. But Bossuet's assertion that there had not been the least variation in the doctrine of the Church since the death of the last Apostle had been designed to underpin gallican arguments against the present claims of the papacy. He told Leibniz, in his Letter XVI, that "it is necessary to believe today what was believed yesterday", but it seemed to Alphonsus that, as Bossuet distinguished between the vocations of St Peter and Benedict XIV, he ensured only that today would be quite unlike yesterday and that nothing was for ever. Alphonsus must, therefore reconstruct the argument for the unchangingness of the Church's doctrine.

It was not a propitious moment for such an attempt. Alphonsus knew that Vico had been interesting Italian intellectuals in the history of their society. That hunting squires were conducting countryside enquiries into the pedigree of a dog and the bloodstock line of a mare. That the keeper's of the king's art collection were asking about the provenance of a statue. And he knew that unpleasant persons were alleging inconsistencies between the first and the present preaching, and that there were, unaccountably, Christians abetting them. Along with this

214

interest in history, there was an equally disturbing expectation of a different future. Tindal in 1730 could cite both Bishop Taylor's remark that "there's no church that is in Prosperity, but alters her Doctrine every Age" and the observation of Vico's correspondent, Le Clerc, that "Theology is subject to Revolutions as well as Empires". Bishop Butler of Durham was suggesting that Scripture might contain "many truths as yet undiscovered" and hoping that divines might by "the continuance and progress of learning and liberty" discover such truths. "Progress", like "alteration" and "revolution", belong to a language that Alphonsus had always deemed to be unCatholic. Contrastingly, the succession of Popes after St Peter had been "constant and perpetual". So he can say plainly, in *Evidence of the Faith*: "It is objected that the Roman church has from time to time defined as of faith what was not of faith before; so she has not remained always the same in her doctrines; I reply, it is true that the Church has defined successively in the course of time doctrines that were not defined before", but that does not mean that she has not remained always the same in matters of faith.[196]

Faith is faith in the Word of God, "the written word of God", and, as Alphonsus goes on to say in his 1769 *Dogmatic Work against Pretended Reformers*, "the unwritten word in the hearts of the faithful".[197] That counter-assertion of "always the same" could be made because the revelation made in the written and unwritten Word of God is always informing the liturgical action of the community. Alphonsus is himself each day making that eucharistic proclamation of the mystery of faith, which is always the same in the Church. And this divine tradition is supplemented by apostolic traditions. Here, again, he refers to the liturgy, instancing the observances of Easter and Pentecost. And by ecclesiastical traditions, such as the recitation of the divine office. At the central moment of the liturgy all these traditions come together. The Roman Canon "is composed", Alphonsus repeats from the Council of Trent in his *Short Explanation of the Mass*, "of the very words of our Lord, of the traditions of the apostles, and the pious regulations of the popes". If, then, there have been definitions from time to time these have been public announcements of truth already active in the liturgical community. It is the papal vocation to make such announcements, "having power from God to resolve all doubts that might arise from time to time", and thus to secure an end to controversy. Bossuet was wrong. Today

215

is just like yesterday. The history of "articles of faith" is a history of that "secret and hidden wisdom" decreed before the ages being now, as in the first Corinthian community, imparted "among the mature".

A Regime of the Secret

Some might wonder why the whole truth was not declared all at once at the foundation of the Church, but Alphonsus had no difficulty about Christians keeping secrets. If anything, it was a difficulty that Christians should have spoken out in the later times. There are, as he writes in the "Paradise" meditation of his *Preparation for Death*, secret words, *arcana verba*, of that intense communion a Christian may enjoy with the Lord "which it is not granted to man to utter". There had been, he knew, such secrets in the community yesterday. He had read St John Chrysostom's account of the initiated Christians shutting the doors "when we celebrate our mysteries". He had been reminded lately by Toland of St Basil's remark that "the Esteem of Mysteries is preserv'd only by Silence". And he knew there were such "communities of the secret" today. He had at the beginnings of his own missioner life, in June 1725, been sent by Torno as a catechist with the Apostolic Missions to the island of Procida.[198] Working under Canon Gizzio's direction, he had been much impressed by a "Secret Congregation" of Christians, clerics and laymen, devoted to a shared pursuit of perfection. Such fraternities, originating perhaps with the French Jesuits of La Fleche in the early seventeenth century, and reaching first to Milan and Rome, had been much encouraged in the Kingdom of Naples by Francesco Pavone (1569-1637); the members were, as Gennaro Sarnelli describes them in his *Reformed World*, attempting to forward each other in the praise of God, the doing of good to their neighbours, and the perfecting of their own souls. The *"Rule of the Secret of the Sorrowful Lady"* of Procida especially encouraged men of the society in their devotion to the service of Mary. Alphonsus' further experience on the mission had, by the time he was writing the *Glories of Mary*, convinced him of the use of such fraternities, particularly in restraining the younger men from vice. He wanted, he said in the *"Exercises of the Mission"*, to set up, wherever it was convenient, such secret congregations of labourers and artisans, and himself wrote a *"Rule of the Secret"* for them, prescribing the devotional practices to be fitted into the workmen's day, from mental prayer, frequent Communion, and avoidance of rude jokes, to visiting the sick and giving assistance to the poor.[199]

Alphonsus could very well appreciate the difficulties of Christian congregations in apostolic and patristic times. His experience in the "evening chapels" suggested that Christians talking, singing, praying together, would always be suspect, especially if they belonged to the under-privileged classes of society. What was being said in his groups could at least be explained to a listening, Christian, magistrate and the arrested ring-leaders would be let out of prison. The first Christians could not expect such an understanding hearing when they were summoned into the courts of imperial Rome. So they would be likely to shut their doors and celebrate in secret. The first communities of Christians at Corinth and Antioch would be like those eighteenth century groups of "the most fervent brothers" who were coming, through their praying and working together in secret, into a deeper appreciation of the mystery of faith and the demand of a moral life. Alphonsus would, therefore, be likely to take the view of those who discerned the workings of "a regime of the secret"in the life of the first Christian communities. Generations of Christians had, according to this version of history, kept silent in the unfriendly society of the Roman Empire about many doctrines which later Christians would teach openly in Christendom. They had not wanted the most holy truths to be dishonoured in the mouths of irreligious persecutors.

There are hints of such a version of doctrinal history in the writings of the Dominican, Melchior Cano (1509-1560), and the Jesuit, Robert Bellarmine (1542-1621), and Alphonsus had the collected works of both these great men to hand while he was working on his *Moral Theology* and perhaps while he was composing his later dogmatic treatises. He was not, I think, acquainted at first hand with the more unpleasant variation of the idea of the secret which was proposed by Isaac Casaubon (1559-1614), who liked to place Christianity among the mystery religions of antiquity. But Casaubon's work was much talked about even a hundred years after his death, and by then both the idea and the language of "a secret of the faith", *arcana fidei*, had been established in general use by a Calvinist theologian, Jean Daillé (1594-1670), in his *Using the Fathers*, 1631. This was quickly appropriated as a "regime of the secret", *disciplina arcani*, by the Belgian Catholic, Emmanuel Schelstrate (1649-1692).[200] In his charming *View of Antiquity*,

1678, and his severer treatise *On the Council of Antioch*, 1681, Schelstrate had been able to deal with a number of nasty gaps in the record of the Church's teaching by appealing to such Christian reticence. His enthusiasm for "the secret" was more largely expressed in his *de Disciplina arcani*, 1685, in the midst of a rancorous controversy with the Lutheran scholar, Ernst Tentzel.[201] The all-purpose character of his thesis became apparent as Schelstrate found himself attacking Arnauld's restrictive notion of divine grace and defending papal supremacy against the criticisms of Bossuet. His exposition of the authority of the pope in the hidden years of the Church was judged to be so convincing that Schelstrate was promoted to be the Prefect of the Vatican Library and Canon of the Lateran.

Schelstrate's thesis would seem the more convincing to those who took part in Neapolitan discussions of these matters once Vico had produced his account, in the *New Science*, of classical societies. Vico had shown that in Homer there are two sorts of assembly: the *secret* at which the heroes consulted about the laws and the *public* at which the laws were published. From this he had gone on to propose a providential history of all societies by which their governments moved from oral custom into promulgated law. So the Romans had a secret curia of the priests and a public assembly of the tribes.[202] He would not himself, of course, suggest the reference of all this to the structures of the Catholic community. But Alphonsus had attended Vico's lectures. He had read Schelstrate's final treatise on ecclesiastical power as it was exhibited in the 1686 decrees of the Council of Constance. And there was a persuasive exposition of Schelstrate's thesis in the writings of his Venetian collaborator. Zaccaria, in an essay on the relation of *Liturgical Books and Theological Questions*, had re-affirmed the liturgical reference of "the secret" during a controversy with the Augustinian, Giovanni Lorenzo Berti (1696-1766), about the valid forms of the seven sacraments. Alphonsus read Berti's pamphlets, too. Or at any rate he kept them on his bookshelf for a while.[203]

None of these writings is likely to be taken off the shelf by a modern-day Christian. Most of us have accepted what Sam Coleridge says of Christianity in *Aids to Reflection*, 1825, as "a Life and a Living Process", and we have accepted Newman's suggestion that that "Life" is like his life. The Church now does not look like or sound like the Church of ancient Corinth, but, taking the growth of ideas in his own mind as the angelic boy grew into the prim Oxford don, and the don into the Littlemore retreatant, to be the paradigm case, Newman proposed that there had been a development of ideas in the mind of the Church from the apostolic times to the nineteenth century. Newman was fascinated by his own history, and by all history. The splendid collections of the Medici in their Tuscan villas, the contemplations of Gibbon in the Roman forum, the excavations sponsored by Charles IV at Pompeii and Herculaneum, show that it was possible to enjoy a like fascination in eighteenth century Italy. But Alphonsus never visited the museum that the king had established at Portici for the display of objects found by Alcubiere. Those evidences of Roman towns which had begun, proceeded, and collapsed, could not rouse much interest in the inhabitant of an unchanging Kingdom. He certainly could not be bothered by Newman's difficulty that, on Schelstrate's thesis so many secrets should have been kept in the Church long after the accession of Constantine. If keeping and announcing the secret had characterized the first community it would always characterize the community.

It is noticeable that as he settled himself more comfortably within the forms of Catholic life, in the Oratorian community and the Hagley Road parish, Newman himself needed to rely less on "development" as he meditated upon doctrine. It is particularly noticeable that he gave up his reliance on his hypothesis of development in the course of meditating upon precisely that doctrine to which Alphonsus gave such lively articulation in the Church. In the 1845 *Development of Doctrine*, Newman was remarking that "there was in the first ages no public and ecclesiastical recognition of the place which St Mary holds in the Economy of grace". In the 1850 apologetic of *Difficulties of Anglicans*, he was still using the historians' language: "The dogmatic truth of the prerogatives of the Blessed Virgin may be said in the lapse of centuries to have grown upon the consciousness of individuals". But by 1866 he was able to tell Pusey in a reply to *Eirenicon*: "I do not allow that the doctrine concerning her has undergone a growth for I believe that it has been in substance one and the same from the beginning". Arguing from the patristic witness to Eve's being "raised above human nature by that indwelling moral gift which we call grace" from the moment of her personal existence, and to Mary's enjoying "a greater grace", Newman concludes, "I do not know how to resist this inference — well, this is simply and literally the doctrine of the Immaculate Conception".[204]

The Glories of Mary

Newman was talking to Pusey as he had talked to Kingsley, one English gentleman to another, and, referring to Alphonsus' "notorious devotion" to Mary, he had put himself at a modest distance from Alphonsus, "it never surprises me to read anything unusual in the devotions of a saint" since "such men are on a level very different from our own, and we cannot understand them". He thereupon admits, perhaps he is even boasting, that "I never read his *Glories of Mary*". This was, I think, a misfortune. Reading that book is likely to assist anyone to a better understanding of both the devotions of the saint and the doctrine of the Church.[205]

Alphonsus never let a sermon pass, or a meditation, without making his chivalric bow to "this most kind lady", and he made it an inviolable rule for his missioners that they too preach a sermon on devotion to Mary at each mission. "We can attest, with all truth, that in most cases, no sermon is more profitable, or produces so much compunction in the hearts of the people." However often Alphonsus sat at his table to re-compose such a sermon, he never rushed the praise of Mary, "my mother, my light, my consolation, my refuge, my hope, amen, amen, amen". The *Glories of Mary* itself was a slowly composed work. Alphonsus set out on his programme of reading patristic and mediaeval authors in 1732 and did not have the book ready for publication until 1750.

Here, as usual, Alphonsus has learned things to say and lively stories to tell, especially in the meditation upon the Feast of the Immaculate Conception on account of "our Congregation's having the Blessed Virgin Mary for its Principal Patroness precisely under this title". The meaning he attaches to this title is beautifully conveyed as he sets his learning and his stories within a Trinitarian structure. We are, he says, to help Mary thank God for the grace of the Immaculate Conception which she receives from the Father, the Son, and the Holy Spirit.[206]

"In the first place", he announces, with a glance towards *Ecclesiasticus* 24:5, the Eternal Father preserved Mary from original sin because "she was his first-born daughter". Alphonsus' interpretation of both text and doctrine is shaped by his experience of the structures of contemporary Neapolitan society. Birth-rights were carefully protected by the members of his class. "While a poor man may become rich by his industry, an ignorant man learned by his study, it is much more difficult for a person of humble origin to enter the ranks of the nobility." There were occasions when Alphonsus himself had taken some pleasure in honouring Mary as a Lady of that aristocratic society. After the Amatrice suit in 1723, the young squire had, as if at a mediaeval tournament, dipped his little court sword to the feet of our Lady of Ransom in sign of perpetual fealty. But now, in 1750, Alphonsus is turning the tables on the little nobility of the bench who boasted of their lineage. Mary is, he says, noble with the nobility of a free spirit. Unlike those aristocrats, she has never been the slave of sin, never needed to be ransomed from that slavery. And that Mary should be thus recognizable as "the first-born daughter" fits with Alphonsus' experience that the one who comes later, as Mary comes after Eve, may enjoy the privilege and responsibility of the first-born. He had ceded his own rights of primogeniture to his younger brother Ercole. It fits, too, with the ordinary workings of his temperament that the historical series should be unable to contain the eternal design of the Father.

Alphonsus' exploration of the doctrine remains within the frame of contemporary social conventions as he meditates on Mary's being the Mother chosen by the Son. Alphonsus returns to *Ecclesiasticus* for an expression of Neapolitan belief that "the glory of a child is from the honour of his parent". He had disappointed his father by refusing to court a princess. His tattered cassock was a further disgrace. And he did not seem to have the slightest notion of how to get himself a bishopric. But he did have a gentleman's understanding that the Son owed it to himself that he should have a Mother worthy of every honour. Who, if he could choose, would choose a slave, a servant, an enemy of God, as his mother? The Son, as a matter of honour, chose for himself a Mother who is a queen, a free woman, who is always a friend of God. Mary is conceived without sin for her Son's sake. "Not that Jesus could have contracted sin, but that he might not be reproached for having a mother who had been touched by it." Of course, Jesus was not simply seconding the social prejudices of the Neapolitan nobility. He could have shrugged off any human contempt for "the son of a poor woman", but it would undoubtedly have been a disgrace to him if he could have heard the devils mutter, "Was not his mother once our slave?" So the Son forestalled such an accusation. He has a nice coda from Nicholas of Cusa, d. 1464, to set the honourable relation of Son and Mother together: "For others he is the Liberator, for the holy Virgin a pre-Liberator".

221

Reading in the Lukan annunciation narrative the angel's declaration that "the Holy Spirit shall come upon thee", Alphonsus understands that "since it was becoming that the Father should preserve Mary from sin as his Daughter, and the Son as his Mother, it was also becoming that the Holy Spirit should preserve her as his Bride". References from his experience as eldest son and man of honour now yield to those of the creative artist. Alphonsus thinks first of the Holy Spirit as a painter making a portrait of his beloved, showing her to the world as the most beautiful of women. He would see to it that his Bride would be "as lovely as it became him that she could be". Alphonsus had tried his hand at drawing and overseen the design of frontispieces for his books of meditations, and had flung red paint at an oil painting of the crucifixion which he thought too bloodless, but he had had more success with words and music. He thinks next of the Holy Spirit as troubadour serenading Mary in his *Song of Songs*:

> *Thou art all fair, O my love,*
> *There is no spot in thee*

and

> *There are numberless maidens*
> *But one is my dove,*
> *My perfect one*

These are delighted affirmations of Mary's Immaculate Conception. And, shifting from poet to critic, Alphonsus warns the reader that the Vulgate Latin text is not at this place quite exact in translating the Hebrew as "my perfect one"; the original, he says, came much nearer to "immaculate". But still, the Spirit proves to be a good baroque poet, juggling conceits with all the exuberance of the Neapolitan favourite, Giambattista Marini (1569-1625). Alphonsus deals delicately with another verse of the *Song of Songs*:

> *My sister, my bride,*
> *Is a walled garden,*
> *A sealed well*

simply noting that St Bernard wanted to add a verse to the poem of the Spirit, serenading their Lady as "a secret bower" into which "the sinner's hand has never reached to pluck the flowers". Alphonsus would not himself be so bold with Scripture, but he is quite prepared to attempt an elaboration of a theologian's text, even of the formidable St Peter Damian. In a moment of unaccustomed enthusiasm, this austere reformer had written that the Holy Spirit was, at the Annunciation about to "carry her off for himself". There is an echo for Alphonsus here of the episode in the tale of Prince Paris which follows immediately upon his making his choice among the three goddesses. He ensures that those who have not been taken line by line through the narrative of the Trojan's carrying off the lovely Helen, or heard Vico lecturing on the social meaning of the story, should get a sense of what is happening in St Peter Damian's exegesis. They should understand that the saint is using the language of *rapio* to convey something of the holy speed of the divine Spirit, eager to make Mary his own before Lucifer should touch her.

St Peter Damian proves to be not simply a lively literary critic but also a precise theologian. He had, in that very passage, identified Mary as at once "chosen and pre-chosen". She is, at the Annunication both being chosen to be the Bride of the Spirit and already pre-chosen, already conceived immaculate, "full of grace as the angel recognizes before the proposal is made." Our poor histories, even the Lucan narrative, have to distinguish between the time of Mary's conception and the time of her betrothal and the time of our saluting her. But Alphonsus' characteristic method of presenting the Church's witness to doctrine allows him once again to break through the barriers of our times, present, future and past tenses coincide as he hails Mary: "I thank, and resolve always to thank, our common Creator, for having preserved thee from every stain of sin".

The cumulative effect of Alphonsus' Trinitarian exposition of the Immaculate Conception is to suggest that this is a doctrine which has been everywhere received in the pre-times and times of the Church. That opening quotation from *Ecclesiasticus* is succeeded by others from *Proverbs*, *I Chronicles*, and *Psalms*, from *I Corinthians*, *Matthew*, and the ever-pleasing *Hebrews*. And the distinct interpretations of *Ecclesiasticus* by Scotists and Thomists serve to introduce citations of Denis of Alexandria, Ss John Damascene, Bernard and Bernadine, Athanasius, Theophilus of Nice, and Basil of Selucia, Augustine and the Augustinian Fr Thomas of Strasbourg, Chancellor Gerson, and, of course, "the learned Suarez". "They all say so." The scholar still, Alphonsus adduces, too, a supportive passage from a tract which Claudius Frassen had recently, in *Scotus Academicus*, VIII, 1720, Pt 2, tr. 1, art. 3, sect. 3, qu.1, para. 5, shown to be the work of St Bonaventure. But everyone has heard that both St Bernard, the great advancer of Marian devotion,

223

and St Thomas, the arbiter of theological argument, remained wary of what these others were saying. This must make a Catholic pause. It is in his examination of these two witnesses that Alphonsus most clearly demonstrates what he can do with Schelstrate's thesis.

At the time he was shaping this discourse for the *Glories of Mary*, Alphonsus was constructing the last *Liber* of the *Moral Theology*. He felt a need to make a place for the Immaculate Conception somewhere in his text-book, and opportunities were becoming rarer as he neared the end. He determined on presenting this doctrine within his treatment of "Excommunication, its causes and effects", as an illustration for his section on how penalties are incurred and how absolutions are to be sought. There is some awkwardness in all this, as Alphonsus must have recognized, but he evidently thought the structural inelegance a price worth paying for the opportunity to celebrate the Immaculate Conception here as in his other writings. In the very first edition, 1748, he placed at *Liber* VII, *Dubium* iv, Article 3, a *"Brief Dissertation"* on the doctrine and the censures attaching to those who do not reverence it.

Reconstructing Busenbaum's account of Law at the start of the *Moral Theology*, Alphonsus had suggested occasions when customary practice had the force of law, and when contrary custom might supercede the authority of enacted law. In this last *Liber*, he was suggesting that there is a custom of belief as well as of law. It is in this context that Alphonsus cites what Aquinas himself says of custom's having an authority beyond that of any theologian, "even of Augustine", and what Torno had taught him about the authority inherent in the belief of "all Catholics". He need not, he says, refer to private revelations, and then, most like a lawyer, he quotes from the revelations made to St Bridget. But he will say that almost every decent dogmatic theologian is of his opinion, all members of all religious orders except the Dominicans, and even 137 of them. And every worthwhile ascetical theologian. He need only refer to his third "golden book", the *Mary, Throne of God*, 1613 of the Neapolitan Jesuit, Pietro Antonio Spinelli (1555-1615), which he had taken as his model at various places of the *Glories of Mary*.

With the all-but universal custom in the theological schools of acknowledging the Immaculate Conception, Alphonsus can, in this *Moral Theology* dissertation, cite a local practice. In the university of Naples, every graduate took his oath to defend Mary Immaculate "even

224

to the shedding of his blood". Alphonsus had taken this oath himself in 1713. Curmudgeonly theologians had been objecting, he knew, to that university oath to defend a doctrine which, not yet being defined as "certain", remained, they chose to say, "uncertain". But the oath-taking was not a merely academic ceremony. It was a manifestation of ecclesial custom in the Kingdom of Naples. It had to be understood within this context. At the parallel place in the *Glories of Mary*, Alphonsus felt free to tell a couple of stories. "In confirmation of this great privilege of Mary, we may be allowed to add the well-known innumerable graces that our Lord is daily pleased to dispense throughout our Kingdom of Naples, by means of the pictures of her Immaculate Conception." "In the diocese of Salerno, where we were giving a mission...", a man had for years sustained a great hatred for one of his neighbours. One of the Redemptorists, being quite unable to argue the man out of his hatred, offered him a little picture of Mary Immaculate. "What use is this?", asked the man with the grudge, but, on his taking it into his hand, he at once agreed to be reconciled with his enemy. Then, when it came to it, in the morning, the man relapsed into rancour. He was offered another little picture and for some time, nervous of its effect on him, he refused to have anything to do with it, but on his reluctantly taking it, "Behold! He said at once, 'let us be quick; where is the Notary?', and was instantly reconciled". Alphonsus leaves unstated the connection of popular devotion to the sacramental order. That a reader is to assume that the rancorous man will go from the lawyer to the confessor is clear from the structure of the companion story. There was "this woman and she came to a house of our little Congregation". She did not know how she might persuade her husband to come to confession. A Redemptorist told her to give the sin-hardened man a picture of Mary Immaculate. On her doing so, he was so thoroughly changed that, after twenty-eight years of staying away, he could hardly wait in patience for the morning to come when he should be able to confess his sins. Such stories witness to the existence of a custom of belief. They do not, however, settle questions about the status of the custom. For their settlement, Alphonsus refers to the authority of liturgical practice. It is from a base in such an authority that he begins, in the *Moral Theology*, his consideration of Aquinas' refusal in the *Summa Theologiae* to go further than saying that Mary is sanctified in the womb after her conception.

Others, he knew, had tried to argue from Aquinas against Aquinas. Torno, in his notes to *"Estius"*, had pointed to an affirmation of Mary's life-long freedom from original sin in Aquinas' own commentary on Lombard's *Sentences* and the specific reference to Mary's being immaculately conceived, in the only editions available to Torno, in Aquinas' commentary on *Galatians*. Torno interpreted Aquinas' language in the *Summa* according to what he read there. The "celebrated and learned bishop" had gone as far as to say that "in truth it is only by the common consent of the faithful that we are assured of the sanctification of Mary in her mother's womb and of her glorious assumption into heaven". Aquinas held both these doctrines as "certain". So, someone should put the question to him: "Why should not the same common sentiment of the faithful make us certain of her Immaculate Conception?" Alphonsus was not much interested in this rather dubious attempt to demonstrate that Aquinas was an inconsistent opponent. His instinct was that Aquinas would prove to be both quite consistent and using arguments that would help other theologians to find out what is always true. So Alphonsus' account concentrates on Aquinas' reason for believing Mary to be sanctified in the womb after conception. It is apparent to him, as he reads the *Summa*, that Aquinas was reasoning from the liturgical practice of the Church. This was authoritative for his conduct of all theological discussion. Aquinas held Mary to be holy at her birth precisely because the Church was celebrating a feast of Mary's birth. He did not hold Mary to be conceived immaculate because there was no authorization of such a feast in his time. The Immaculate Conception was then still an element of the known but undeclared secret of the community. But since 1476, when Sixtus IV authorized the Mass and Office, and 1570, when St Pius V issued his revision of the Roman Missal and laid it down that for the feast the liturgical texts of the Nativity of our Lady should be used, changing only "Nativity" to "Immaculate Conception", and 1708, when Clement XI extended the celebration of the feast to the universal Church, this secret was open. It is according to the principles of St Thomas' own understanding of the Church and doctrine and liturgy that now, when the community is clearly celebrating Mary's Immaculate Conception, the doctrine is to be received as certain.

Alphonsus' references to Popes and their bulls restore a balance to the discussion. He is pointing to there being a *disciplina* as well as an *arcanum*, a regimen as well as a secret. It was for evidence of the exercise of papal authority that Alphonsus had consulted Schelstrate's book on the Council of Constance along with the fourth "golden book", *The*

Power of the Pope of Giovan Battista Noghera (1719-1784).[207] He was now demonstrating that Aquinas had been obedient as well as consistent in his observing the terms of the liturgy as it was authorized in his time. This consideration for obedience in Alphonsus' version of Schelstrate's thesis is discernible even more clearly in his dealing with an objection based on Letter 174 in the Migne edition of St Bernard's works.

St Bernard had written to the Canons of Lyons cathedral censuring their celebration of a feast of the Immaculate Conception. Some scholastic theologians thought to deal with this embarrassment by setting up a nice distinction. St Bernard, it could be said, understood conception in a passive sense. He thought of Mary's being conceived as the result of her parents' action while sin was still reigning. But the doctrine of the Immaculate Conception refers to Mary's own active enjoyment of grace from the very first moment of her existence. So St Bernard was not objecting to the doctrine. But to Alphonsus it was apparent that the saint was not making a comment on the doctrine itself, only on the irregularity of the Canons' action. They had converted an element of the secret into a public liturgy. This feast, unlike, as St Bernard properly said, feasts of the Nativity and Assumption of the Virgin, had not yet been approved. At this point in the *Moral Theology* Alphonsus' decision to treat of the Immaculate Conception in a section dealing with censures does not appear quite so arbitrary as it did at the start. The Canons had put themselves in danger of an ecclesiastical ban by their disregard of liturgical norms. Alphonsus brings Bellarmine along to confirm that "if St Bernard were to see the feast of the Immaculate Conception being celebrated in the Church by the authority of the Roman See, he too would willingly join in the celebration". Alphonsus can now refer to the penalties incurred by those who make an inadequate estimate of the liturgical feast, or who say or write that this pious belief of so many Catholics can never be defined as a doctrine of the Church.

He puts what he wants to say about that "definability" very plainly in his 1769 account of what the Council of Trent had said about Original Sin. He devotes more than half his exposition of this decree in *Against the Heretics* to considerations of the status of the doctrine of the Immaculate Conception. This time he had "many other universities" and 133 Dominican supporters waiting in the corridor. He refers again to Bishop Torno's cheeky questioning of Aquinas about "the common consent of the faithful". Then, decisively, he moves to "another argument still more convincing" which is "taken from the celebration of the festival of the Conception of Mary". Alphonsus has shaped what Aquinas was saying in the Third Part of the *Summa* into a knock-down liturgical syllogism: The Church cannot celebrate anything which is not true and holy; but the Church does celebrate the Immaculate Conception; therefore... The present liturgical celebration so far opens the secret as to render the doctrine, in the language of professional theologians and their lawyers, "Proximately definable" as an article of faith. Alphonsus has secured that Schelstrate's thesis should apply not only to *Genesis* and *Luke* and Aquinas and the bishops at Trent, to Torno and Spinelli and himself, but to Pius IX. The doctrine of the Immaculate Conception could be defined on 8 December, 1854.

"And that is the promise..."

Pius IX in proclaiming "a singular privilege" of Mary put an Alphonsian emphasis on the communal significance of her vocation. Mary is conceived immaculate, full of grace, so that she may be a mediatrix of grace. St James, on Mary's Assumption, comes to thank her "for all the comfort she had given the apostles while she was on earth".[208] That comfort is now given to each of us. Adopting in the first section of the *Glories of Mary* commentary on the "Hail, holy Queen", a precise reading of *John* 19:27: "He said to the disciple, Behold thy Mother", Alphonsus bids the reader note that "Jesus Christ did not address himself to John but to "the disciple", in order to show that he then gave Mary to all who are his disciples, that is to say, to all Christians, that she might be their Mother". This is a planned prologue to his citing much further along in the *Glories of Mary*, in his meditation on the Assumption, Mary's own last words, as St Bridget overheard them. The Lady said to "this disciple who had served her so well", as she prepared for her death in John's house, "Do not forget me. In all thy wants call me to thy aid. I will never forget thee".[209] Because we have been shown already that each of us is "this disciple", there is an encouragement in all this for each of us now to take an active part in the conversation of the Kingdom.

There is a "courtesy of love" still. "He who salutes Mary will be saluted by her." St Bernard once heard a statue of the blessed Virgin reply "Hail, Bernard" to his "Hail Mary".[210] There is an exchange of charity:"the blessed Virgin, being unable to thank our Lord for all the

228

gifts he has bestowed on her, rejoices greatly when her children help her to thank him".[211] Alphonsus printed with his *Glories of Mary* a little Trinitarian chaplet of such assisting prayer: "I thank you, Eternal Father, for the power given to Mary, your daughter; I thank you, Eternal Son, for the wisdom given to Mary, your mother; I thank you, Eternal Spirit, for the love given to Mary, your bride". This is a small sign of the give and give of charity in the Church and our shared thankfulness. There is, most especially, a eucharistic thankfulness."Do not forget" and "I will never forget" receive their meaning in the context of the remembrance of the Lord's death. While Christians now "say, or hear, or have said, Mass in honour of the Virgin", she will, as the Council of Trent says, be speaking for them to God. This is her part in the gracious conversation. She is a tower of strength. "My mother, help me to love Jesus Christ." She reflects the divine care of us. Alphonsus hands on her comforting messages. On every matter. "Tell that wretched hiccough from Mary Immaculate that it must go away at once and not any more torment Don Saverio." And the dying man was cured.[212]

This cheerful eucharistic conversation with Mary is maintained as we sing her litany while the Blessed Sacrament is exposed. We call her "Tower of Ivory". We call her "Mirror of Justice". It was, therefore, a matter of amazement for Alphonsus, as he remarks in one of his last pamphlets, *"A reply to Abbate Rolli"*, 1776, that any Catholic should protest against the custom of singing the Litany of Loreto during the "Forty Hours". Rolli challenged "a part of the public worship of the Church" and what is being done "with the approval of many Pontiffs". There was something peculiarly repugnant in this Catholic liturgist's justifying his "New Project" by a specious re-appraisal of what "for so many ages" had been "recited and sung in all churches". The arguments of both Medici and Hapsburg litigants were being alleged together against what is always true. But Alphonsus did not have to stay to argue this time. "For my part, I cannot understand how it is unbecoming to ask the Mother of God to offer her prayers for us to Jesus, exposed in the Blessed Sacrament."

All his life as a missioner, he had been bringing others to appreciate the eucharistic community as that Kingdom of the Lord where Mary and angels and ourselves enjoy eternal life together. This has been his aim in every piece of ascetical, moral, and dogmatic writing, making itself apparent even in the midst of controversy with the most aggravating opponent. Indeed, it is in the course of rebutting the accusations of the impious Bayle[213] that Alphonsus most powerfully identifies the angel's announcement of the Kingdom to Mary with the Lord's own announcement of the Eucharist to us: "The holy Gabriel said to the blessed Virgin Mary; *And of his kingdom there shall be no end.* And that is the promise that the Lord made to those who receive the holy eucharist: *Whoever eats my flesh... has eternal life*".

NOTES

1 Instructions for the People, Pt I, IV, ii. 34.

2 Sermon XXXVI for the seventh Sunday after Pentecost, "On the education of children", II, 8. cf. *Truth of Faith*, II, XIX, Marietti 671b: "Fathers of families must be very attentive to see where their children go to learn, so that, in acquiring good letters, they do not also take in vices and errors. I would hope that this disaster has not happened in our city of Naples but I fear to God that such things have happened in many cities of Europe, where modern errors have got a hold".

3 *Considerations for those called to the Religious State*, I, *Exercises of the Missions*, VII, viii, 2. Letter to Andrea Villani, 25 August, 1774,

4 *True Bride*, XI, ii.

5 *Glories of Mary*, Pt I, I, i.

6 *Ibid.*, Introduction, 'which should be read'.

7 *True Bride*, XXIV, vi.

8 Christians should meditate "without labouring to represent in the mind the peculiar features of our Saviour, his face, his height, or complexion", *True Bride*, XVI, iii.

9 cf. Hoegerl, *op.cit.*, 25-33.

10 29 October, 1730.

11 *True Bride*, VII, iv.

12 cf. Hoegerl, *op.cit.*, 75f.

13 *Discourses for the Novena of Christmas*, IX, Introduction.

14 cf. Hoegerl, *op.cit.*, 111, 124, 127, 177.

15 *Ibid.*, 84.

16 *Short Explanation of the Mass*, II.

17 cf. Hoegerl, *op.cit.*, 70, 156 and 179ff.

18 *Refutation of a Book "On Preaching"*, 2.

19 Jones, *op.cit.*, 67. I think we might add, even at the distance of letter-writing, the painstaking Giambattista Remondini. But a couple of such friends cannot be reckoned as demonstrating Alphonsus' conviviality.

20 At the very start of the eucharistic celebration, "Before going to the altar", he notes in his *Short Explanation of the Prayers of the Mass*, "the priest says to the people, 'The Lord be with you'" and at their answering 'And with thy spirit' we hear "the faithful union of priest and people in Jesus Christ". It is entirely in character that his *Visits to the Blessed Sacrament* should begin with an appeal to each of his eucharistic friends, and that he should be assured that our friendship transcends all temporal limitations: "I ask, my

dear reader, that, whether I be dead or alive, you will recommend me to the most Holy Sacrament each time you use this little book, and I promise to pray for all who do me this act of charity, every time I celebrate the holy Mass".

21 *True Bride*, XXII, viii, *Glories of Mary*, Introduction and Pt I, IX, *Visits*, XXXI, *Practice*, V and IX. 8, *On the Passion*, XI, i, *Preparation* XXXV, ii.

22 Alphonsus was very sensitive to the deliberate structuring of such speeches; cf. "as Thomas à Kempis makes her say…", *Glories of Mary*, Pt II, Discourse V.

23 cf. Hoegerl, *op.cit.*, 75ff and 230ff.

24 *Practice*, IV, ii, 1.

25 *Life of Paolo Cafaro*, XI.

26 cf. Hoegerl, *op.cit.*, 156ff.

27 *Considerations for those called to the Religious State*, XII.

28 *On the Passion*, I, ii.

29 *Life of Gennaro Sarnelli*, X.

30 *Discourses for the Novena of Christmas*, VIII, 2.

31 cf. Hoegerl, *op.cit.*, 253, 257, and 285ff.

32 *Pious Reflections*, II, xiii.

33 *Discourses for Novena of Christmas*, VIII, 2.

34 His experiences of assisting condemned men at the gallows in Piazza del Mercato and at the cross-roads approaches to the city inform the little tract, *Advice to Priests assisting the Dying*, 1757, which he wrote to guide others in this ministry.

35 *Treasury*, Pt II, Instr. IV, ii, 1 and Pt I, IX, 3.

36 Alphonsus always refers to his tutor as "Torni" but the researches of Domenico Capone have established that in official documents the illustrious doctor is every time "Torno"; cf. his essay, *Le Citazione nelle opere ascetiche di S Alfonso*, in *Opere Ascetiche, Introduzione Generale*, 343, note 1.

37 cf. *Theologia Moralis*, Lib. III, Tract. II, cap.I, 130; Lib.III, Tract. VI, cap. III, 1027 and Lib.VI., Track. III, cap.II, dubium ii. art. 1.257.

38 "From his toenails", he said: cf. Cicero, *Epistulae ad Familiares*, I.6.2, and Horace, *Carminae*, III.6.24. Both of them are using *"tenero ungui"* proverbially to mean "from childhood".

39 Not only at every place in *Theologia Moralis* from Lib. I, Tract.I, cap.I, 1, 2, and 3 onward, but also recurringly in his ascetical works, especially in *True Bride* and the *Glories of Mary*.

40 *Glories of Mary*, Pt I, VIII, iii. It was particularly pleasant for Alphonsus to point out, at huge length, to Salvatore Ruggieri that Aquinas had already said, *Summa* I, 2, *quaest.* 67, *art.* 6, that our love of God "is the same" here and in Paradise, "remains (please note) identically the same" *in via* and *in patria*, for here and in Paradise we know and love "the same divine Goodness". 22 July, 1776.

41 Abelly advertised his *Medulla* as expressing the moral doctrine of 'the holy Scriptures, Councils, Papal decrees, Fathers and learned men'. He was a consistent defender of *Le Pouvoir du Pape*, 1654, and of *L'honneur de la sainte Mere de Dieu*, 1666, and the enthusiastic biographer of his master, S Vincent de Paul, 1664. Several commentators have let themselves be a little misled by Boileau's reference to Abelly, *Lutrin*, IV, as a smooth man, into thinking him a rather too indulgent moralist. Alphonsus citations, egr. *Practice*, VII, and *Treasury*, Pt I, X, iii, suggest that he esteemed Abelly to be as severe as a decent anti-Jansenist could be. Abelly is always "reasoning wisely", *Theologia Moralis*, Lib. I, Tract I, cap. ii, 25, and then offering "the very best" advice, *Ibid.*, cap. iii, 65. Alphonsus thought

Abelly's greatest virtue was his capacity to write clearly. He was "that clear author", "that clear and methodical and concise author". His *Eclaircissements* of the Catholic truth of the Eucharist and of Penance, 1661 and 1678, showed missioners how they should announce the eternal, for it was such clarity that would result from their avoiding both "new" and "antiquated" terminologies. cf. letter to Giovanni Mazzini, 27 November, 1746, and *Exercises of the Missions*, VII, iii. Alphonsus consulted Abelly's *Episcopalis sollicitudinis enchiridion*, 1672, when preparing his own *"Useful Reflections for Bishops"*, and kept Abelly's devotional work, *Sacerdos christianus*, 1656, handy to the end of his life.

42 Genet had been commissioned by Bishop Le Camus to produce a text book in the *casus conscientiae* tradition. He put together in his *Théologie morale* the cases he was presenting in his lecture course at the seminary in Aix. And for fear that he might have slipped into something irregular, Genet sent the book to be proof-read by Antoine Arnauld at Port-Royal. His work was properly described by Le Camus in 1678 as "a book for country curates", if it had been anything else, as the Bishop said, "it would have been of no use to me".

43 *Apologetic Rejoinder concerning the Equi-probable Opinion*, 16 January, 1764.

44 *Théologie morale*, VIII, Bk.I, 'On civil law', 29.

45 *Ibid.*, VIII, Bk.I.3, 'On the rights of persons', 51 and I, Bk.V, 'On Legacies', 629f.

46 *Ibid.*, I, II, 'On contracts in general', cap.II,Qu.2,Resp. and V, 'On exchange', III, Qu.9, Resp. and VI 'On Games', Qu.4.

47 *Ibid.*, I, Tract. 1, cap. III, Qu.2, Resp.

48 *Ibid.*, I, Tract. 1, cap.V, 'On the Equally Probable Opinion', Qu.2, Resp. cf., the discussion in J. R. Pollock, *Francois Genet: The Man and his Methodology*, 179-185.

49 *Apologetic Rejoinder*, 16 January, 1764.

50 No copy of the original printing survives but Alphonsus' considered version occurs at *Theologia Moralis*, Lib.III, Tract. II, cap.1.130ff.

51 *Theologia Moralis*, Lib.VI, Tract. IV, cap.1, dub. ii.2.452ff; *Instructions* cap.V; *Homo Apostolicus*, Tract. ult., cap. unicum, I ff; *Treasury*, Pt II, IV, ii.4.

52 20 October, 1774.

53 17 November, 1755; 22 June, 1755.

54 cf. Preface to 1st edition of *Theologia Moralis*, quoted by Gaudé, I, xiv. Busenbaum's *Medulla*, Munster, 1650, was thought by its author to be exhibiting "an easy and clear method of dealing with cases of conscience brought together from a variety of sound authors".

55 Lacroix's 4 volume work, 1707-1714, was itself subtitled 'a Commentary on H. Busenbaum's *Medulla*'. Zaccaria's *Liber Prodromos* occupied 230 double-columned pages of Lacroix's first volume quarto.

56 Lib. IV, cap.II, art.ii; Lib.I, Tract. II, cap.IV, App.I; Lib.VI, Tract.IV, cap.I, art.ii. At the very places where Alphonsus makes these references to the *Medulla* instances it is noticeable, however, that Busenbaum's descriptions of hypothetical situations and the definitions of moral action derivable from these descriptions are re-directed into a discussion that is entirely Alphonsus' own invention, and which is introduced as of especial interest: *"Magna agitur Quaestio"*, Lib. III, Tract. V, cap. III, dub.vii; *"Hic oportet quaestiones discutere scitu maxime necessarias"*, Lib.IV, Tract. II, art ii.91.

57 *Theologia Moralis*, Lib.I, Tract.I, *de Conscientia*, cap.1, 12.

58 Letter to the Rector of Caposele, 15, July, 1757, and "to the Fathers and Brothers of the Congregation", 8 August, 1754.

59 *Theologia Moralis*, Lib.I, Tract.I, *de Conscientia*, cap.I, 11: *"de qua longiorem oportet habere sermonem"*. cf. "Let me explain myself", *"Me explico"*, in the discussion of invalid contract, Lib.I, Tract.I, *Morale systema*, 69.

60 *Newman's Apologia Pro Vita Sua*, ed. Wilfrid Ward, 1913, 363.

61 *Ibid.*, 444.

62 He thought it necessary, time and again, to explain this irritating mode of production to Remondini, cf. Letters of 10 February, 1759, 24 May, 1760, 19 June, 1760, 24 July, 1760, 20 July, 1761 and so on until June 1768.

63 Alphonsus quotes *Illud dicitur licitum, quod nulla lege prohibetur* from Aquinas, *In 4 Sent.* dist. 15, qu.2, art.4. solut. 2 at a variety of places in *Theologia Moralis*, egrr. Lib. I, Tract. I, cap. II, 26 and cap. iii, 61 and Tract. II, cap. i, 97. He nicely demonstrates the thoroughness of Torno's tutorials and Domenico Campanile's university lectures on the history of this topic in the Law Schools by foot-noting a reference to *Corpus juris civilis*, 5 vol., Lyons, 1548-1550, and the *Glossa* in *1 Necnon* ff, *Ex quibus causis majores*, V. *Prohibeant*. The reference to Heinecke's *Elementa juris naturae et gentium* is, equally, evidence of his keeping up with current literature. Heinecke was popular enough among Naples lawyers and moral theologians for his *Opera* to be put out by a local publisher in 12 volumes, 1759-1775. Alphonsus' reference is to Lib. I, cap. I, para. 13, in Vol. VIII. He is careful to indicate in *Theologia Moralis* that Heinecke's argument about liberty is not based on one knock-down scripture text but relies for its further validity on a clutch of citations from canon and civil law.

64 *Theologia Moralis*, Lib.I, Tract.I, cap.III.54.

65 *Ibid.*, Lib.I, Tract.I, cap.III, *alterum corollarium*, 73ff; *Morale systema*, 54; 66ff and 72. For a short review of the principles of equi-probability, *vide* the letter to Pietro Paolo Blasucci, November, 1768.

66 *Theologia Moralis*, Lib.I, Tract.I, *Morale systema*, 56.

67 *Ibid.*, Lib.I, Tract.I, cap.III, *corollarium primum*, 64. For the long-running controversy with one who was "certainly a learned man" but, "unlike God and the Church", not infallible, Letter to Giambattista Remondini, 31 March, 1764, see Patuzzi's *La Causa del Probalismo*, Naples, 1764, and *Apologia dell' Illustriss. e Reverendiss. Mons. D. Alfonso de Liguori*, 1764, to which Patuzzi replied with *Osservazioni teologische* "on the Apology of A. de Liguori, Ferrara, 1765. That these *Osservazioni* were also published by Remondini allowed the publisher to show his opponent's work to Alphonsus in proof and he could thus be ready with his reply immediately upon Patuzzi's pamphlet's appearing. Alphonsus revised critique of this "little work" in *Theologia Moralis* at Lib. I, Tract. I, cap. iii, *Alterum corollarium*, 74 and *Monitum* I, 85ff. Alphonsus was not averse to the scrap. "I have looked again at the Reply of Fr Patuzzi", he wrote to Remondini in mid-July, 1764, "and I am very glad that he has written against me. I see that he does not in the least weaken either my System or my individual propositions. A reply of this sort can only result in showing my System in a better light." He next assured the anxious publisher, on 28 September, 1764, that "when my *Apology* makes its appearance, Fr Patuzzi's work will have a larger sale", so he would profit from both sides of the controversy. Looking back on these events in a letter to Villani in November, 1773, when he was getting ready to enter another dispute, Alphonsus could say that in 1765 "my remarks were universally applauded by the learned". After all, "I used only the teaching of St Thomas".

68 Letter to Blasucci, November, 1768.

69 *Homo Apostolicus*, I, 267.

70 Charles Kingsley (1819-1875), had been looking at the *Theologia Moralis Universa, 1847*, of Pietro Scavini (1791-1869) and the *Compendium Theologiae Moralis, 1841*, of Dieudonné Neyraguet (1798-1867(?)).

71 *Newman's Apologia*, ed. Ward, 46. Neither Scavini nor Neyraguet seems quite to warrant Kingley's ferociousness in attack. Both are rather careful to keep within scriptural limits. Thus, in his discussion, Lib.II, Tract.V, Disp.1, cap.III,85 and *Adnotationes*, 239, Scavini begins from *Ecclesiasticus* 37.20 and the odiousness of the clever speaker, points to a restriction that is not purely mental being allowed even by *rigidiores* if there is *justa causa*, and then argues that a confessor should countenance nothing which would disrupt human social relations or put Christian simplicity into question, and comes at last to the 'let your *yes* mean *yes*' of *Matthew* 5.37. Similarly, Neyraguet, in Tract.VII, cap.II, App.1 begins from "No, I am not Elias", refuses, again, to countenance any purely mental reservation, but again, admits *ex justa causa* a restriction that is not purely mental, like "I am not going up to the festival", by which we may allow another to deceive himself, and defines *justa causa* in terms of *"finis honestas"*.

72 *Newman's Apologia*, ed. Ward, 273.

73 *Ibid.*, 449. In the *Homo Apostolicus*, Alphonsus begins his considerations of *aequivocatio* by indicating the different senses of words, "literal" and "spiritual" and "mystical", with a clear reference to the exegetes' distinctions in their talk of the layered meanings of Scripture, cf. Tract.V, cap.2.15.

74 Alphonsus seems to have developed for himself the example in *Conversing Familiarly*, III, iii, 1, of Jesus "making as if" he knew nothing of Lazarus' death until the Magdalene told him of it.

75 *Théologie morale*, VI, Tract.III, cap.II, qu.8. The discussion of *aequivocatio*, *Theologia Moralis*, Lib. III, Tract. II, cap.II, dub.iv, is another place at which Alphonsus suggests that the confessor look at the cases presented in Busenbaum's *Medulla*. Having asked whether it is ever lawful to use "equivocation", Busenbaum answers that it is allowable "only when there is just cause" and "only when the truth is being hidden without recourse to a lie. Everything, again, depends on "just cause".

76 *Homo Apostolicus*, Tract.V, cap.II, 16.

77 des Rotours, *Saint Alphonsus Liguori*, 1916, 145, note 3.

78 *Theologia Moralis*, Lib. III, Tract.II, cap.II, dub.iv.162.

79 *Ibid.*, Lib.VI, Tract.VI, cap.III, dub.ii.1050f. and Lib.Iv,Cap.III, art.iii.202.

80 *Simple Exposition*, XII, i.

81 23 February, 1769.

82 *Theologia Moralis*, Lib.III, Tract.II, cap.II, dub.iv.154.

83 *Ibid.*, dub.iv, 156.

84 It always remains for the confessor to judge, in his dealings with an individual penitent, if the oath taken in ambiguous terms was indeed *"ad servanda bona spiritui vel corporis utilia"*, Lib.III, Tract.II, cap.II, dub.iv.151. There is no quick way of establishing *"justa causa"*.

85 cf. Letter to the Royal Chamber of Santa Chiara, March 1777.

86 cf. Jones, 181.

87 cf. *Newman's Apologia*, ed. Ward, 274.

88 *True Bride*, XVIII,i.

89 *Newman's Apologia*, ed. Ward, 50, 52, 55, 53, 45 and 58.

90 *Fidelity of Vassals*, II, 7.

91 *Theologia Moralis*, Lib.I, Tract.II, cap.I. dub.ii.107.

92 *Ibid.*, dub.iii.136 Alphonsus is here quoting Busenbaum and citing Vasquez, Suarez, and Molina. But even the discussion of papal authority requires that he make some careful distinctions. Writing in 1769, at just the completion of the necessary ten-year period,

Alphonsus noted in his *Rubrics of the Mass* that "in 1759 Pope Clement XIII ordained that on all Sundays which have no Preface of their own, the Preface of the Blessed Trinity must be said", and also that "the custom which has the force of law" favours the Preface of the Octave to be said on the Sunday within the Octave of a feast. He would have the clergy observe that this custom has the force of law precisely because it obtains "in Rome" and thence, generally, "in other places".

93 *Ibid., dubium* ii.110ff.

94 *Ibid.*, 124,6.

95 Adolf von Harnack, *Lehrbuch des Dogmengeschichte,* Leipzig, 1886ff., English trans. 1894ff, cf. vol. III, 677f.

96 *Interior Trials,* I and II, Sermon XXV for the fourth Sunday after Easter. For equally emphatic appeals to *"directoris judicio"* in a quite different context, see *Theologia Moralis,* Lib. I, Tract. I, cap. i, 12, where St Antoninus, St Bernard, Chancellor Gerson, St Philip Neri, St Francis of Sales, and St Ignatius Loyola, throng to repeat what Alphonsus has been saying about "Obedience to the judgement of a wise director".

97 Celeste Crostarosa, *Autobiography,* cited in S. Majorano, *L'Imitazione per la Memoria del Salvatore,* 55.

98 End of March, 1733.

99 Letter to Bartolomeo Corrado, 28 June, 1781.

100 Letter to Francesco Antonio de Paola, 25 November, 1780.

101 Letter to de Paola, 18 October, 1780.

102 *Treasury,* Pt II, Instr. iv.

103 But see James A. Cleary, 'Did St Alphonsus ever refuse absolution?', *Irish Ecclesiastical Record,* LXII, 1943, 389ff for the suggestion that Tannoia's remark does not constitute a claim that Alphonsus never deferred absolution, only that he did not, in his old age, remember deferring. cf also *Theologia Moralis,* Lib.VI, Tract.IV, cap.1, 453ff and *Praxis* para. 69.

104 *Treasury,* Instr. IV, i.

105 *Exercises of the Missions,* VII, i, 3.

106 Daniello Bartoli, *L'eternita consigliera,* Pt I, iii,36; *Preparation,* XIV,ii.

107 *Glories of Mary,* Pt I, VI, iii.

108 Alphonsus, clearly, had also in mind the incident at *Acts* 5.1-11. These things are always the same.

109 *Letter to a Religious on the Manner of Preaching.*

110 *Exercises of the Missions,* VII, iii.

111 *Letter to a Religious, Exercises of the Missions* VII, iii, and *Treasury,* II, Instr.IV

112 *Truth of the Faith,* III,XI,9; Marietti, 783b; *Letter to a Religious; Exercises of the Mission,* VII,iii; *Refutation of a Book "On Preaching",* 2.

113 Charles Burney, *A General History of Music,* IV vols., 1776, Vol. IV, ch.viii, 'Progress of the Musical Drama at Naples, and an Account of the eminent Composers and School of Counterpoint in that City', 546ff and 550ff.

114 cf. Oreste Gregorio, *'Un discorso giovanile di S Alfonso', L'Osservatore Romano,* 1 January, 1960, p.4.

115 *Exercises of the Missions,* VII,iii.

116 *Ibid.,* VII,i.

117 These stories have made some readers uneasy. The translating Grimm actually removed some of them from Alphonsus' text as offensive to pious ears. Giuseppe Cacciatore, in his essay for the *Introduzione Generale* to the *Opere Ascetiche*, 1960, "*Le Fonti e I Modi di Documentatione*", Excurses B, 285ff, Giuseppe Orlandi, in his article, "*L'Uso degli "Exempla" in S Alfonso Maria de Liguori*", *Spicelegium Historicum*, XXXIX, 1991, 1-39, and Frederick Jones in his 1992 biography, all resort to ameliorating talk of "understanding things in their historical context". But in that context, a Provincial Synod of the Naples Archdiocese and its dependent dioceses, 1699, had warned local preachers against an uncritical use of local tales. There were, it seems, naughty preachers who, 'in order to move the common people', were making up miracle narratives, and even pretending that some of their stories were taken from Scripture. Anyone who based his announcement of the Kingdom on such untruths would, the Synod declared, be sinning mortally, (Tit.I, cap.iii, *De Praedicatione verbi Dei*'). And while Busenbaum might hope that such things could often be excused 'on account of ignorance or mere simplicity', (cf. *Theologia Moralis*, Lib.III, Tract.I, cap.i,3.5), he has to refer the confessor to the severer judgement of the redoubtable expert, Tomas Sanchez (1550-1610), in his *in praecepta decalogi*. Alphonsus noted the careful directive of the Synod. He kept the 1723 Parma edition of Sanchez on his shelf. He went on telling his sort of story. In our days, when "magical realism" is again a respectable literary genre, we may, surely, both enjoy a story and take its meaning.

118 Alphonsus advised those priests who felt themselves to be less than adequate in the pulpit that they should at least do good in their parlour and market-place conversation and keep telling stories which 'inculcate some maxim of eternity', *Treasury*, Pt I, IX, iii.

119 *Meditations for all Times of the Year*, LXVIII, *Glories of Mary*, Pt I, I, iii, *True Bride*, VII, vi, *Meditations*, LXXXIV.

120 There are indications of some general civilized conversation, in which Alphonsus is taking a part with Cornelius a Lapide (1567-1637), and Jean le Crasset (1618-1692), and Cardinal Celestino Sfondrati (1644-1696), in the resonances of *Lear* at *True Bride*, XIV,i and *Meditations for all Times of the Year*, XXXIV, of *Hamlet* at *Preparation for Death*, XIII, and *Prayer*, Pt II,1,3, and at the instructions to preachers about word and action, art and natural gesture, *Exercises of the Missions*, VII, iv, 2, of *As You Like It* at *Preparation*, XIII, and of *Merchant of Venice* at *Glories of Mary*, Pt I,V,ii, where our hero, having signed a bond is rescued from the bargaining Jew by a skilful lawyer Lady.

121 *Examples of the Infant Jesus*, II.

122 *Glories of Mary*, Pt II, VI, ii, and iii.

123 Hoegerl, *op.cit*. In a general letter to the Congregation in 1744, Alphonsus was already trying to prevent the establishment of 'any fixed rule' for the opening of a mission.

124 Tannoia, IV, 29.

125 Sermon XV for the First Sunday of Advent. Perhaps as many as three dozen of these sermons had their origins in Alphonsus' missioner preaching. But, as he was very keen to point out in his *Letter to a Religious*, there is, always, a vast difference between the preached and the printed versions of any sermon.

126 *Hints to the Catechist*, 2, II.

127 *Exercises of the Missions*, Introduction.

128 *Instructions for the People*, Practical Introduction.

129 *Exercises of the Missions*, III, Preparing Children for Confession, 3: "Here is narrated in a few words an example of the mercy of God. The most touching is that of the prodigal son".

130 20 October, 1776. They were reading their own sermons *For Times of Calamities* which, even though professedly undeveloped, have lively stories of the dancing princess Salome

who fell through the ice and in struggling to escape severed her head from her body, of the sick man who threw his medicine bottles out of the window, of King Robert and the crucifix, of Lucifer and the dawdling demon, II, III, IV.

131 *True Bride*, XIII, i.

132 *The Mass Hurriedly Said*, 2.

133 *Treasury*, Pt I, VII, III, 3.

134 *Treasury*, Pt I, VI, I, *Examples of the Infant Jesus*, 3, *True Bride*, VII,ii.

135 *Glories of Mary*, Dolours, II.

136 *Treasury*, Pt I, VI,i.

137 *Glories of Mary*, Pt I, VIII,i.

138 Jones, *op.cit.*, 248.

139 *Ibid.*, 252.

140 *Meditations for all Times of the Year*, LXVIII, *Glories of Mary*, Pt I, I, ii, and VIII, iii, Pt II, I.

141 *Conversing Familiarly*, V. The Venerable Serafina turns up again at *True Bride*, XII, iii, and again returns as the ghost at the convent grill at *True Bride*, XVI, i. Alphonsus had clearly enjoyed reading that *Life* which he recommends along with those of St Teresa of Avila, St Maria Maddalena de Pazzi, and a small clutch of other exemplary religious.

142 30 April, 1760.

143 *Treasury*, Pt I, VII, *Glories of Mary*, 'Practices of Devotion', V,5.

144 *Account of the Miraculous Finding of the Blessed Sacrament*, 1772.

145 *True Bride*, IX, ii, *Practice of the Love of Christ*, X, II.

146 *Treasury*, Pt I, IX, ii, *True Bride*, XIX and XVIII, iii.

147 *True Bride*, VII, i and v, and VIII, iii.

148 *New Science*, 667, 712, 715, 757.

149 *Glories of Mary*, Pt I, III,ii.

150 *Glories of Mary*, Pt II, II. Alphonsus had many such things from the famous Jesuit mariologist. Francesco Pepe (1684-1759), was a great collector of marvellous and improving stories for his *Della Grandezze di Gesu Cristo e di Maria*, 1744-1749, and besides thus providing both an exemplar and a resource for Alphonsus' *Glories of Mary* enterprise, Pepe was employed by Alphonsus to keep King Charles IV content with the Redemptorists, and was the prime mover in the project to erect the Giuglia dell'Immaculata outside the Gesu Nuovo in 1747 which showed that Naples could celebrate Mary's privilege as generously as Rome.

151 *Glories of Mary*, Pt I, V, I, cf. *La Véritable dévotion*, Pt I, I, qu. 5.2. This anti-Jansenist Jesuit preacher, who had devoted his energies to the pastoral care of domestic servants, artisans, and illiterate workmen, must seem most attractive to Alphonsus on several counts. Besides the great *Véritable dévotion envers la sainte Vierge*, 1679, which Arnauld wanted condemned by Rome, Alphonsus had also read le Crasset's *Histoire de l'église du Japan*, 1689, *Treasury*, Pt II, Instr. VII, 2. For a further use of this language of the spheres by an author who was read with approval and pleasure by Alphonsus, *vide Il divoto di Maria Vergine* by Paolo Segneri, (*senior*, 1625-1694) and the citation at *Glories of Mary*, Pt I, V, II, 2.

152 *Glories of Mary*. Pt I, V, i.

153 *Ibid.*, Pt I, VI, i.

154 *Ibid.*

155 5 July, 1759.

156 Alphonsus made the same sort of bad joke at the expense of Baruch ("Benedetto") Spinoza. *Brief Dissertation,* I, ii; Marietti, 445b.

157 *New Science,* 375, 1091.

158 *Ibid.,* 334, 1095.

159 Falcoia to Alphonsus, Letter 49, July 1734, *Analecta,* 1932, 364.

160 *Letter to a Bishop about the Missions,* para 5, *True Bride,* III,iii, VIII,iii,X,i,XI,iv; *Visits to the Blessed Sacrament,* Introduction, *Treasury,* Pt II, Instr.Ix.2; 'On the Utility of Missions'; *Glories of Mary,* Pt I, VIII,i, *Instructions for the People,* Appendix, "Melancholy Examples", V.

161 *Truth of the Faith,* II, I,5; Marietti 576a.

162 *Ibid.*

163 *Ibid.*

164 *Truth of the Faith,* III, II, 6; Marietti 685b: Charles de Rochfort, *Relation du l'isle de Tabago,* 1665; Jean Baptists Du Tetre, *Histoire des Indes dans l'Amerique,* 1654; Gabriel Sagard, *Le grand Voyage du Pays des Hurons,* 1632.

165 Several times in his correspondence with Remondini, Alphonsus suggests that he has culled "all that other authors have said" on his topic, that he is giving succinct and lucid answers to "all the objections of the heretics", and that "everybody will be pleased"; the *Truth of the Faith,* for instance, was, he thought, "almost a complete Dogma", cf. their correspondence between 29 December, 1765 and 21 August, 1769, 12 February and 28 August, 1776.

166 cf. Thomas Hobbes, *Leviathan,* Pt I, 2, in *English Works,* vol.3, ed. W. Molesworth, 1839.

167 *Truth of the Faith,* 1, VI, 44 and I, I, 2; Marietti, 570a and 538a.

168 *Brief Dissertation,* II, II; *Truth of the Faith,* II,I,4; *Reflections on the Truth,* I, 12; Marietti, 453b, 576a, 474b.Vico had noted such language. He was much troubled by those who were still popularising Orphic tales of "an adulterous Jove", who even burns with "wicked love for Canymede", and, worse, "transforms into a swan to lie with Leda". The god had been made, on this licentious perversion of the myth, into a self-justifying representation of the outlaw. Vico intended, by his scientific account of these things, to demonstrate that the original myths offered worthy exemplars for those who were responsible for european civilization. cf. *New Science,* I, xxii. 80f.

169 *Evidence of the Faith,* I; Marietti, 492a.

170 cf. the *"Emilio"* quotations and references in *Reflections on the Truth,* I, 2 and 32, III, 44, 46 and 50, and *Truth of the Faith,* I,VI,ii.23; Marietti, 471a, 480b, 481a, 484a, 486b and 564b. Alphonsus had also read carefully Rouseau's *Discourse on Inequality,* see, especially, *Truth of the Faith,* I, VI, 10; Marietti, 56ab.

171 29 December, 1765 and 7 January, 1766.

172 *Christianity not Mysterious,* xiii, 53, and 55.

173 *Letters to Serena,* III.

174 cf. the argument conducted in terms of a living memory in the community recorded by the scriptural authors, *Reflections on the Truth,* I, 16; Marietti, 475a-b.

175 Letter to Giuseppe Remondini, 15 November, 1776.

176 *Christanity as old as Creation,* 375, 417, and 8. Alphonsus notes with some suspicion that it is on the assumption that every father pardons every penitent son that Tindal says it is unnecessary to resort to notions of some 'special redeemer'. God will, of course, pardon his creation. It may be, says Alphonsus, all very well to entertain such a comforting

view of fathers but we require, as the great myths and the Hebrew scriptures and Christian parables show, that certainty of the Father's forgiveness offered in the revelation made in Christ. cf. *Truth of the Faith*, II, I, 14; Marietti, 579b.

177 *Christianity as old as Creation*, 92, 385, and 87.

178 *Ibid.*, 233, 46, 363, 311, 169, 315, 210, and 90.

179 cf. Letters of 26 January, 11 and 20 February, 1764; *True Bride*, XXIII, VII, i; *vide* also letters of 26 September, 1736, 1 August, 1763, January, 1768, and 29 August, 1769.

180 *Practice*, I, 3.

181 *Affections* XVI, iv, *Glories of Mary*, Pt I, II, ii, *Victories of the Martyrs*, Pt I, LVI.

182 *Counsels concerning Religious Vocation*, III, 1, "Secrecy", *True Bride*, XVI, iii, *Times of Calamities*, III, *Conversing Familiarity*, III, V, *Discourses for Novena of Christmas*, VI, i.

183 *Conversing Familiarly*, V.

184 *True Bride*, XVI, iii, *Glories of Mary*, Pt I, II, ii.

185 *Visits to the Blessed Sacrament*, Introduction, I, cf. *Preparation for Death*, XXXIV, 3, and *Practice*, Introduction, II, ii.It may be evidence of some contemporary Neapolitan interest in matters Bohemian that in 1721 Paolo de Mattheis was painting *San Giovanni Nemomuceno davanti a Re Venceslao* for the Royal Apartments. As for the sources of Alphonsus' story, the Bollandists' *Acta* for 28 September omitted the pleasing detail of the follower and the warming footprints, but it is possible that, among other *Lives*, Alphonsus had read H.R.E. Charles IV's *Vita* of St Wenceslas.

186 *Conversing Familiarly*, V. Alphonsus' work is, as he acknowledges, 'taken from a small French work'. This is the *Méthode pour converser avec Dieu*, 1684, of Michel Boutauld, 1607-1688, which was on the Index of Forbidden Books from 1723 to 1910.

187 *Divine Office*, Sunday Matins.

188 *Octave of Corpus Christi*, Meditation II, *Visits to the Blessed Sacrament*, X, *Prayer*, Pt I, III, *Preparation for Death*, XXXV, 2, *Practice of the Love of Jesus Christ*, Introduction, III, *Meditations for all Times of the Year*, LXIX, *True Bride*, XVIII, III, 9.

189 *True Bride*, XVI, I.

190 *Affections* III, iii, and IX, iii, *Glories of Mary*, Pt I, VIII, iii, and II, i, *On the Passion*, XIII, ii, *Rule of Life*, 1, II, 3.

191 *True Bride*, XVIII, i and XVI, iii.

192 Letter to Luigi Capuano, 7 September, 1773.

193 *Preparation for Death*, VII, 2, *On the Passion*, 'To the Reader', *After Holy Communion*, V.

194 *True Bride*, XII, ii.

195 *Meditations for all Times of the Year*, LXVIII.

196 *Evidence of the Faith*, cap.III; Marietti 503b. "*da tempo in tempo dichiarati*" suggests that the Church is making that clear and clarifying announcement of the eternal which Alphonsus thought a reading of Abelly would encourage in his student preachers.

197 *Dogmatic Work against the Heretics*, IV, 8.59; Marietti, 851b.

198 For the Procida mission, cf. '*De apostolata S.P.N. Alphonsi in insula Prochyta olim exercito*', *Analecta*, X, 1931, 41ff.

199 *Exercises of the Missions*, VIII, ii.

200 Schelstrate was just Alphonsus' sort of civilized scholar, an editor of the *Aeneid* and a careful repairer of cracked books.

201 The change of usage may indicate that Schelstrate thought more highly than Alphonsus of Rossignoli's *Disciplina perfectionis christianae*.

202 *New Science*, 624, cf. 667, 712, 715, 757.

203 In April, 1772, Alphonsus was much vexed by the ecclesiastical censor, Canon Giuseppe Simeoli (1713-1779), and put his raising objections against his *History of the Heresies* down to "that blessed" Simeoli's "holding tenaciously to the doctrine of Berti". G. Lorenzo Berti (1696-1762), was, like Simeoli himself, a drudging professor of theology, and his chiefest ambition was to get his eight-volume *De theologicis disciplinis*, 1739-1745, acknowledged as a suitable text-book for dogma classes. For a carefully mounted attack on Berti and the specious principle *Qui probabiliter agit, prudenter agit*, see *Theologia Moralis*, Lib. I, Tract. I, cap. iii, *corollarium primum*, para. 65.

204 *Development*, 145, *Difficulties of Anglicans*, I, xii, 7, 323, *Reply to Eirenicon*, 28 and 48.

205 Perhaps Newman, in his reference to what was 'notorious' in Alphonsus' writing, was thinking of the *Acclamations in Praise of Mary* which were, in the nineteenth century often placed at the close of the *Glories of Mary*. Perhaps a member of the Birmingham Oratory had quoted them in a "Doubt" one evening as part of the community's usual exchange of learning after supper. But the *Acclamations* were appended to printings of the *Glories of Mary* only after Alphonsus' death and they are not his work. cf. *Opere Ascetiche*, VI, 437.

206 *Glories of Mary*, Pt II, I "The Immaculate Conception".

207 Noghera had produced a series of books that pleased Alphonsus: *On Modern Eloquence*, 1752, *On the Infallibility of the True Church*, 1775, *On the Infallibility of the Pope*, 1776, and *The Power of the True Church*, 1778.

208 *Glories of Mary*, Pt II, VIII.

209 *Ibid.*, Pt I, I, II and Pt II, VII.

210 *Practices of Devotion*, V, I, "The Hail Mary". cf. the delicate moment, recorded at *Octave of the Epiphany*, Meditation V, when Mary and Joseph "courteously informed the friends whom they had made in that country" that they were leaving Egypt to return to Palestine.

211 *Ibid.*, X, I. This courtesy has its rubricional dimension. On his consecration as bishop of S Agata dei Goti, Alphonsus refused to apply for the usual indult to wear his skull-cap at the celebration of the Eucharist: "Am I to pay twenty-five scudi for the privilege of being bad-mannered to our Lord in the Blessed Sacrament?", cf. Jones, *op. cit.*, p 365. Alphonsus' carefulness in keeping Vico out of all troublesome controversy was, it must seem, a particular instance of this charitable courtesy exercised "everywhere" and "always".

212 Letter to Pasquale Caprioli, 20 May, 1754.

213 *Truth of the Faith*, II, XIX, 13; Marietti, 668b.

A Note on Books and the further reader

Every reading must, of course, begin from Alphonsus' own writing, for example, from the *Preparation for Death* meditations: "Whoever examines well this little work on Death will certainly purchase it", he encouraged Tannoia, who had been sent to sell them during Lent at d'Iliceto in 1789. Or from the *Way of Salvation* which "in my opinion", Bishop Alphonsus told Remondini in 1767, "is very useful for all classes of people, for priests, nuns, and laity: I use it continually and have it always at hand". To get a workable text of these little works, as of all Alphonsus' ascetical writing, I have looked back and forth between the *Opere Ascetiche* edited by O. Gregorio, G. Cacciatore, and D. Capone, *Introduzione Generale* and 10 volumes so far, Rome, 1933ff., and the translation of the indefatigable Eugene Grimm for the "Centenary Edition", 22 volumes, New York, 1886-1894. While usually quoting from Grimm's translation I have attempted at some places to give Alphonsus' meaning a less nineteenth century turn of expression and at others to restore something of the liveliness of Alphonsus' tone, at the tellings of those miracle stories, for example, which seem to have made Grimm a trifle uneasy.

A reading of his moral or dogmatic or, more likely, of his ascetical writings, may prompt an interest in the events of Alphonsus' life and in the ways that others have interpreted his work. A. M. Tannoia's great account *Della Vita ed Instituto del Ven. Servo di Dio Alfonso Maria de Liguori*, 3 volumes, Naples, 1798-1802, was, on an English version's being made in 1847, for the *Saints and Servants of God* series, from the 1842 French translation of the Dutch Redemptorists of Wittem, thought to be too revelatory of the depravity of the Church in the Kingdom of Naples. This objection has not, I think, been raised against Raimundo Telleria's collection of exciting materials, *San Alphonso Maria de Ligorio*, Madrid 1950 and 1951, or against the most recent biography, *Alphonsus de Liguori* by Frederick M. Jones, Dublin, 1992, corrected reprint 1994, whose subtitle, "The Saint of Bourbon Naples" declares an at least equal interest in the context of Alphonsus' work. This is a fine work of scholarship, a pleasure to read and re-read. With these, I have kept Harold Castle's two volume translation, Edinburgh, 1906, of the French *S. Alphonse de Liguori* of Auguste Berthe, Paris, 1900, on my work-table with the more popular *Monsignore se diverte* of Oreste Gregorio,

Modena, 1962, reprinted Naples, 1987, and Théodule Rey-Mermet's *Le Saint du siècle des Lumières*, Paris, 1987, translated for the American edition, New York, 1989, by Jehanne-Marie Marchesi as *St. Alphonsus Liguori, Tireless Worker for the Most Abandoned*. Along with these, I have had Carl Hoegerl's *Founding Texts of Redemptorists*, Rome, 1986, a most useful handbook to "the mind of the Congregation" from 1732 to 1747 which gives the proper emphases to the shaping intelligence of the Venerable Celeste Crostarosa and Bishop Tommaso Falcoia, and the first volume, *Le Origini, (1732-1793)*, of the new *Storia della Congregazione del Santissimo Redentore*, edited by Francesco Chiovaro, in *Studia et Monumenta Congregationis SS Redemptoris*, Rome, 1993.

The publication of *Studia et Subsidia de Vita et Operibus S Alfonsi de Ligorio* as volume XIII of *Bibliotheca Historica Congregationis SSmi Redemptoris*, Rome, 1990, has made things much simpler for anyone who wants to know about Alphonsus and responses to his theology. With Giuseppe Orlandi's account of work in progress for a new edition of Alphonsus' letters, H. Arboleda Valencia's register of the Alphonsian manuscripts in the archive of the Roman Generalate of the Redemptorists, and the catalogue of printed editions of Alphonsus' writings made by Fabriciano Ferrero and Samuel J. Boland, the volume offers a critical review by Otto Weiss of the large number of biographies of Alphonsus and a listing by Weiss and Ferrero of over 400 additions between 1978-1988 to the 1938-1978 Bibliography of André Sampers.

Since I must make a short selection from this vast range of critical writings, I would recommend these seven Redemptorist works as having variously aided my own effort to understand Alphonsus' enterprise:

Capone, Domenico: *Sant'Alfonso missionario*, Naples, 1987.

Johnstone, Brian: "The Significance of the Moral Theology of St Alphonsus", *Studia Moralia*, Supplement I, 1990.

Marcelli, Ezio and Raponi, Sante: *Un Umanista del '700 Italiano*, Rome, 1993.

Orlandi, Giuseppe: "*S. Alfonso e i laici e la fondazione della Congregazione dell' Addolarata (o dei 'Rossi') di Procida*", *Lateranum*, N.I.S., 55, 1989.

Rey-Mermet, Théodule: *Le Morale selon St Alphonse de Liguori*, Paris, 1987.

Verdes, L. Alvarez and Majorano, Sabatino: *Morale e Redenzione*, *Quaestiones Morales* 1, Rome, 1983.

Vidal, Marciano: *Frente al rigorismo moral, benignidad pastoral Alfonso de Liguori,* Madrid, 1986, Italian translation, *La Morale di Sant'Alfonso, dal rigorismo alla benignita, Quaestiones Morales 7,* Rome, 1992.
I have read with profit and pleasure three Alphonsian dissertations:
Anderson, Mark: "Alphonsus de Liguori and the Option for the Poor", University of Kent at Canterbury, 1986.
Freda, Ambrosio: *De Institutione et Eruditione Juridica S. Alphonsi M. de Ligorio,* Pontificium Institutum Utriusque Juris, Rome, 1939.
McCabe, Gerard, "Alphonsus de Liguori: A Theology of Prayer", University of Kent at Canterbury, 1983.
The Freda dissertation *"ad lauream"* was revised for publication as *"S Alfonso universitario"* in *S Alfonso De Liguori, Contributi Bio-bibliografici,* edited by Gregorio, O., Capone, D., Freda, A., Toglia, V., Brescia, 1940, and the McCabe dissertation for *Readings in Redemptorist Spirituality 4,* edited by J. O'Donnell and Kevin Dowling, Rome, 1991.

Important to those who mean to keep up with contemporary Alphonsian studies is the *Spicelegium Historicum* which had, for example, in 1991, a splendid article on Alphonsus' story-telling sources by Orlandi: *"L'uso degli 'Exempla' in S Alfonso Maria de Liguori",* and to *Studia Moralia,* also published by the Alphonsian Academy, Rome, which, from Capone's commentary on Alphonsus' notes about probability and conscience in the first three issues, 1962-1965, to Louis Vereecke's essay in December, 1993, on Alphonsus as jurist is maintaining a lively conversation about important matters, and to *Apostolicum* published in Mayfield, New South Wales, which has published not only Brian Johnstone's fine article "St Alphonsus and the Theology of Conversion" but William Nayden's English translation of the 1972 pastoral letter of Albino Luciani (later to become Pope John Paul I), "St Alphonsus and Today's Priest", in the 1978 and the 1979 issues.

In attempting to place Alphonsus in relation to some of his contemporaries, I have enjoyed reading two affectionate studies of Celeste Crostarosa, Majorano's *L'imitazione per la memoria del Salvatore,* Rome, 1978, and Joseph W. Oppitz's *The Mystic Who Remembered,* Suffield, 1979. A properly more critical look at his subject was taken by Gregorio in *Mons. Tommaso Falcoia, 1663-1743,* Rome, 1955. There is a helpful study of the condition of contemporary moral theology in James R. Pollock, S.J.: *François Genet, The Man and his Methodology,* in the

Analecta Gregoriana series, 1984, and of the European discussion of dogmatic matters in Robert E. Sullivan: *John Toland and the Deist Controversy* in Harvard Historical Series, 1982. For the shaping of Alphonsus' characteristic turn of mind, the wide sweep of Giambattista Vico's Law School lectures seem to me to have been at least as important as any particular notion which occurred to him in a reading of contemporary moralists and dogmatic deists. From the ever-increasing number of Vician studies in English, I would recommend Donald Phillip Verene's essays on *Vico's Science of Imagination*, Ithaca, 1981, and *The New Art of Autobiography*, Oxford, 1991, and Peter Burke's excellent little handbook, *Vico*, Oxford, 1985, in the *Past Masters* series.

Index

247

252